Zachary Isrow
The Spectricity of Humanness

Zachary Isrow

The Spectricity of Humanness

Spectral Ontology and Being-in-the-World

DE GRUYTER

ISBN 978-3-11-152071-1
e-ISBN (PDF) 978-3-11-069099-6
e-ISBN (EPUB) 978-3-11-069114-6

Library of Congress Control Number: 2022938366

Bibliographic information published by the Deutsche Nationalbibliothek
The Deutsche Nationalbibliothek lists this publication in the Deutsche Nationalbibliografie; detailed bibliographic data are available on the internet at http://dnb.dnb.de.

© 2024 Walter de Gruyter GmbH, Berlin/Boston
This volume is text- and page-identical with the hardback published in 2022.
Cover image: Nataliia Yankovets / iStock / Getty Images Plus

www.degruyter.com

Man's relations to man do not captivate my fancy. It is man's relation to the cosmos – to the unknown – which alone arouses in me the spark of creative imagination.

– H.P Lovecraft (2007, p. 56)

Il est dangereux d'avoir raison dans des choses où des hommes accrédités ont tort.
– Voltaire (1817, p. 1071)

Acknowledgements

There are plenty of those whom deserve recognition for their support in the working of this manuscript. I offer them sincerest thanks below:

To all my colleagues and friends past and present who have shaped my way of thinking both by listening and by challenging – it can only ever serve to benefit. Though there are too many of you to name I would especially like to thank: Frank Karioris, Aflie Bown, Rosangela Barcaro, James Besse, Nathan Wiley.

To my advisors, professors and teachers who, taught me what I know, which so ever often was at odds with what I thought I knew, and who pushed me to continue to expand my ambitions: Jason Troka, Andrew Orgler, Graham Harman, Mark Walter, Rok Svetlic, Wendy Doniger, David Tracy, Michael Turner, Jean-Luc Nancy, Lenart Skof, and Janko Lozar.

To my family who made me who I am, but who always encouraged me to not settle for that state of being, but to rather be who I wanted to be and to always do my best.

Above all, however, I wish to acknowledge my wife Karolina for unwavering encouragement. For this I note:

In a world of billions, if I had never met you, I would most certainly have met someone else to live out my days with; how grateful, then, am I, that it was our paths which have crossed with each other amongst all the others.

Contents

Preface —— XIII

Introduction —— 1

Chapter One
The Rise of the Speculative and the Problem of Humanness —— 11
    Speculative Realism and The Problem of Emergence —— 12
    Correlationism, Relations, and Emergence —— 18
    Speculative Nominalism —— 21

Chapter Two
Dethroning the Speculative —— 26
    Object-Oriented Ontology as Nominalistic —— 28
    Non-Flat Models —— 31
    Focus on Universals —— 32
    Re-enter Relationality, Correlationism Revived —— 34

Chapter Three
The Search for the Grounding of Metaphysics —— 39
    The Problem of a Complete Ontology —— 42
    Fundamental Ontology as a Groundwork for a Future Metaphysics —— 43
    The problem of the source of Fundamental Ontology —— 45

Chapter Four
The Ontical Modes of Dasein —— 47
    Finitude —— 49
    Nonfinitude —— 55
    A Commentary on the Limits of Pure Reason as Opposed to Sensible Reason and the Nonfinite Nature of Pure Reason —— 75

Chapter Five
The Ontological Modes of Dasein —— 77
    Infinitude —— 77
    Transcendental —— 81

Chapter Six
Metaphysics of *Dasein* —— 92
    The Worlds of *Dasein* —— 92
    World in Kant —— 93
    The Worlds of Kantian Thought as Articulated through the Antinomies —— 95
    Kantian Worlds Overview —— 98
    The Two Worlds Interpretation —— 99
    The Two Aspects Interpretation —— 103
    The Two Relations Interpretation —— 106

Chapter Seven
Heidegger's Being-in-the-World —— 113
    Attunement and Care —— 115
    The Way Which We Relate to the World: Ready-to-Hand vs. Present-at-Hand —— 118

Chapter Eight
The Systematic Expression of Humanness —— 124
    Exposition on the Origin and Implementation of the Question of Humanness —— 126
    The Historical Articulation of the Question of Humanness —— 128
    The Analytic of Humanness as Differentiated from The Existential Analytic of *Dasein* —— 130
    Elucidation of Being —— 132
    Beginning the Question of Being —— 132
    Being as Nothingness —— 135
    Being as Nature —— 137
    Being as World —— 139
    Being as Worldhood —— 142
    Unveiling the Categorization of Beings in the World —— 143
    Subject-Object Orientation (Tools) —— 144
    Object Orientation —— 148
    Object-oriented ontology —— 152
    World —— 153
    World Itself —— 158

Chapter Nine
The Systematic Transcendental of Humanness —— 162
    A Case for the Distinctiveness Between Worlds —— 163

A Case for the Multiple Aspects of Beings —— 164
A Case for Ontological Prioritization of Existence —— 165
Objects and their Nonbeing —— 166
Aptitudes, Forms, and Emergence —— 169
Spectricity of Humanness —— 173
A Brief Note on Spectricities —— 179
The Pathway to Philosophical Anthropology —— 181
The Fundamental Structure of the Critique of Humanness —— 183
The Continuing Procedure of the Critique of Humanness —— 187

Bibliography —— 192

Index —— 211

Preface

The Emergence of the Problem of Humanness

Insofar as the problem of humanness is taken to be philosophical, it has emerged out of a recognition of the misdeeds committed by contemporary musings under the guise of modern academic philosophy. What now passes for philosophical originality provides little to no insight into the depths of knowledge once sought. It is a consistent failing so blinding that it has caused outcries against humanistic inquiry; Stephen Hawking and Leonard Mlodinow (2010, p. 1) went so far as to proclaim that "philosophy is dead" with science being the new torch-bearer of truth.

Of course, it was philosophy which gave rise to what we now distinguish as scientific inquiry, though a very different sort of philosophy. "Philosophers have failed to stay abreast with modern science" Hawking and Mlodinow posit, a statement with which one can largely agree (ibid.).[1] Nonetheless, there is something to be said for philosophical investigation; it drives into the very heart of all inquiry – no question posed is off limits. That is to say, although Hawking has a point which must be recognized, it does not render philosophy moot. Instead, it poses a challenge to philosophy which echoes the sound of the following message: "speak like a science". Notably, Heidegger calls scientism into question as he argues that Being cannot be spoken of at all, especially not scientifically or logically.[2]

The message understood properly, however, clearly differs from 'be more scientific'; it is not a call to become experimentalists – though some have attempted exactly this, though it is beyond the scope of the philosopher's work to do so. This call to arms resounds with a necessity of the treatment of philosophy *as* a science; indeed, it came first, after all. This treatment of philosophy as a science requires nothing other than the complete devotion to the utilization of mod-

---

[1] Christopher Norris, however, in fact disagrees, and while one can understand why, I believe to completely undermine the assertion that philosophy has not remained in consistent conversation with other sciences would be unwise, since this largely seems to me to be the case. For Norris' explanation of his position, see Christopher Norris (2011) "Hawking Contra Philosophy".
[2] Heidegger notes this difficulty most articulately in *Introduction to Metaphysics*. See, See, Martin Heidegger (1961). However, for a good work on the notion of silence in *Being and Time* see, Brandon Absher (2016), "Speaking of Being: Language, Speech, and Silence in Being and Time". Contrary to this, is Carnap's assertion that "Logic is the last scientific ingredient of Philosophy; its extraction leaves behind only a confusion of non-scientific, pseudo problems" (1934, p. 22).

ern science as a starting point. That is to say that philosophers cannot seek answers to questions which have already been satisfactorily answered through the means of science. Philosophy's purpose in the modern world is not to be the discoverer of truth – in fact, truth itself was never the goal of philosophy, not in the sense of uncovering knowledge – but instead to be the bearer of wisdom. Philosophy must aim to supplement the current science through this act of bearing wisdom.

What does it mean to bear wisdom without regarding truth? Does having wisdom not mean to have truth? Rather, I think one will find that two very different meanings are invoked by the nouns "truth" and "wisdom", though cautious of definitions.[3] In the case of truth, we speak of knowledge such that the action or activity associated with truth becomes knowing; as regards wisdom, we speak of possession, that is, the act of "having". For example, we say one *knows* the truth or that they *know* what is true, and that one *has* wisdom. Indeed, even when we say that someone *is* wise, we mean precisely that they possess wisdom, whereas what *is* true, is a claim on the judgment of its Being. Thus, "is" means different things in these different propositions. In the former, Being means having the *character of* and in the latter, it means having the static *nature of*.

This is clear in science when one thing has been stated as truth which is no longer regarded as such; we say that it has "been proven false", which means precisely that it was never actually true but merely appeared so. On the other hand, the lovers of wisdom have the task of setting forth the parameters of questions. Herein lies the problem of philosophy: setting the parameters requires an impartiality towards truth rather than a reliance on strict adherence to ancient models. Thus, the influence of philosophy on this work stems from a proposed revitalization of its method, not a disposal. That is to say, we need not eschew metaphysics, but reconsider from where that metaphysics springs. The father of *Dasein* is correct to determine this foundation as a fundamental ontology, but he descends quickly into strict phenomenology with speed bumps of unoriginal[4] metaphysics – namely, the metaphysics of Being as such.

But if fundamental ontology is concerned with the metaphysics of *Dasein* (that is, to put it differently, the ontological foundations of human nature or *Dasein*), then it is not with an analytic of *Dasein* that it must commence. Rather, it is

---

[3] Cautious because of the words of Quine: "The word 'definition' has come to have a dangerously reassuring sound" (1953, p. 26).

[4] "Unoriginal" here means simply that it begins as most metaphysics does – the question of Being. A more "original" approach is that taken by Hans Blumenburg (2010) in his work *Paradigms for a Metaphorology*. For more on this methodology see, David Adams (1991) "Metaphors for Mankind: The Development of Hans Blumenberg's Anthropological Metaphorology".

through a delimitation of that ontological foundation, that humanness of *Dasein*, and this requires a passage into philosophical anthropology. Insofar as previous philosophical accounts do not originate and spring forth from fundamental ontology, one rooted in the question of humanness, we may rightfully say that there has as of yet been no true philosophical anthropology, but merely philosophical and anthropological accounts of the human being. Indeed, sometimes these two approaches come to be mixed, but merely mixing the approaches of philosophy and anthropology or considering aspects from each does not itself account for philosophical anthropology. Instead, philosophical anthropology must be its own methodology as a dialectic between the two approaches which originates in the problem of humanness.

It is therefore important to note that the following work is not itself intended as a philosophical anthropology, but rather as a preliminary guide or groundwork for a philosophical anthropology, since the focus here is on the problem of humanness itself. Once this is addressed, philosophical anthropology may prosper. Contemporary philosophical anthropology fails in its matter of investigation, not in its quality of inspection. Whether that undertaking is one of culture, human nature,[5] the phenomenology of *Dasein*, or the philosophy or anthropology of the human being, I do not intend here to dismiss these efforts as being invalid. I prefer to use the word "misguided" for their current avoidance of the question of humanness as I treat the term. The current work thus aims at reorienting philosophy towards a new fundamental ontology (which I will call *spectral ontology*), that emerges out of the question of humanness and lends itself primarily towards a rethinking of philosophical anthropology.

Brief Note on the Background of the Work

I would first begin working on the notion of humanness at the age of fourteen. I recognized in the Kantian transcendental system a concern not simply with epistemology, but with the human condition itself, an ontology – or, more specifically, what Martin Heidegger calls fundamental ontology. Kant's system, his three *Critiques* (among other works), were laying the foundation for a *Critique of Humanness*.

---

5 According to Donald E. Brown, human nature is interconnected with history and therefore 'human nature' here should be treated as if including historical studies. For more on Brown's thoughts on 'human nature', see Donald E. Brown (1999) "Human Nature and History".

At the age of fifteen, I would first start to write this *Critique*, some of which has found its way into this work in modified forms. In the process of its writing, it was clear that any such "critique" of the concept of humanness could only be fulfilled following a very specific, though I would argue accurate, reading of Kant's system – a reading which begins with the Heideggerian reading of Kant – as laying this groundwork for a fundamental ontology, confronts the distortion of the Kantian system established by the speculative realist movement, and object-oriented ontology in particular, derived from the desire to eliminate correlationism when in fact it is essential to the recognition of objects as objects, and finally, a reading which produces a new ontological model, which I term spectral ontology. It therefore became clear that what was first necessary was to make clear in what way Kant's system can be read as a system focused on humanness, and indeed, a very particular conception of humanness.

That is the position of this work; it is an attempt to locate a particular conception of humanness within the Kantian system and as an outcome of recent scholarship in speculative realism, especially object-oriented ontology. In setting up this notion of humanness, it is then possible to turn back to the critique of it, and examine it in even greater depth in the form of a philosophical anthropology.

Insofar as this work is indebted to the many scholars (not just limited to Kant, Heidegger, and Harman) past and present featured throughout, as they have all shaped my thought in various ways, I do feel I have come to understand the famous metaphor: *nanos gigantium humeris insidentes*.[6] Admittedly though, despite the great influence of each, the "world" of scholarly activity, of mainstream academic inquiry, has always felt removed from my work; like a gathering to which I was never invited. My work has garnered criticism at the many conferences at which I have presented and is met with skepticism by Heideggerians, Kantians, and Speculative Realists alike. It is with that uncanny feeling of intellectual isolation that I begin this work:

> And for these words, thus woven into song,
>   It may be that they are a harmless wile,—
> The colouring of the scenes which fleet along,
>   Which I would seize, in passing, to beguile
>   My breast, or that of others, for a while.

---

[6] Although made famous by Issac Newton, the first use of the phrase seems to be due to John of Salisbury, who used the phrase in reference to Bernard of Chartres. The whole phrase in translation reads: "Bernard of Chartres used to say that we were like dwarfs seated on the shoulders of giants. If we see more and further than they, it is not due to our own clear eyes or tall bodies, but because we are raised on high and upborne by their gigantic bigness" (Taylor 1919, p. 159).

Fame is the thirst of youth,—but I am not
So young as to regard men's frown or smile
As loss or guerdon of a glorious lot;
I stood and stand alone,—remembered or forgot.
I have not loved the world, nor the world me;
I have not flattered its rank breath, nor bowed
To its idolatries a patient knee,—
Nor coined my cheek to smiles, nor cried aloud
In worship of an echo; in the crowd
They could not deem me one of such; I stood
Among them, but not of them; in a shroud
Of thoughts which were not their thoughts, and still could,
Had I not filed my mind, which thus itself subdued.

(Lord Byron, *Childe Harold's Pilgrimage* 1885, p. 137)

Introduction

Philosophers often consider first principles as the fundamental building blocks of the *kosmos*.[7] They are, in totality, what account for everything that is, and are responsible for the formulation of the world. However, the best means through which we can discover these principles is the existing philosophical debate which has continued for centuries. Some, such as the Pre-Socratics and Heidegger, find the most crucial question of philosophy – in its attempt to uncover the secrets of the first principles – to be a metaphysical or an ontological one. Others, Socrates himself for instance, found ethics to be the most crucial element of philosophy. Still another large group have selected epistemology as the fundamental science of first principles, since how can one know first principles if they cannot even understand what it is to know and be knowable?

Immanuel Kant, widely considered to be one of the most influential philosophers of all time, is commonly read primarily as either a metaphysician or an epistemologist. However, were these his central concerns? In his most famous work, *The Critique of Pure Reason*, Kant is seemingly concerned mostly with epistemology, though metaphysical issues arise and are dealt with in detail as well. Elsewhere, however, he concerns himself with ethics, religion, and even the *kosmos* itself as the topic of contemporary science.[8] Nevertheless, he himself notes that none of these approaches is central in philosophy, though each is important. There is instead, he argues, a more primary science that unifies the other sciences, one that should really be commanding our attention: namely, philosophical anthropology.[9]

Martin Heidegger later offered a position that was contrary to this, though also perhaps reflective of it. Inspired by Husserl's phenomenological approach, which was influenced more directly by Kant, Heidegger took the Kantian discussion of space and time and turned it into an analytic of the being which possesses *pure reason*, namely *Dasein*.

---

[7] Cicero once noted *"Nam efficit hoc philosophia: medetur animis, inanes sollicitudines detrahit, cupiditatibus liberat, pellit timores"* (1834, p. 14).
[8] For more on the influence of Kant on modern science see, Daniel F. M. Strauss (2000) "Kant and modern physics—The synthetic a priori and the distinction between modal function and entity" and David E. Leary (1982) "Immanuel Kant and the Development of Modern Psychology" in *The Problematic Science: Psychology in Nineteenth-Century Thought*.
[9] For more on Kant's interest in philosophical anthropology, and more specifically, on the question of what makes a human being what it is, see Kant (2013) "Anthropology from a Pragmatic Point of View" in *Anthropology, History, and Education*.

In this work, I argue for the necessity of a critique of humanness: that is, that which makes us what we are, in the hopes of delimiting the ontological foundations of philosophical anthropology. In so doing, I hope to reorient philosophy towards a closer consideration of humanness. Through a consideration of Heidegger's philosophy, insofar as it serves as a reading of Kant, I suggest that a critique of humanness is what both philosophies have been lacking to make them complete. By exploring concepts as they relate to the human condition,[10] such as finitude, infinitude, nonfinitude, and the transcendental, I make the case that through a reinterpretation of Kantian worlds (phenomenal and noumenal), and with the influence of object-oriented ontology, a rethinking of *Dasein* is not only possible, but necessary. I hope in this text to expound upon this problem and articulate a response that not only remains truer to the Kantian system, but which also stays relevant to contemporary philosophical discussions by bringing philosophical anthropology to the forefront of inquiry.

Since Kant's *Critique of Pure Reason* posited the separation of things-in-themselves and things as they appear, and additionally asserted the existence of noumena, a major debate has occupied the field of continental philosophy. Kant's student Fichte claimed that noumena were unnecessary for an idealist system, and since this assertion, noumena have largely been forgotten and rejected from contemporary philosophical systems.[11] When Heidegger undertook his analytic of *Dasein* he did so while rejecting the distinction between Kantian worlds. Thus, he positioned *Dasein* as *in-der-Welt-sein*. This interprets that *Dasein* is primarily "in the world."

However, "world" for Heidegger was a series of interactions, interconnections, and relations. As such, *Dasein* was said in fact to be the only entity with a "world" for Heidegger, as only *Dasein* engages with its world in its own particular way. Recently Graham Harman, among others, has criticized this claim to ontological priority of *Dasein* and instead argued for what is called "object-oriented ontology" (Harman 2002). This treats all objects, not just *Dasein*, as beings with a "world". The problem this creates for *Dasein* is that *Dasein* can no longer be understood primarily as *in-der-Welt-sein*; all beings become beings-in-the-world under this model. Instead, there must be a more primary mode of being-in of which *Dasein* is a part. I argue that by revisiting Kantian worlds, that is, through the reimplementation of noumena into the analytic of *Dasein* there is a more primordial mode of being-in that we can grant to *Dasein*.

---

10 Human condition here means not *vita activa* as in Hannah Arendt's use of the term, but rather as *vita perfectum totus*. For Arendt's use of *vita activa* see, Hannah Arendt (1958) *The Human Condition*.
11 Although not from scholarly works on Kant.

Transcendental Idealism, the Kantian systematic philosophical position, has received both the highest praise and the harshest criticisms. During Kant's own life his philosophy was widely discussed and much was published on it, whether supportive or critical. Additionally, many of his letters were preserved. From everything we have, it is clear that the philosophical system of *transcendental idealism* was a topic of great interest even during his own lifetime.

Heidegger too, most notably his major work *Sein und Zeit*,[12] has been subject to much discussion, especially in more recent philosophy. Commentaries on *Sein und Zeit* are easily found and often enter into conversation with other commentators or with the text itself. Heidegger's extraordinarily detailed analytic of *Dasein* requires true dedication if one is ever to fully understand it.

What is less commented on, however, though I would argue it is certainly more fundamental, is Heidegger's lectures on and interpretation of the Kantian system and the problem of metaphysics in Kant. What Heidegger often refers to as "the Kantian problematic" is the distinction between noumena and phenomena, in particular *appearances* and *things in themselves*.[13] As stated earlier, Heidegger was far from the first person to note the difficulties with this distinction. In fact, in referring to it as the Kantian problematic, he does not insinuate or delve into the problems of it, but only indicates that this is Kant's main agenda – which Heidegger will call a "fundamental ontology."

Among Kant's earliest supporters was one of his former students, Karl Leonard Reinhold. In proposing a theory regarding the process of representation in his work *A New Theory on the Human Capacity for Representation*, Reinhold defends the Kantian system. He contends, and correctly so, that the Kantian system is so unique that "it must be accepted or rejected in its entirety" (Reinhold 2011, p. 7). Due to its systematic structure, this is indeed the case. Reinhold also addresses the multitude of claims that the *Critique* is, as he notes, "incomprehensible" or contradictory. Though his refutation of these and other claims made against Kantian philosophy are not worth noting, what is important in his defense of Kant are two claims, the first controversial, the second subtle.

The latter claim builds a strong case against many who attacked the Kantian system. This is, notably, that "every philosopher who writes assumes something universally accepted" (Reinhold 2011, p. 30). This of course seems to be true and should not raise much alarm. However, in relation to the arguments

---

12 While it is *Sein und Zeit* which receives most consideration, Heidegger's other texts, in particular his work on art and on technology, have become increasingly popular as they offer a different perspective from the earlier works.
13 For a good overview of Kant's description of things in themselves, but which offers an interesting and refreshing interpretation, see Robert Merrihew Adams (1997) "Things in Themselves".

against Kantian philosophy, this claim pierces to the core. It is often assumed that something universally accepted must also be universally understandable – how can it be accepted if it is not understood? If, however, we consider that there are few if any universally accepted principles, would this not lead to the conclusion that it is difficult to recognize the universality of a principle when it is first proposed or claimed to be universal?

Indeed, novelty does not prosper immediately; confronted by a universal principle, one does not necessarily recognize its universality, this requires time and careful intellectual investigation. As Friedrich Schlegel wrote, "The mind understands something only insofar as it absorbs it like a seed into itself, nurtures it, and lets it grow into blossom and fruit" (1971, p. 241). Thus, by asserting this claim, Reinhold effectively suggests that critics do not understand Kantian philosophy, and more so, that Kant's philosophical system is meant to be incomprehensible until it is comprehended in its entirety. In other words, until the principles articulated in the *Critique* are recognized as universal, Kant's system cannot be understood.

For the purpose of this work, the first of these claims is more important. Reinhold calls into question everyone's understanding of the *Critique* and the claims made within it. He writes that "it is not *absolutely impossible* that the *Critique of Pure Reason* has been misunderstood just as much by its supporters as by its opponents" (Reinhold 2011, p. 10). This could be seen as quite a contentious claim; yet is it not always the case that supporters of a theory always believe that its opponents lack a complete understanding, and that they support it because they are in possession of this understanding? Recognizing the irony of doing so, this work also proposes that the *Critique*, and thus the entire Kantian system, has been misunderstood by supporters and opponents alike.

In fact, the present work intends a more contentious claim: that *Kant himself* misunderstood his system. That is to say, that the seeming contradictions of the Kantian system are due to a lack of consistency and follow-through, resulting from a resolution left unrecognized, yet present within the system. This will be discussed later, but suffice it here to note that while this work suggests new ideas and a novel approach, it also contends that these are only the outcome of a strict following of the Kantian system, and that had he himself stayed the course, Kant would have articulated much of what it contains.

Although some of Reinhold's own theories were considered important on their own merits, his work did not accomplish the task of defending Kant from his intellectual adversaries, though it is responsible for much of the success that the *Critique* received. In fact, by the time of Fichte's writings, which critiqued the Kantian system and in particular the *Ding an sich*, the Kantian system had already been considered to be positively refuted and shown to be contradictory by other writers, with perhaps the most influential of these being Gottlob Ernst Schulze.[14] Nevertheless, Fichte's works removed any lingering doubts that while Kant's transcendentalism could be praised for its attempt to systematize philosophy, it was not coherent, and as such new attempts must be made towards a systematic philosophy. Thus Fichte is rightly considered to be the father of German Idealism. Though the present work is not intended to be a survey of German Idealism, a quick glance at the treatment of a few central concepts from Kantian philosophy through his successors will help to establish the relationship between Kant and Heidegger, on which this work relies. These concepts are those of (a) the noumena/phenomena distinction and thus the thing-in-itself, as well as (b) consciousness.

With the notion of a noumenon, and more specifically a thing-in-itself, having been considered disproven by the likes of Schulze, Fichte seeks the grounding of consciousness elsewhere. In fact, Fichte holds that the grounding of consciousness is consciousness itself and that it needs no external *Ding an sich* to be grounded. Consciousness is grounded within and arises out of a recognition of itself. This conception of the "I" and its self-positing nature remains relatively stable in German Idealism and can be found up through Hegelian self-consciousness, particularly in reference to the dialectical nature of consciousness. Though the dialectical structure may have originated in Kant's and Fichte's writings, Hegel's development of it was certainly most crucial.[15] While Fichte's dialecticism left the synthesis in abstract form, Hegel's offered a negation, a rejection of the abstract, and left the synthesis in what he properly termed a concrete form. This concretization of the synthesis establishes a unity of self-consciousness and accounts for the very possibility of subjectivity.

Interestingly, however, Fichte did not reject the Kantian notion of a transcendental ego.[16] Fichte's so-called *pure ego* is very much like the Kantian transcendental ego. However, using the definition of *pure* from Kant, Fichte's ego is entirely abstracted away from empirical experience; it is, in essence, a proposal for

---

14 Schulze, an early critic of Kant, is most known for his work *Aenesidemus*, which was originally published in 1792. See, Gottlob Ernst Schulze (1996), *Aenesidemus, oder, Über die Fundamente der von dem Herrn Professor Reinhold in Jena gelieferten Elementar-Philosophie: nebst einer Verteidigung des Skeptizismus gegen die Anmassungen der Vernunftkritik*.
15 A wonderful discussion of Hegel's development of the dialectical structure can be found in Robert R. Williams (1992) *Recognition: Fichte and Hegel on the Other*.
16 What makes this intriguing is in Kant's systematic philosophy, the transcendental ego is not explicitly discussed, but rather is made clear and can be easily inferred from his conception of *noumena* and more precisely *positive noumena*. With Fichte's rejection of *noumena*, it would seem out of place to suggest a transcendental ego.

the *positive* noumena, which Kant suggests we lack, or at least he makes no claim of its existence. With this step, Fichte did two major things for the history of philosophy, and the development of Kantian philosophy in particular. On the one hand, he cemented the elimination of the thing-in-itself and noumena. Contrary to popular treatments, we will see that these are two distinct concepts in Kant.

Fichte rejected both; on the other hand, he emphasized the importance of a transcendental ego. By virtue of and in the process of the latter, Fichte also idealized the Kantian system, leading to the continuation and dominance of the idealism that Kant sought to fight. That is to suggest, then, that any philosophical system which keeps a transcendental ego in the absence of noumena, and specifically the *Ding an sich*, is necessarily idealist in its conception. This was the trend which persisted up until Heidegger's rejection of what he took to be the idealism of his teacher, Edmund Husserl. As George Nakhnikian articulates in his introduction to Husserl's *The Idea of Phenomenology*, Husserl claimed "that nothing can exist if it is not dependent for its existence on the transcendental self" (1964, p. xx). It was Heidegger's rejection of this principle which finally ended this idealist tendency, though certainly not entirely.

Yet it is important to recognize the necessity of the thing-in-itself, rather than simply discarding it as nonsensical or contradictory to the systematic philosophy which Kant devised. A closer reading of Kant, much indebted to Heidegger's own reading, reveals the non-contradictory nature of the thing-in-itself, and instead shows it to be not only coherent, but necessary. Thus, it can be said, the idealist trend of keeping the transcendental ego goes astray only insofar as it finds the grounding source of the transcendental ego to be unnecessary and so eliminates it; whereas Heidegger, in rejecting the transcendental ego as well, avoids this.

The question can very well be posed as to why Heidegger is at the heart of this work, though he may not take up the majority of its pages. Heidegger presents us with, what is in my opinion, the most complete manner of thinking about the kind of being we are.[17] Yet, due to his rejections of the Kantian system as stated previously, he envisions our being as a being in its immediacy. By defining this being as *Dasein* and providing the definition of "world" as one that is necessarily relational to this being as the description of "*da*," that is as to "where" this being is in terms of its "thereness," Heidegger's analytic is confined only to this world as he defines it. How would this analytic of *Dasein* look if the task was undertaken with the presumption of Kant's two worlds of noumena and phe-

---

17 A good commentary on Heidegger's conception of *die sache des Denken* can be found in John D. Caputo (1983) "The Thought of Being and the Conversation of Mankind: The Case of Heidegger and Rorty".

nomena? Or else, how would it be different if both the transcendental ego and *Ding an sich* were left intact?

It should hopefully be clear then that I am not aiming in this work simply to defend Kant's conception of a *Ding an sich* from being cast off, but to argue that in noting its necessity and finding how to fit the thing-in-itself back into contemporary philosophy, particularly through Heidegger's analytic of *Dasein*, we may be better positioned to complete Heidegger's task regarding *Dasein*. That is to suggest that had Heidegger, rather than simply breaking with the idealist trend through rejecting the transcendental ego, reconsidered the necessity of the *Ding an sich*, his analytic of *Dasein* would be entirely different from its current form.[18] Rather than an analytic of *Dasein* as *in-der-Welt-sein*, *Dasein* must be something more; *Dasein* is also, and most primarily so, *in-der-Weltlichkeit-sein*.

Thus, there are two central objectives which I intend to accomplish in Part One. The first is to show the necessity of the thing-in-itself in the Kantian system of transcendental idealism. The second is to argue that Heidegger's analytic of *Dasein* is incomplete since it deals only with an analysis of *Dasein* insofar as *Dasein* is ontic, that is, relational. In Part Two, an attempt shall be made to render a rethinking of the ontological foundations of humanness in setting up the possibility for a future philosophical anthropology.

Despite the aim of drafting an ontological analytic of *Dasein*, the only ontological claim regarding *Dasein* is, as it were, *Dasein* itself. That is to say that *Dasein* insofar as it is *Dasein*, exists in such a way as to be *in-der-Welt-sein*. However, the way in which *Dasein is in the world*, is ontical. *Zuhandenheit* and *Vorhandenheit* are both ontical relationships to the world, which I will argue is also necessarily relational in Heidegger, and as such ontic. Although Heidegger himself only treats *Zuhandenheit* as relational, *Vorhandenheit* must also be in constant relation. Insofar as we may treat the world as containing beings, it also contains the possibility of relationality and is, in fact, relationality itself. I hope to make clear in the following work that the world is itself relational, and as such, anything which can be said to be within the world necessarily stands in relation to everything else within the world. Therefore, even the mode of *Vorhandenheit* articulates some form of relationality. Heidegger's main analysis of *Dasein*, by placing *Dasein in the world*, is necessarily composing an analytic of the relationship of *Dasein* to the world – a world of relationality, an ontical one. This is due in no small part to Heidegger's conception and treat-

---

[18] David Carr provides an excellent commentary on the relationship between Heidegger and transcendental thought. See, David Carr (1994), "The Question of the Subject: Heidegger and the Transcendental Tradition".

ment of *world*, a solution to which can be found in a revisitation of Kant's *Ding an sich*.

By combining these two claims and re-envisioning the analytic of *Dasein* with the additional consideration of the thing-in-itself, I believe a truly ontological examination of *Dasein* is possible; that is, a fundamental ontology may well be completed. Nevertheless, this project only becomes possible upon successful integration of the thing-in-itself into the Heideggerian project on *Dasein*.

Although perhaps no longer at the forefront of philosophical debate, the problem of the thing-in-itself is certainly still very prominent. It permeates contemporary scholarship – even those whose intention is not to invoke the subject often find themselves doing so, or if not, they remain in conversation with the concept nonetheless. One particular movement of note, object-oriented ontology, brings noumena back into the conversation through a rejection of the anthropocentrism of Heideggerian philosophy. This specific philosophical position has been gaining popularity (either in agreement or in critique) in recent scholarship, mainly amongst Heidegger scholars, but also with Kant scholars.[19] Object-oriented ontology, however, has a major impact on philosophical anthropology, a field which is also receiving a fair share of attention in recent publications after remaining relatively sidelined for some time. This work finds itself well-positioned in both approaches, as it seeks not only to revisit Heidegger in light of object-oriented ontology and its efforts to retain noumena, as well as to serve as a groundwork for a philosophical anthropology.

The First chapter will begin with an introduction to speculative realism and object-oriented ontology and will confront the problem of emergence as it gets exemplified in these traditions. Following this, chapter Two will seek to further illustrate some of the problems with the rejection of correlationism which is fundamental to both the speculative realist traditions as a whole, and to object-oriented ontology as well. Emerging from the discussion of these first two chapters will be the conception of a new ontological model, spectral ontology, which, though sharing in many of the principles of object-oriented ontology, is rooted in a very different reading of Kant (and Heidegger), and which *requires* correlationism rather than seeks to eliminate it. In order to fully articulate the differences between object-oriented and spectral ontology and to make a case for the latter, it will be necessary to reevaluate humanness and correlationism through Heidegger and Kant, *vis-à-vis* the search for a fundamental ontology.

---

19 See for example, Andrew Cole (2013) "The Call of Things: A Critique of Object-Oriented Ontologies" and Peter Wolfendale (2014) *Object-Oriented Philosophy: The Noumenon's New Clothes* among others to be discussed later.

In the Third chapter, "The Search for the Grounding of Metaphysics", I aim to articulate Heidegger's concern with addressing "fundamental ontology" in particular as to its presence in the Kantian system. Heidegger claims in *Kant and the Problem of Metaphysics*, that Kant's system, especially in the first critique, is not, at its core epistemological, but rather ontological (1997). Furthermore, he argues that a fundamental ontology can be developed out of this system and its grounds. The question then becomes: where can this ground be found in Kant?

It must be remembered that a fundamental ontology is that ontology of *Dasein* which accounts for *Dasein's* being *Dasein;* it is the why, of the how, which is articulated through the very notion of *Dasein*. Thus, while it may initially seem to be the case that, if the theme of "world" and a new interpretation of Kantian worlds is the central goal, we may altogether avoid Heidegger's *Dasein*, it becomes all the more clear when dealing with the subject of a fundamental ontology, that *Dasein* cannot be removed from the discussion. As such, it is not as simple as illustrating the focal point of a fundamental ontology within the Kantian system and in the *Critique of Pure Reason*. Rather, the source of fundamental ontology in Kant must come through an analysis of Kant and his system, prior to the exploration of this fundamental ontology. It is only after this analysis of where a fundamental ontology can be drawn out of the Kantian system that one can evaluate *Dasein* as treated by Heidegger, and in doing so, recognize the need for a critique of humanness.

This Third chapter will therefore accomplish three goals. Initially, it sets forth the overall arc of investigation: namely, why a critique of what Heidegger calls the "finitude of reason" is necessary. Next, it examines the very preconditions of the phenomenology of *Dasein* that is found in Kant, predominantly, though not exclusively, space and time. Finally, it introduces the need to critically examine the various components of *Dasein* which stem from these preconditions: the finite, the infinite, the nonfinite, and the transcendental, which is the focus of chapters Four and Five.

The chapters Four (on the ontical modes of *Dasein*) and Five (on the ontological modes of *Dasein*) seek to locate within the Kantian system the way in which *Dasein* is fundamentally; that is to say, how does *Dasein* get articulated in Kant? From a close reading of Kant, it is clear that a finitude of *Dasein* is expressed insofar as reason relies on the sensible. In this way, *Dasein* is seen as a phenomenon. However, *pure reason* stretches beyond the sensible and towards an infinite, and thus it may be said to articulate the infinitude of *Dasein*. Additionally, through introducing noumena, Kant proposes an aspect of *Dasein* which is nonexistent in Heidegger's *Dasein*. It is, as Heidegger would note, *in the world,* yet it is not a phenomenon and as such non-sensory. It can therefore be called non-finite. Finally, *Dasein* can be said to be transcendental, insofar as a transcendental ego exists.

This rethinking of *Dasein* in terms of its finitude, infinitude, nonfinitude, and transcendental aspects leads to the discussion of the "Metaphysics of *Dasein*", the focus of Chapter Six. It is in this chapter that the various components of *Dasein* in Heidegger's articulation, such as *Sorge*, *zuhanden*, and *vorhanden*, are evaluated. However, this apparent review of Heidegger's analysis of *Dasein* aims not at summarization, but at setting up discussion of *objects* and *world*. Thus, at its end, Chapter Three accomplishes its task of leading to the discussion of humanness in Part Two by rethinking objects and the very concept of world.

Chapter Seven takes as its starting point the concept of humanness. The chapter explores the notion of "world" and the way that objects can be said to relate to the world. Furthermore, it seeks to examine how objects might also be nonrelational. To do so, object-oriented ontology will be explored and evaluated as a possible solution or at the very least a new starting point. It is in this chapter where I propose a nonrelational nonbeing which I call aptitudes.

Chapter Eight develops the concept and engages in a delimitation of it with the aim of formulating it into a new method of doing philosophy; a new methodology which begins from a philosophical anthropology and extends outward. The outcome of the chapter is the proposition and the prospect of a complete philosophical anthropology, from which this new philosophical system may originate.

Chapter One
The Rise of the Speculative and the Problem of Humanness

Celui qui n'a égard en écrivant qu'au goût de son siècle songe plus à sa personne qu'à ses écrits: il faut toujours tendre à la perfection, et alors cette justice qui nous est quelquefois refusée par nos contemporains, la postérité sait nous la rendre.
– Jean de La Bruyère (1836, p. 37)

The concept of humanness at first appears to be rooted in philosophy of the person, or philosophical anthropology and to be of little to no consequence to the problems of "world", "correlationism", and of "object" which are found in most all philosophical treatises of the last two decades. For these problems are the problems of ontology and epistemology, primary fields of study upon which all other philosophical questions can be phrased, answers sought, and thoughts formed. Humanness as a concept poses no possible threat to these problems and needs little to no attention paid to it until we have first set forth our questions and postulations of the ontological and epistemological groundings for such other concerns.

This is what one might believe if they were to pick up any of the great works on these problems which have been written since the time of Descartes, originating in his thesis of mind-body dualism. Indeed, it is something which was not only believed and accepted, but assumed and which permeated throughout philosophical works over the last several centuries since. Even those who broke with the Cartesian separation between thought and extension, such as Spinoza who noted "*Et consequenter quod substantia cogitans et substantia extensa una eademque est substantia*" (1905, p. 32–33), were nonetheless committed intimately to the concern of subjectivity and so thus Descartes' influence lived on through the subject-object distinction. Heidegger broke the reliance on the Cartesian way in his *Sein und Zeit* as he examined "world" and critically dismantled the subject-object distinction, revealing instead that, we too, are objects. Although Heidegger's phenomenological approach to 'world' resulted in an overturning of a centuries long reliance on Cartesian dualism, it nonetheless could not escape one of its primary features: privileging the human being. This is clear throughout Heidegger's work, but comes to the front in a very particular passage in which the human serves as the interpreter of Being:

> *We are too late for the gods*
> *and too early for being*
> *being's poem, just begun, is man.*
> (Heidegger 2001, p. 4)

Philosophy was once again overturned at the end of the 20th century when Graham Harman, in his 1999 thesis *Tool-Being*, noted this Cartesian heritage of Heidegger and argued that when the human being is privileged, there can be no undoing of the dualism of Descartes in any real way.[20] In other words, so long as we are privileging *Dasein*, we are never truly escaping the subject-object distinction, even if we attempt to position ourselves against it by eliminating the subject and treating everything as an object. If we want to break from the tradition, if we want to make everything an object, we must do away with the traditional roles of "world" and "interlocutor" as well. In short, Harman sought to even the playing field, establishing a flat ontology of objects.

Not quite a decade later, there was another thinker cast on the philosophical "hot seat" awaiting trial. This time it was Kant who was seen as a propagator and introducer of a related but different thread woven within philosophical systems since his transcendental idealism influenced many in its wake. In 2008, Quentin Meillassoux published *After Finitude*, in which he termed this thread "correlationism" and articulated its presence in post-Kantian thought, but also expressed the necessity of eliminating correlationism in order to completely eradicate privileging subjectivity. This spawned the re-dawning of realism cast in a new light – one that is purely speculative.

Speculative Realism and The Problem of Emergence

Correlationism was defined by Meillassoux as "the idea according to which we only ever have access to the correlation between thinking and being, and never to either term considered apart from the other" (2008, p. 5). This position

---

[20] Others had of course emphasized the need to eradicate anthropocentric frameworks. Jeremy Bentham in *An Introduction to the Principles of Morals and Legislation* (1879, p. 311) wrote: "A full-grown horse or dog, is beyond comparison a more rational, as well as a more conversable animal, than an infant of a day or a week or even a month, old." Stephen Jay Gould (1992, p. 91) advocated that one of the main benefits to scientific exploration is that "it reformulates our view of the world by imposing powerful theories against the ancient, anthropocentric prejudices that we call intuition." However, Harman's fight is not just against anthropocentrism but against the subject-object distinction as a whole – that is, against the privileging of any object over the other in their ontological footing in the world.

results in the Cartesian mode of thought that privileges the human orientation of the world; what can be known about the world is only as it appears to the perceiver – subjectivity reigns supreme.[21] In rejecting this interpretation of Kantian philosophy grounded in the German Idealist tradition, Meillassoux denies the idealist thesis in favor of a realist one in which the world outside of the perceiver is itself independent. But like the idealism of Fichte, Schelling and the like, it is *speculative*.

Thus speculative realism seeks in general, whether it be Meillassoux's speculative materialism, Harman's object-oriented ontology or any of the other renditions of the movement, to reduce the anthropocentrism of post-Kantian philosophy (and even philosophy since Descartes). But what is the root of the correlationism that Meillassoux, Harman, et al., find problematic? Cartesian dualism is certainly one aspect of correlationism, however, it is also more closely found in the problem of emergence.

Emergence is a central concern for speculative realist philosophies, and is often discussed in terms of its ontological influence in relation to how rethinking emergence allows for a more descriptive flat ontology. In considering more in-depth the relationship between emergence and correlationism, it becomes clear that with the problem of emergence, there is more at stake than simply ontology – it offers an epistemological problem rooted in correlationism and Kantian philosophy as well. Meillassoux begins *After Finitude* with the claim that sensible qualities (secondary qualities) are merely *relational* qualities, as opposed to qualities of the object. Let us too, begin there and seek out the meaning of this for Meillassoux, how it ignites correlationism, and recognize the flaw in Meillassoux's conception of *relation* as it ignores emergence.

Insofar as any encountered object in the world has properties of which it is composed, be they primary or secondary, such an object is its properties. Each object is precisely its mass, its extension, etc., and also, it is its color, flavor, size, etc. While it is true, as Locke noted,[22] that secondary qualities do not belong to the thing itself on a general level – redness does not belong to "apple" – it is

---

21 As Kierkegaard noted: "it is only in subjectivity that its truth exists, if it exists at all" (2019, p. 116).
22 In his *Essay Concerning Human Understanding*, Locke discusses the relationship between the secondary qualities and the object in terms of "power" and "degree". He also notes that it is not possible to determine the nature of the coexistence between the two, indicating that secondary qualities do not belong as such to the object itself. He writes (1824, p.109): "or of all the qualities that are co-existent in any subject, without this dependence and evident connexion of their ideas one with another, we cannot know certainly any two to co-exist any farther than experience, by our senses, informs us."

nonetheless inaccurate as it explains the world of particulars: redness does in fact belong as an essential property to a particular apple. As we can well note by considering any particular object, what property might be nonessential to the category of objects to which that object belongs, it remains entirely essential to that object itself.

Here we can imagine a book. Two identical copies of a book in terms of its primary qualities (same mass, same content, etc.) but different in their secondary qualities (more or less pages, different translation/language, different cover) result in the two copies being different "books" even if they are the same "book" (i.e., the same text). It is the same in the general sense but not in the particular. So Locke is only partially correct in his assertion of the essentiality of primary qualities and the nonessentiality of secondary qualities. But it is here that we encounter the problem of emergence and in many ways an explicit origin of correlationism, which predates the speculative idealism of the 19th century. For we now must consider the origin of these secondary qualities, how they came to be, and to examine the relevance of these qualities to the thing itself.

It was, for Locke, the case that secondary qualities were nonessential properties of objects because they can change without the object itself altering in any significant way. As already noted, Locke was thinking of general categories of objects, since changes in these qualities do indeed change the object. But we can further this by noting that secondary qualities are not qualities of the object but of the perceiver. Color, for instance, is nothing more than the way an object is being perceived and has little to no value to the object itself – it does not belong to the object but is impressed upon it by the perceiver who, in their mode of perception, recognizes this or that color as being a property of the object, though its origin rests only with themselves.[23] This is precisely why it is an essential quality of the perceived object. To change a secondary quality is to change the perception of the object, and to therefore change the perceived object.

Locke is entirely correct then, to assert the essentiality of primary qualities to objects themselves, but wrong to claim secondary qualities too, belong to that same object. An object can only ever have primary qualities – an object is what it is because of the primary qualities that make it so. There are no such elements to call secondary qualities. Any quality which belongs to an object is pri-

---

[23] Or as we read in Douglas Adams' novel *Mostly Harmless*: "'Everything you see or hear or experience in any way at all is specific to you. You create a universe by perceiving it, so everything in the universe you perceive is specific to you'" (1993, p. 111).

mary insofar as it makes it the object that it is.[24] There are, however, two different objects with which we must distinguish: the object itself and the perceived object.

Not unlike Kant's own distinction between the *Ding an Sich* and the appearance of that thing to a perceiver, here we speak of objects only to better fit with the contemporary work following the speculative turn in realism by the likes of Harman, Meillassoux, Garcia, and others. The object itself is only ever what it is and any *thing*, or any property, that belongs to it by virtue of its being what it is, is a necessary and essential property which we call primary in Locke's sense. Any property of an object itself is by necessity and is therefore primary insofar as each property of the object itself is essential to the object being as it is.

That which we have, until now, called secondary qualities (or properties) do not belong to the object as essential, as has been the case since Locke. But to further this to the extended view articulated here, that those properties which we term secondary qualities do not belong to the object *at all in any case*, we need to reconsider the perceived object. When an object is perceived by a perceiver, there arises from this perception a new object, a *perceived* object. Attached to this perceived object are not merely the primary qualities of the object itself which are perceived as they are picked up by the perceiver, but also qualities which are subsequently added to the object *vis-à-vis* perception and representation. What we used to term secondary qualities then, are in fact primary qualities; they belong essentially to the perceived object. To alter any of these qualities will by necessity change the perceived object in a very essential way – if a perceived object, for instance, a green apple, was changed red, the perceived object would be a red apple as opposed to a green apple.

Although these are the same *object* they are different *perceived objects*. The "red apple" as a perceived object is fundamentally different from a "green apple" as a perceived object, even if the object itself is the same on a fundamental level. To make this distinction more clear we must consider two additional factors: 1) How the perceived object differs from the object itself and 2) is this distinction the result of a distinction between objects, properties of objects, or something else entirely?

For Meillassoux, the perceived object is different from the object itself simply because it is precisely the representation of the object itself from a subjective perception. The object itself stands alone, independent of perception, but the

---

24 Issac Newton indicated something similar in *Opticks* in discussing light rays and color: "For the rays, to speak properly, are not coloured. In them there is nothing else than a certain power and disposition to stir up a sensation of this or that colour" (1704, p. 90).

perceived object requires it – the perceived object is only ever the product of a relation between the subject and the object, the object and the perceiver. The relationship between the object itself and the perceived object becomes at best like that of Platonic Forms, in that the perceived object is an imperfect copy of the object itself, it lacks the whole being of the object itself. At worst, the perceived object becomes nearly imaginary.[25]

Yet, if this distinction is the result of *relations*, and the object itself is simply the object as it is on its own, without being perceived by a perceiver, there arises a problem in dealing with emergence. How do emergent properties of an object arise from an object itself? Emergent properties are usually bound by relationality – they either arise out of necessity or adaptability, and sometimes even spontaneously.[26] But in every circumstance an emergent property is a relational one – regardless of a perceiver separate from the object itself.

Meillassoux, and others who follow this path, have two options to confront the problem of emergence. It is an impractical solution to assert that there are no emergent properties, which leaves only one possible way out: potency. Emergent properties must be always already within the object itself, a potency that becomes actualized. In such a case, an object itself, without the necessitation of a perceiver or any sort of relationality, can have emergent properties which are at first contained within its own being and which are brought out by the entirety of its being when taken as an object in itself. That is to say, it is a property that is simply *dormant* in the object itself, but which emerges within relations. Such a solution might provide an acceptable account of emergence if it did not rest on a hidden relation overlooked.

Any emergent property is by necessity a relational property. There can be no emergent property of an object outside of relations. Even a dormant emergent property, can only be rightly called a property if it is present as relation. Insofar as emergent properties become *activated* only through relation, they must also only ever be properties of an object in relation. An emergent property that is a potency is not really a property of the object at all, until it becomes actualized. Potencies are not properties – an acorn does not have the properties of an oak tree, even though it does have those properties as potencies. Nonetheless, within the acorn itself, these potencies are not properties.

If emergent properties become properties only ever when actualized in the object of which they are emergent properties, and emergent properties are by ne-

---

[25] Of course, we must also keep in mind Emerson's words that "Science does not know its debt to imagination" (1904, p. 10).
[26] "*Mais quand une règle est fort composée, ce qui lui est conforme, passe pour irrégulier*" writes Leibniz (1907, p. 33)

cessity relational, then the object itself can have no emergent properties. We can take, for example, lungs. Lungs are made up of many individual cells, none of which have the property of holding oxygen and sending it through the bloodstream. However, in combination, all of these individual cells as a lung holds this property as emergent. But here we have two objects: cells and lungs. Furthermore, we can say that the cells have the potency for the emergent property of containing and transmitting oxygen, but not that the cells as an object possess such a property. This emergent property is actualized only in the amalgamation of cells as a lung, the cell as an object itself does not have such a property.

Yet, the lung is an object distinct from the cell. Simply because it is the combination of smaller objects, the lung too is an object itself. If the lung as an object itself has the emergent property of transmitting and holding oxygen, then Meillassoux avoids the problem of emergence. But when we think more critically of an emergent property, does the lung *have* this property independent of its relationality, as an object itself? Should a lung be placed on the table in front of you, does it contain the property of holding and transmitting oxygen? Surely it has the potential for such a property to be actualized, if it were to be put inside a body. Yet, on its own, as an object itself, it possesses nothing of the sort. Emergent properties are relational properties, not properties of objects in themselves. If emergent properties are, like secondary qualities, rooted in relation, what problem does this pose for Meillassoux and the other speculative realists?

To identify this problem we can turn to object-oriented ontology frontrunner, Graham Harman. For Harman and object-oriented ontology in general, accounting for emergence is a central concern. It could, in fact, be seen as one of the most primary concerns as indicated by the length at which it is discussed in theories of speculative realism. In the case of Harman, emergence arises as a concern in rejection of what he terms undermining. Undermining occurs when objects are seen as reducible to smaller substances which underlie them, which Harman argues treats objects as secondary and those underlying substances as primary (2011, p. 8-10). If all objects are reducible to smaller "parts" or substances,[27] and are thus treated as secondary, it not only devalues the object itself, but also, according to Harman, does not allow for an account of emergence on this smallest

---

27 Harman's concern here can be traced to the influence of Aristotle, who in the *Metaphysics* also noted that when amalgamated, parts become a new whole: "For all things that have more than one part, and of which the sum is not like a heap, but a whole that is something over and above the parts" (2002, p. 163). The original Greek reads "πάντων γὰρ ὅσα πλείω μέρη ἔχει καὶ μή ἐστιν οἷον σωρὸς τὸ πᾶν ἀλλ' ἔστι τι τὸ ὅλον παρὰ τὰ μόρια" (*Metaphysics* 1045a 8–10).

scale. The smallest substance underlying any object would need to have all essential properties of the object, leaving no room for any account of emergence.

Any speculative realist approach, then, must be wary of the trap of undermining any object. Although theorists in this tradition go to great lengths to give an account of emergence which aligns with the basic principles of speculative realism, the aim of accounting for emergence and avoiding undermining seems to run contrary to the aim of eliminating correlationism. To recognize the contradictory aims requires only a reconsidering of the meaning of correlation as Meillassoux defines it in the post-Kantian philosophical oeuvre, and the way emergence works in its actualization within the whole of an object as dictated previously.

Correlationism, Relations, and Emergence

Correlationism as defined by Meillassoux is often considered to be a reflection of philosophical thought post-Kant, beginning with Fitche's elimination of the *Ding an Sich* and the turn to idealism following this trend. Nonetheless, Kant himself recognized the essentiality of correlationism – for Kant did not reject the basic principle of correlationism, but only had the addition of the "real", thing-in-itself, to his correlationist system. Objects for Kant are always filtered through perception and the relations within which they are perceived. The object itself is never available to the perceiver and so his system is ultimately limited to the correlation between thought and being.

The reintroduction of the object itself in speculative realist traditions seeks to overturn the reliance on correlationism. Yet what is overlooked in the 'speculative' turn, is the trade-off necessary to account for the dismantling of correlationism. Absent correlationism, there is no way to account for emergence that does not rely on some form of undermining of the object. We can here briefly recount what has been said about emergence to recognize the limitations that can be found in the speculative path.

Emergence, as before stated, relies on relation – emergent properties are necessarily relational properties, not properties of the object itself, but rather properties which emerge from its relations. It may at first appear that in a realist tradition eliminating correlationism has no impact on emergent properties of objects as they stand in relation, since that relation is independent of the *thought* behind correlationism (thought thinking being). Regardless or independent of the *thought*, the emergent properties of the object *are*. However, reflecting on our previous example of a lung will make it clear that doing so requires *undermining* the object in favor of its relations.

As already stated, a lung that is made up of many individual cells exhibits the emergent property of taking in, holding, and circulating oxygen throughout the bloodstream, despite none of the individual cells determining its make-up possessing such a property. Emergence and emergent properties ought to stand as a signifier of an object itself, distinguishing it from the undermining that often begets it as object. For what is a lung other than what it is made of – many tiny individual cells? Such a designation is deeply entrenched in the undermining of the lung as an object. But the emergent property of the transmission of oxygen offers a different approach to distinguish the lung from the cells of which it is made, a method of its being determined an object on equal footing.

But what is such an emergent property is not merely another undermining of the object of which it is an emergent property? For the emergent property is not the object itself but merely a function of the object. This type of reductionism – which is the opposite of the other form – Harman calls overmining. Although the rejection of correlationism escapes undermining the object, it remains tightly bound with overmining, if indeed it seeks to hold any account of emergence. Meillassoux's speculative materialism here gets entrapped, yet Harman's object-oriented ontology offers an attempt at reprieve – an account of emergence that avoids overmining the object. Unfortunately, as we will see, Harman's account of emergence arises new issues which Harman cannot, nor can any speculative realist, address without rethinking ontological foundations.

In his battle against overmining, Harman notes that doing so leaves no room for emergence. What does Harman's object-oriented ontology offer instead? In some sense Harman returns to the notion of primary and secondary qualities, though he terms them *real* and *sensual*.[28] Every object (*real or sensual*) possesses both *real* and *sensual* qualities, just as Locke might note all objects hold primary and secondary qualities. The real qualities are those that can be recognized and intuited only via intellect, whereas sensual qualities, Harman argues, can be experienced. If indeed Harman offers an account of emergence that is able to truly avoid overmining, it must be as a property of a real object with sensual qualities.

It cannot be the case that emergence falls within the pairing of a real object and real qualities – although the real qualities which are attributed to real objects assist in differentiating real objects such that object-oriented ontology can maintain all objects on an equal footing, emergent properties are not merely intuited via the intellect. That said, emergent properties also therefore cannot be a part of a sensual object with real qualities. As stated emergent properties must be

---

[28] Although I will be discussing this manifold of object-oriented ontology throughout this work, for Harman's own detailed treatment see *The Quadruple Object* (2011, p. 49–50).

sensual, not real. In any case, with the pairing of sensual objects and real qualities, Harman accounts for underlying structures of objects of experience, something which first requires emergent properties to be previously accounted for.

The only remaining option would be sensual objects with sensual qualities, but this too requires emergent properties to have already been accounted for, since this pairing is mostly regarding classifications of experience. In other words, it is this pairing that enables us to truly navigate the world of objects around us as each sensual object's sensual qualities creates "profiles" of that object, a way to classify it. Without classification of objects in the mind, we could not make sense of the world and would have no way of making our way in the world. Absent this pairing of sensual objects and sensual qualities, which in many ways grounds our perceived "real world", we would be left to return to the words of the Romanian-French poetic Princess[29] "*Il n'est rien de réel que la rêve et l'amour*" (1901, p. 163).

In the case of a real object with sensual qualities, an object which is akin to the Kantian thing-in-itself, has qualities that are translated into those which can be sensed *vis-à-vis* either the intellect or an action. Kant himself was reluctant to give things-in-themselves any ability to be sensed, even indirectly as in the case here with Harman. Yet if emergent properties can be accounted for, it would only make sense that it is the emergent properties of a real object which are made sensible, thus allowing for the pairing of a real object with sensible qualities.

But does this really overcome the problem of overmining or undermining? Does it address the problem that was noted above in primary and secondary qualities? Although Harman's real object with sensual qualities might provide a necessary account of emergence, it fails to recognize the limitation of sensual qualities for real objects. Emergent properties are, as mentioned, relational properties, and sensual qualities are relational qualities – relational, in this case, to other objects real or sensual. Yet this defeats the entire push of Harman and speculative realists to overcome idealism.

Insofar as a real object with sensual qualities can account for emergent properties, which themselves must stand in some relation with other objects, such properties drag real objects themselves into relation – for if the emergent properties are properties of the object and yet stand in relation, than so too must the object be in some relation. The real object then, cannot be said to es-

---

[29] The Romanian-French poet Anna de Noailles was born Princess Anna Elisabeth Bibesco-Bassaraba de Brancovan. The line quoted is taken from her poem "Chanson du Temps opportun" from her first collection *Le Cœur Innombrable*.

cape relation if there is to be an adequate account of emergence in object-oriented ontology or in Speculative Realism.

In such a case, there are two options:
1. object-oriented ontology and speculative realism must disregard emergence as a purely relational aspect of objects and as such it holds no place among the real object;
2. object-oriented ontology and speculative realism do not offer what is promised – a realist ontology.

Considering the importance of emergence, the former will also pose further problems that object-oriented ontology and speculative realists would need to address. As such, I will here focus on the second option, which I believe to be more accurate.

Object-oriented ontology and speculative realism have claimed that objects can exist independent of relations, specifically in rejection of the thesis of correlationism: thinking equals being. Yet the rejection of this thesis does not result in a realism to separate thinking from being, nor does it give an opportunity to treat the being as independent of that which thinks it. This basic premise of object-oriented ontology and speculative realism is flawed. Even though it seems as if this severance would be required, it is in fact, the other way – the correlation is necessary. Realism is not to be found absent correlationism, but within it, spawned from it. Correlationism provides the necessary foundation for realism to be grounded and without it, realism cannot be footed.

As I will here argue, it is not possible to have a *speculative realism*, but rather only a *speculative nominalism*. To arrive at a realism we must first *dethrone* the speculative. It will be the spark that lights a fire. "*Poca favilla gran fiamma seconda*" as Dante wrote in *The Divine Comedy, Paradiso* (1921, p. 4).

Speculative Nominalism

It is imperative to first show that what is called speculative realism is in fact, merely speculative nominalism. Nominalism as a metaphysical position holds that only particulars and not universals have a true reality. It will undoubtedly be argued that the speculative realist position, and object-oriented ontology in particular, has a clear *résistance* to nominalism – a claim which I do not here seek to deny. There are indeed many claims and arguments in object-oriented ontology and speculative realism which reject nominalist positions. However, what I aim to show here is that there are contradictions within these positions, and ultimately speculative realism and object-oriented ontology cannot escape the binds of nominalism with their current line of thought.

In his article "Materialism is not the solution" (2015), Harman specifically argues against two different approaches to materialistic thought: nominalistic and holistic. In referencing Lake Michigan as an object he writes against nominalism that "The scientific lake would treat it nominalistically as just a nickname for a series of varying collections of water that have enough family resemblances over time that we can call it 'Lake Michigan' in a loose and only a loose sense" (Harman 2015, p. 97). Here Harman attacks nominalism as a form of reductionism – or undermining – as it treats the object of "Lake Michigan" entirely as the individual bits of water droplets from which it is composed. When enough droplets are added to a location we term it a lake, puddle, river, pond, ocean, etc. A number of small objects combine into a larger object, something Harman would not reject if it did not diminish the treatment of the larger object at hand.

But likewise, focusing entirely on the larger object, be it lake, river or puddle, is a holistic approach that remains materialistic and as such, reductive, for Harman. He writes on this "the holistic position would treat it as just a zone of relative lakeness, one that is basically continuous with neighboring lakes and with the shore" (ibid., p. 97). This leaves "Lake Michigan" as merely the object "lake", indistinguishable save for perception from those other objects which share in such a designation of "lake". Any particular lake is only individualized insofar as it is perceived in one instance, whereas another lake is so only in another. Nonetheless, any and all entities which fulfill the criteria for a designation as an object "lake" are thus reduced to being the generalized object of "lake" without any individuated consideration. The ocean is a more interesting case since it is both plural and singular. There are several oceans, but all of them are merely one ocean divided only by determined boundaries and language. Of the ocean(s) we may say: "*Vieil océan, tu es le symbole de l'identité: toujours égal à toi-même*" (de Lautréamont 1874, p. 24).

Harman summarizes his critique of these two forms of materialistic reductionism in the following way:

> What both materialisms miss is the way in which the lake cuts itself off from its neighbors and its own causal components, allowing a certain degree of entry and exit to all the forces of the non-lake, but remaining a form that endures for some time even if not eternally. The lake endures until other entities actually do the significant and not inevitable work of destroying or changing it (Harman 2015, p.97).

Given what Harman notes here, which also appears in his other work as well, it is clear the critique that is offered against nominalism (namely that it is reductive and unfairly treats the object). How then, and in what way, does object-oriented ontology nevertheless fall into nominalist tendencies?

In no way should Harman be read in what is quoted above as stating that only "Lake Michigan" is the object worthy of being labeled and considered as such. To state such would be against the main agenda of object-oriented ontology, which is to equally treat all objects. In the above effort to critique the two materialist positions, Harman offers the middle ground not in contradistinction to the two (though it is argued in such a way that it appears so), but as an addition. For object-oriented ontology, it is true that "Lake Michigan" is itself an object that must be treated independently of the amalgamatory droplets of water which comprise it. Yet, it must also be the case that the individual water droplets composing the object "Lake Michigan" are also objects; they are objects of equal importance and standing, neither "Lake Michigan" nor "water droplet" holding a privileged position of esteemed consideration as objects.

Here it might be worthwhile to explicate however briefly on the disagreement between Harman and Meillassoux in this regard. As mentioned, speculative realism, as it has been termed, shares a distaste for correlationism, but this does not mean all under its banner think alike. In fact, even with the posed problem of correlationism itself Harman and Meillassoux are on different paths. Meillassoux escapes correlationism only by indirectly confronting the thing-in-itself which is ultimately equated with primary qualities and for Meillassoux this means mathematical properties. A determined idealist, Žižek criticizes Meillassoux on this very aspect claiming instead that there is no escaping correlationism and rearticulates its thesis (and the one offered by Kant in the *Critique of Pure Reason*) that by thinking the thing-in-itself, you bring it into relations and it ceases to be a thing-in-itself. Žižek writes that "it is not enough to oppose transcendental correlation to a vision of reality-in-itself–transcendental correlation itself has to be grounded in reality-in-itself; i.e., its possibility has to be accounted for in the terms of this reality" (2012, p. 643).

Harman, however, critiques Meillassoux as a comrade against correlationism through an extension of this Kantian paradigm; Harman concedes the unknowability of the thing-in-itself absent human "thing-in-itself" relations, but takes it further to suggest that objects themselves remain a mystery from one another. The object itself (here to be read as a thing-in-itself), so long as it remains so and as such absent relations, is unknown not only to the human perceiver, but also to the object perceiver. In other words, for Harman, the world is comprised of a bunch of objects themselves which are mysterious and unknown to the world of objects at large, apart from the way they engage with those other objects through relationality.

Returning to "Lake Michigan" and "water droplet" as objects both worthy of treatment as objects in themselves, we must also note, in consideration of Harman's critique of Meillassoux *vis-à-vis* extension of the Kantian thesis on the thing-in-itself, that the two objects themselves remain untethered to one another: they remain unknown the one from the other. Even when the "water droplet" is added to "Lake Michigan", the former does not become, if Harman's position is to hold consistent, a part of the latter except in terms of the sensual object "water droplet" which through relations entered into with "Lake Michigan" becomes recognized as a part of "Lake Michigan". Yet, the objects themselves ("real objects" in Harman's terminology) remain forever distinct, untouched, and unknown; they are as distant from each other as if they always were even before their sensual counterparts entered into relations at all.

This position at the heart of object-oriented ontology has been called by Harman himself "weird realism" for obvious reasons. But if this is a realism, it is beyond weird – it is something else altogether, a non-realist realism, a contradiction.[30] We have already discussed the problem of emergence as it relates to speculative realism and object-oriented ontology, and where it must be found in Harman's division of sensual and real objects and qualities. It would not require much to take what has been said and apply it to Harman's example of "Lake Michigan" above to see the problem faced as previously articulated. As such, I will leave this to the reader and instead focus on two different, more difficult and interesting problems arising from the above example, leading me to suggest it positions Harman in a less realist manner than he, and other speculative realists, believe.

My claim here is simple: speculative realism and object-oriented ontology are both forms of nominalism. In truth, this is a partially unfair claim against the two, particularly against object-oriented ontology, as they do make realist claims within their given positions; however, their system as a whole appears quite nominalistic. This is why object-oriented ontology and speculative realism appear as a "weird" form of realism – "weird realism"[31] might simply be a misnomer that could more accurately be termed nominalistic realism (a contradiction, as noted above). I here wish to note that my objective is not to entirely uproot object-oriented ontology and speculative realism generally, since I myself fall into a parallel camp that shares the same general foundations and objec-

---

30 Although contradiction can be helpful and embraced, it must be recognized and called-out as such for it to be so. Left unrecognized it becomes an error. Instead, contradiction, if we are to allow for it, should be met with as Whitman meets with it in "Song of Myself" from *Leaves of Grass:* "Do I contradict myself? Very well then I contradict myself" (1882, p. 78).
31 The title of Harman's 2012 book is *Weird Realism: Lovecraft and Philosophy*.

tives. Indeed, there are many claims within object-oriented ontology and speculative realism that I find myself drawn to and which pave the way for my own thought. Instead, I seek here only to consider the seemingly contradictory treatment of objects, the reasons for this arisen contradiction, and to offer a resolution, a different path – one departing from a point of agreement between myself, Harman, and other speculative realism thinkers, but which avoids this mistaken treatment of objects.

Chapter Two
Dethroning the Speculative

In the preceding chapter I have made the claim that speculative realism and object-oriented ontology are ultimately nominalistic-realist systems and never venture into the true realism that they aspire to. In this chapter I will examine the source of this claim and how we might circumvent the trap in order to develop the central theses of speculative realism and object-oriented ontology into a realist system. Let us begin then by first considering how object-oriented ontology can be read as nominalistic. It was shown that Harman in *The Quadruple Object* rejected nominalistic thought as a form of reductionism, a claim that is understandable given the emphasis on particularity in the nominalist position. However, I do not think nominalism to be reductionist as Harman claims and his belief that it is so, might ultimately lead object-oriented ontology into its own form of nominalism anyway.

Nominalism as a system of thought emerged among ancient Greek philosophers against the realist system proposed through the medium of Platonic forms. Chrysippus, a stoic following and expanding upon the tradition of Zeno, is generally considered as the forerunner of nominalism – though it appears in Stoicism at large. For these philosophers, universals were nothing but illusory conceptions born of the mind and only the particulars were considered real. Objects are encountered via sense perception which then enables the object to be presented to the mind. Many things can be presented to the mind but only the objects which stand as particulars have an existence external to the mind – *this* person, *this* tree, *this* apple, etc.[32] The Platonic realism of forms, of universals (*personness, treeness, appleness*, etc.), was vehemently argued against.

Yet, for all the appearance of Platonic thought which object-oriented ontology seems to find itself intertwined with, it is not a Platonic system. There are many facets of Platonic ontology which object-oriented ontology does not find agreeable. One of these aspects lies in Platonic forms – that which makes Platonism realist and in favor of universals. Considering the way Platonic forms appear to be "withdrawn" from relations, existing in the perfect world of forms, one might assume that these forms are akin to Harman's real object. Although the

---

[32] Nietzsche, perhaps counter-intuitively, held views that contrasted with this. In "On Truth and Lying" he wrote: "if we had, each taken singly, a varying sensory perception, we could see now like a bird, now like a worm, now like a plant; or if one of us saw the same stimulus as red, another as blue, while a third heard it even as a sound, then no one would speak of such a regularity of nature" (1989, p. 253).

two share some commonalities, there is a major distinction to be made: forms are distinct from the object itself, whereas the real object is nothing but the object itself.

We must keep in mind that for Harman there are real objects of two sorts, with sensual or real qualities. The former is more akin to Platonic forms, since they do have sensual qualities otherwise we would not recognize them in the sensual objects we experience for Plato. This is why forms seem similar to real objects, they are indeed a type of real object, but they are "real objects with sensual qualities". In other words, they are not truly withdrawn to the extent of Harman's real object with real qualities.

The real differentiation between Platonic forms and Harman's real object with real qualities is not merely the sensual, relational qualities. Harman's object-oriented ontology, to the extent that it can be called Platonic, can also be noted for its Aristotelian influence, which might even be stronger in many ways. *Contra* the Platonic structure, Harman writes in *Tool-Being*, Aristotle "famously contends that the substance of a genus or species is *not* separate from that of its individual" something not unfamiliar to object-oriented ontology's structure (2002, p. 270). Yet of course object-oriented ontology is a post-Heideggerian project and so, as Harman summarizes the foundation of object-oriented ontology against its predecessors, "Heidegger aims to pay tribute to the concealed second world of tool-being, while Aristotle wants to implode Plato's second world into the first" (2002, p. 271).

Harman paves a different route to confront the realist position of Plato, merging Aristotle's and Heidegger's aims. Although object-oriented ontology favors Heidegger to Aristotle, it is worth noting that Harman, like Aristotle, seeks to bring the one into the other – real objects (regardless of whether they have real or sensual qualities) are a part of this world. There is nothing like a Platonic world of forms in object-oriented ontology which serves as the 'home' of real objects. The infrastructure of the world "must be made up of *tools in a vacuum*", Harman (2002, p. 296) writes in closing his work. Yet, this "vacuum" is not *otherworldly* as the world of Forms, or as in the two-worlds interpretation of Kantian things-in-themselves, nor the many worlds of dreamers mentioned by Heraclitus.[33] It is the vacuum of this world, the world when relational qualities are vacuumed up – the real object is what remains.

---

33 Frag. B 89 in Diels' *Die Fragmente der Vorsokratiker Griechisch und Deutsch* reads: "τοῖς ἐγρηγορόσιν ἕνα καὶ κοινὸν κόσμον εἶναι, τῶν δὲ κοιμωμένων ἕκαστον εἰς ἴδιον ἀποστρέφεσθαι" (1903, p. 79)

What Plato offers is what Harman critiques as a holistic theory. So in the example from chapter one of "Lake Michigan" as an object, the holistic approach treats this object as a representation of "lakeness", or in the case of Plato, the form of "lakeness". Despite Plato offering a realist position, it is not one which Harman accepts, and in rejecting holistic approaches, object-oriented ontology is left as a realism that rejects certain forms of realism if they fall victim to the undermining or overmining of objects, part of its "weird" realism.

However, I would venture to propose a different reason to term it "weird": object-oriented ontology is ultimately anti-realist as a nominalistic realism. This seemingly contradictory position is most fitting of object-oriented ontology in its treatment of objects. We shall continue with Harman's own example of "Lake Michigan" to further illustrate this point. Upon revealing precisely how object-oriented ontology articulates a nominalistic position, with realist tendencies, it will then be possible to articulate a method of circumventing the problem that gives rise to this position.

Object-Oriented Ontology as Nominalistic

It was already noted that just as "Lake Michigan" is an object, so too are the tiny droplets of water ("water droplet"). Both of these objects are equally sensual objects and real objects and as such each is mind-independent – object-oriented ontology's essential thesis offers a realist position. In fact, Harman even holds that fictional entities are equally real objects that are mind-independent. It would be hard to find a more realist claim than this as many, such as Henri Poincaré,[34] would find the assertion that fictional entities are mind-independent problematic. Yet, object-oriented ontology does not hold a realist account of universals, despite its realism about mind-independent existence of objects themselves.

For Aristotle, Heraclitus was a monist – a realist position in that there is a singular underlying substance of everything that can be said to exist. This singular substance is necessarily mind-independent. It is also a claim about universals – the singular substance is that which all particulars share in common. We see here in Heraclitus's claim something akin to the realism of Platonic forms. Forms are mind-independent "objects" and act as universals. In considering realist po-

---

[34] Poincaré wrote in *The Value of Science:* "a reality completely independent of the mind which conceives it, sees or feels it, is an impossibility" (2001, p. 193).

sitions, the mind-independent objects also form universals that are found in the particulars of the world (sensual objects).

Object-oriented ontology's realism does not, however, offer such in its system of objects. Real objects do not act as universals of which particulars take part. Real objects are, themselves, particulars amongst an ocean of other particulars. With object-oriented ontology's devotion to treating all objects on an equal ontological footing, it must necessarily also treat everything as particulars. If object-oriented ontology did not do this, then it would lose the ontological equality it seeks to establish. This is clear in reconsidering the droplets of water in lake Michigan. Each droplet is a particular object continuing particulars. Although there are universal qualities of the tiny droplets, these cannot be distinguishing factors between one droplet and another.

If the universals were the focus, "water droplet" would be the object of concern for object-oriented ontology and there would not be "this droplet" and "that droplet" of equal ontological grounding. Yet, object-oriented ontology maintains that each particular water droplet has claim to this ontological equality, and so therefore, object-oriented ontology must focus on those qualities that distinguish one object from another; it must center its approach on particulars. In doing so, however, object-oriented ontology largely removes universals from central importance – an ultimately nominalistic, and anti-realist position. The "water droplet" gets swallowed by the lake, just as Arnold's droplet of dew "slips Into the shining sea" (1898, p. 221).[35] This becomes even more clear when considering the distinction between real qualities and secondary qualities in object-oriented ontology in greater detail.

Real qualities and sensual qualities are distinct from one another in a way keeping with the tradition of the primary and secondary qualities of Locke. The former are intuited intellectually whereas the latter are experienced directly. However, when paired with the classification of objects as *real* or *sensual,* the combinations that are yielded reveal the non-realist pattern embedded within object-oriented ontology.

The most interesting of the pairings in object-oriented ontology is the real object/real qualities pairing. Harman notes that this pairing "grounds the capacity of real objects to differ from one another, without collapsing into indefinite substrata" (2011, p. 50). The combination of a withdrawn object, a thing-in-itself, and real qualities that can only be known indirectly through the intellect, results in the real qualities being particulars not universal properties of an object. This is clear when considering further the other pairing featuring real

---

[35] This is a reference to Sir Edwin Arnold's work *The Light of Asia*.

qualities – sensual object/real qualities. In this case, the object that is directly experienced, is cognized and brought into consciousness through the process of representation, consists of intellectually intuited properties.

In order to have objects that are represented to the mind (sensual objects), the emphasis must be on the particular qualities of said object in order that it can be cognized in a way that differentiates it from another object. If for example, in the conscious experience and representation of an object to the mind, only yellowness is represented, as in a tapestry[36] where one thread is lost to the whole, one is unable to discern that the sensual object that is being represented is a tennis ball as opposed to a sunflower. So in this case, the qualities cognized must be particular qualities which are "real" qualities.

The same issue arises with the previous pairing of real object/real qualities. If this pairing is meant to avoid infinite reducibility, then those qualities must be particular to the object itself, and therefore cannot be universal qualities. Ultimately then, all qualities that we can call real qualities, in the sense Harman and object-oriented ontology use it, must be particular qualities, not universal qualities. Again we see that universals no longer hold central importance, but rather it is the particulars which are the focus in object-oriented ontology's flat model. Although this goes largely against the typical principle of realism, and borders – if not outright crosses into – the realm of nominalism, object-oriented ontology and Harman are not absent realist positions.

Harman, of course, is aligned with the central tenet of realism asserting the existence of mind-independent objects, and so cannot be fully considered anti-realist. However, there are undoubtedly anti-realist principles at work in object-oriented ontology, which is what makes it "weird". But is it possible to offer a truly rationalist position starting from the same point as Harman's object-oriented ontology? If so, what would that require? I believe that the problem object-oriented ontology has, as mentioned above, is its focus on particulars in order to establish its flat ontological model rather than remaining with universals. Below I will outline the three main ways that this can be dealt with as well as the problems associated with each from the perspectives of Harman, object-oriented ontology generally, and the speculative realist tradition.

---

[36] Carson McCullers' novel *Reflections in a Golden Eye* includes a wonderful description of color akin to the claim here: "The mind is like a richly woven tapestry in which the colors are distilled from the experiences of the senses, and the design drawn from the convolutions of the intellect" (2000, p. 90).

Non-Flat Models

The most common approach in realist philosophies, but one which is the center of Harman's critique and which is what object-oriented ontology aims to move away from, is the *use* of a dualistic or otherwise non-flat model. Of course the model that has had the most influence over the last millennia is Cartesian dualism, separating mind and body, but which resulted in the broader division between subjects and objects. This approach, which is a form of indirect realism, was critiqued by both Kant and Heidegger long before Harman's object-oriented ontology – Heidegger really is the source of the removal of this distinction, in the West.[37] Kant rejects Cartesian dualism because of its assertion that we do not have an immediate reference point of an external permanent existence in time from which we can recognize our own self as existing *in* time, not external to it. Nonetheless Kant retains some semblance of dualism in his *noumena/phenomena* distinction, though it is not entirely clear – and I would argue that it is not the case – that these reflect on two different substances.

In *Being and Time*, Heidegger makes the case for an ontological model that treats all things as objects, including ourselves, rather than allowing for the division that Harman (and I think correctly, if not also with a bit of humor) terms "humans vs everything else". Heidegger, though, falls into a similar issue in that his anthropocentric system still pits humans against all other objects: it privileges the human. In other words, Heidegger offers a flat ontology of objects, but with humans removed and placed "above" the objects because of our manipulation of, and engagement with, our world.

There are other forms of realism which rely on some form of dualism. Platonic realism of course offers the metaphysical dualism distinguishing forms from

---

37 As mentioned, this dualism has its strongest roots in Descartes, and was fully embedded in cultural states of mind. The subject-object distinction found a home in Shakespeare's *Love's Labour's Lost*:
"As love is full of unbefitting strains,
All wanton as a child, skipping and vain,
Form'd by the eye and therefore, like the eye,
Full of strange shapes, of habits and of forms,
Varying in subjects as the eye doth roll
To every varied object in his glance" (1899, p. 212).
Perhaps even more interesting than Harman's object-oriented ontology, in which the subject is all but eliminated in favor of equal ontological treatment of objects, is Emerson's devotion to dissolving the object: "Thus inevitably does the universe wear our color, and every object fall successively into the subject itself. The subject exists, the subject enlarges; all things sooner or later fall into place" (1903, p. 79).

everyday things that represent those forms as two distinct objects. Aristotelian realism, on the other hand, is a form of monism that treats universals as dependent on the particular things through which they manifest. But even without the subject/object distinction that is derived from dualism, monism does not offer a flat ontology. In order for a flat ontology to hold the same meaning as it does in object-oriented ontology, it is not useful to simplify everything into a singular substance; rather than a flat ontology it merely creates a vertical lined ontology. In other words, by reducing everything to a singular substance monism avoids the distinction between objects and thus cannot properly give each object its individual and equal ontological claim, for it would be less than that of the singular substance from which it is itself derived.

It is not surprising that most realist positions do not leave room for the flat model interpretation of objects as they tend to place importance on universals. One way then to counteract the issue of particulars taking on more influence in object-oriented ontology, would be to reconsider the flatness of its model. Of course, this would be to reject the foundational position of object-oriented ontology and though it would make for a better fit with other realist positions, it would greatly diminish the positive directional shift in realism that object-oriented ontology has brought about. Thus, we turn to the remaining options to deal with the lack of universals in central importance.

Focus on Universals

So long as we are to retain the essentiality of a flat ontology, another option would be to continue the realist tradition of emphasizing universals. This would make object-oriented ontology far less 'weird' than as it currently stands. If we are to shift the focus from particulars to universals while still remaining as a flat ontology, the question becomes: how this might work? As previously noted, universals seem to be at odds with object-oriented ontology's desire for a flat ontological model. However, we must here penetrate into object-oriented ontology and speculative realism to determine if there is a way to rectify the apparent contradiction between a flat ontology and the focus on the central importance of universals that is found in most realist positions.

I believe that no such option exists within Harman's object-oriented ontology as it stands, nor in the speculative realism of Meillassoux. However, there might be a possibility to locate something akin to this in the thought of Timothy Morton. In the work *The Ecological Thought*, Morton describes the term *hyperob-*

jects, something which is not found elsewhere in object-oriented ontology.[38] These are objects which move beyond their spatiotemporality specifically because they are so embedded in space and time. That is to say they, in a sense, transcend any particularity that they might have.

If the issue at hand is to insert the centrality of universals into object-oriented ontology, hyperobjects might be a solution. Since they transcend their particularity, they are universals outright – indeed they do not really have any particularity. There is no *this* or *that* climate change, but rather it just is what it is, as it is, universal without particularity. For Harman, objects like climate change fit into the object-oriented ontology ontotaxonomy, but retain particularity which is what seems to also allow for the retaining of a flat ontological model. But does Morton's model do away with object-oriented ontology's flatness?

There is no way that hyperobjects can fit into object-oriented ontology's flat model without readjusting the ontotaxonomy. Morton's hyperobjects, absent their particularity, are not "withdrawn" objects. For Harman, and object-oriented ontology, withdrawn objects are essentially particulars. On the other hand, hyperobjects are wrapped up in and are hyperactive in their spatiotemporality which is what ultimately enables them to also transcend that very spatiotemporality of which they are a part. This in fact, poses a different issue for Harman's version of object-oriented ontology.

Objects such as climate change, these hyperobjects, cannot fit into Harman's model not only because they do not align with the ontotaxonomy, but more importantly because of where they would have to be input in order to be accounted for. More specifically on point, climate change could not be an object; objects for Harman can withdraw from their relations ("real object"). Climate change, and the other hyperobjects, cannot do so – they are, in many ways, a byproduct of, or just otherwise embedded with, their relationality.

Yet, for Harman, there are no indications of an object which cannot "withdraw" from its relationality, since that is an essential feature of what an object is under object-oriented ontology. Hyperobjects then cannot resolve the issue of Harman's object-oriented ontology as they contradict the fundamental pillars of that model. However, this does not mean that hyperobjects cannot fit into a flat ontology, but rather simply that they do not fit into the ontotaxonomy of Har-

---

38 Although not found in other object-oriented philosophies, the term *hyperobjects* does appear in Terrence McKenna's *Archaic Revival:* "there is a belief that there is a hyperobject called the overmind, or God, that casts a shadow into time… There is both the forward-flowing casuistry of being, causal determinism, and the interference pattern that is formed against that by the backward-flowing fact of this eschatological hyperobject throwing its shadow across the temporal landscape" (1992, p. 93; p. 100).

man's version of object-oriented ontology. Hyperobjects would require a completely different onto-taxonomological approach in order to fit into a flat ontology.

Re-enter Relationality, Correlationism Revived

Considering hyperobjects, though, does indicate a potential option that could not only resolve the issue of universals in Harman's object-oriented ontology, but also bring hyperobjects into the model as well. However, it would require rethinking the very foundation of not just object-oriented ontology but also the entire speculative realist tradition. This approach would be to focus on relationality, rather than seeking ways to remove it. Specifically, in this case, reconsidering the rejection of correlationism that is the source of the speculative realist movement and which is found consistently among the adherents and supporters of object-oriented ontology and other speculative realist systems.

What is interesting here to note is that speculative realism and object-oriented ontology are both traditions that emphasize relationality, yet also aim to remove objects from their relations. This seemingly contradictory stance is actually quite useful and draws incredibly on the Kantian distinction between the thing-in-itself and the appearance of the thing – the former being what is removed from relationality and thus the "real object" for Harman's object-oriented ontology, for example. The issue with the speculative realism and object-oriented ontology treatment of this distinction is arrived at when the rejection of anthropocentrism in philosophical inquiry resolves into outcasting the human nearly altogether through the rejection of the correlationism that is found in Kant and the post-Kantian traditions.

Although the rejection of correlationism as the integration of thought and Being is pragmatic in speculative realism and object-oriented ontology in that it keeps them closer to realism by asserting that objects have a Being outside of thought, it nonetheless results in two issues that both have failed to overcome. The first of these is what has been mentioned above, namely, that speculative realism and object-oriented ontology in particular seem to lessen the importance of universals. This is a direct result of rejecting correlationism.

Universals require some amount of correlationism in order to retain the sort of predominance over particulars – a main feature of realism. This is because universals – such as color – are often not primary qualities. Primary qualities, such as mass or extension, are more commonly particulars rather than universals. This is perhaps one of the reasons why Kant saw it necessary to note that it is primary qualities which, although often seen as belonging to the object itself as opposed to just its appearance, must be called into question as well, when he writes: "the remaining qualities of bodies also, which are called primary, such as extension, place, and in general space, with all that which belongs to it (impenetrability or materiality, space, etc.)—no one in the least can adduce the reason of its being inadmissible" (2007, p. 92). Universals require some form of correlationism in order to establish the categorization of being a universal, i.e., grouping objects into those which share in the universal of redness.

In the case of Harman's object-oriented ontology, abstract entities such as "redness" have a real nature to them as well, and as such, Harman would suggest that universals do not require correlationism insofar as they exist independently. While I am inclined to agree with the sentiment that "redness" can be a universal quality that a group of objects partake in, even absent correlationism, this categorization as such does not. Furthermore, what is lacking in object-oriented ontology's account on this matter is the assignment of universals to the status of "real" completely. "Redness" *ought* to be part of what makes the object what it is, which is accurate in object-oriented ontology, and *ought* to be considered a "real object" in and of itself, which does not seem to be the case in object-oriented ontology as "redness" is a sensual object. Should "redness" be considered as a "real object", the complete rejection of correlationism is possible. However, in considering the experience of art and "art objects", it becomes even more clear that treating "redness" as a real object is both important, but also detrimental to aesthetics, and as such, "redness" is both real and sensual, resulting in the inability to completely reject correlationism. In a similar way, Badiou wrote that *"L'art atteste ce qu'il y a d'inhumain dans l'humain"* (2005, p. 224).

We can imagine an art gallery with a variety of paintings, drawings, sculptures, and other forms of art. Each painting, drawing, sculpture, etc., has a variety of reds, greens, blues, and other colors. Each painting, drawing, sculpture, etc., also has a variety of circles, squares, rectangles, and other shapes. Although the landscape, portrait, or abstract form as a whole can be taken in, it is the colors and shapes, i.e., the very structure of the art, which gives it an aesthetic quality (Isrow 2017). Regardless of any thought or mind to perceive it, if colors, shapes, etc. are "real objects" and as such hold a mind-independent reality, the art has an aesthetic quality by virtue of its taking part in "colorfulness", "shapeliness", and the like.

The main reason for the *Speculative Turn*,[39] as mentioned in chapter one, is to assert a mind-independent reality to the objects in themselves; to bring the

---

[39] The title of a 2011 edited collection of essays on Speculative Realist philosophy by Graham Harman, Nick Srnicek, and Levi Bryant.

Ding an sich back into philosophical inquiry absent the necessity of the *thought-Being* correlate. Although it is the later post-Kantian trajectory that yields strong correlationism, the principles are at work already in Kant since he viewed the *Ding and sich a*s unknowable, even though it exists and has a mind-independent reality to it. In the example above, we can find the mind-independent existence of the aesthetic quality of something even as abstract as art. But it is when we add correlationism that we add something additional to the aesthetic quality of art: interpretation.

Interpretation is subject-dependent and is an instance in which the object of interpretation, that is the interpretation as an object itself, emerges from the correlate of thought and Being. Yet, the interpretation as an object does not alter the object in and of itself that is being combined with thought to form a new object, the interpretation of the object. The art object as a "real object" independently exists apart from any thought-Being correlate, and when perceived by a subject with interpretation added to it, nonetheless remains the "real object" yet also exists as a new object, a sensual object which consists of the art object and the interpretation of it by the subject. In short, the thought-Being correlate does not in any way diminish the "real object", it does not take anything away from it. Rather it only creates a new object, a sensual object which the perceiver engages with. Experiencibility is an essential part of art, and in many ways of all objects worthy of the name.

As such, it is unclear to me what the genuine reason for the elimination of correlationism would be, though I understand the motivation behind it offered by Harman, Meillassoux, and the others in this line of thought. Still it seems to be a misguided motivation. One of the main things that we would perhaps gain from the removal of correlationism is the ability to assert the knowability, the cognizability, of the *Ding an sich*. Kant is clear that the thing in itself is not known to us, but only recognized as it appears to us once cognized via the sense apparatus. It could be suggested that by eliminating correlationism from Kant's system there is an ability to grant access to the thing in itself so that its knowability is not tied up with sense, that is, with a perceiving subject. It would reject Kant's thinking that "The understanding can intuit nothing, the senses can think nothing. Only through their unison can knowledge arise" (2007, p. 93).

But this is not what has been done with the claim to remove correlationism – I do not think it would be a great claim anyway. It is unclear what is actually gained from the elimination of correlationism in many of the speculative realism and object-oriented ontology accounts. In the case of Harman, the opposite end is the goal. In Harman's object-oriented ontology we do not actually gain anything in terms of access to the thing in itself, we simply push it further into the realm of the unknowable since for Harman the thing in itself is unknown not only to us but to other objects as well.

The benefits for Harman's model that this claim provides are obvious: it fully evens the ontological "playing field" of "real objects". Rather than attempting to make a much more difficult claim – which would not really serve the cause at any rate – that by eliminating correlationism we can open access to things in themselves, Harman removes all knowability from things in themselves by leaving relationality unexhausted for objects. While I think the focus on relationality is crucial, if it is in fact essential to place relationality at the forefront, correlationism is also essential. We do not need to claim that Being emerges *only* from thought, but to discard the thought-Being correlate altogether seems just as flawed – we can recall the words of Dewey here[40] – as we move from one extreme to another.

Of all the speculative realism and object-oriented ontology thinkers, I believe that Harman provides the most compelling model for rethinking the trajectory of the thing-in-itself, largely because of his reworking of the Heideggarian tool analysis to more accurately account for many of the aspects of the Kantian system that are found in object-oriented ontology. The problem with Harman's account is the use of the thing-in-itself ("real objects") and the removal of correlationism. I believe this issue stems from a common reading of Kant, but one which misses much of the intricate nature of the system as a whole.

For Kant, the thing in itself is unknown to us because of a lack of relationality, we cannot relate to it in a way that allows us access to know it (it lacks spatiotemporality). The thing-in-itself is not cognizable for Kant not because it is not cognizable as an object ("real object" in Harman's terms), but because of a "flaw" (or lack of relationality) in our cognition of the thing in itself. When we consider the Kantian system as a whole, blended with Harman's unique reading of Heidegger that gave rise to object-oriented ontology, it becomes clear that the necessary ontological model is not just flat, not just a simple line, but rather is a spectrum and as such can be termed *spectral ontology*.

Ultimately, the difference between Harman's line of thought and my own can be articulated in the following way: object-oriented ontology emerges out of Harman's unusual – and often contentious – reading of Heidegger (who in turn offered a unique reading of Kant), whereas *spectral ontology* arises from my own, admittedly unusual reading of Kant. Although Heidegger forms a large part of its

---

40 Dewey writes: "the individual butterfly or earthquake remains just the unique existence which it is. We forget in explaining its occurrence that it is only the occurrence that is explained, not the thing itself" (2008, p. 112).

background as well, it serves mainly as a middle-man and as my reading of Heidegger is aligned with Harman's, the true difference, I believe, rests with the different readings and interpretations of Kant that we hold. If Harman had offered a more uncommon reading of Kant to be paired with his interpretation of Heidegger, I believe that Harman's object-oriented ontology might look more akin to what I here call *spectral ontology*. Harman's object-oriented ontology and my spectral ontological model are rooted in the same fundamental idea of a flat ontology. However, spectral ontology allows for greater depth in the treatment of objects.

Before proceeding, then, to an articulation of what I term spectral ontology, it is important to first address these different readings of Kant. It is only by recognizing the missing elements of Harman's, and many others', reading of Kant that it will be clear precisely in what way an alternative reading, more true to the system as a whole, could provide an ontological model that resolves the problems Harman, Meillassoux, and others in the speculative realism tradition find in correlationism of Kant and post-Kantian philosophers. Since object-oriented ontology is mainly devised out from an attempt to rethink the tool-analysis of Heidegger as a way of approaching the elimination of correlationism and anthropocentrism, I will here indicate how the different approach to Kant that I offer in turn alters Heidegger's analytic of *Dasein* such that Harman's critique of the tool-analysis nevertheless applies but is carried out into a different ontological model. As the aim of this work is to advocate for a new ontological model that can build upon the work of Harman's object-oriented ontology, while still maintaining the central importance of humanness, we must begin with the search for a fundamental ontology.

Chapter Three
The Search for the Grounding of Metaphysics

Of all the philosophers in the modern period, Immanuel Kant stands out as having had the most profound impact. After devoting the vast majority of his early work to science, then called natural philosophy,[41] Kant re-emerged from a silence of several years with what is now considered his magnum opus. *The Critique of Pure Reason*, often considered to be one of the most influential texts in the history of philosophy – though also one of the most difficult – is the work that secured Kant's status as perhaps the most important philosopher since Aristotle. Though one of the most important texts in contemporary philosophy, it is also one of its most debated. Disagreements, not just in the form of critiques of his philosophical system and positions, but also over Kant's meaning in various aspects of his philosophy, have circled since Kant's own time, as can be seen in his letters as well as in published works on his philosophy from scholars of his era, such as Karl Leonard Reinhold[42] and Johann Gottlieb Fichte[43] among others.[44]

To this day debates continue to spring forth from various interpretations of Kant, his system, and its influence on the continued development of philosophy, as with German Idealism.[45] Much of this has been against the Kantian system, seeing it as fundamentally flawed or self-contradictory. This is perhaps not helped by the many noted inconsistencies between the three *Critiques* themselves.[46]

---

41 Some examples include: Immanuel Kant (1976) *Allgemeine Naturgeschichte und Theorie des Himmels, oder, Versuch von der Verfassung und dem mechanischen Ursprunge des ganzen Weltgebäudes nach Newtonischen Grundsätzen abgehandelt,* and Immanuel Kant (1807) *Monadologia physica.*
42 See Karl Leonard Reinhold (2011) *Essay on a New Theory of the Human Capacity for Representation.*
43 See Johann Gottlieb Fichte (1994) *Introductions to the Wissenschaftslehre and Other Writings.*
44 Marcus Herz and Johann Gottfried Herder most famously. See, Eric Watkins (2009) *Kant's Critique of Pure Reason: Background Source Materials.*
45 For a good text on tracing the influence of Kant's *Critique of Judgment* through the German Idealist tradition, see John H. Zammito (1992) *The Genesis of Kant's Critique of Judgment.*
46 For more on the self-contradictions within Kantian philosophy, see Friedrich Heinrich Jacobi (1976) *Friedrich Heinrich Jacobi Werke (1815) Vol. 2,* Arthur Schopenhauer (1969) *The World as Will and Representation,* Gordon G. Brittan (2015) *Kant's Theory of Science,* and James Van Cleve (1999) *Problems from Kant.*

In fact, as early as 1792,[47] a mere eleven years after the first *Critique* was published and two years after the appearance of the third and final *Critique*, came the publication of *Aenesidemus* by Gottleib Schulze.[48] This work began a trend that remained strong in the debate: namely the contradictory nature of, and need to dispose of, the *Ding an sich*. Thus even Fichte, a supporter of the Kantian system, ultimately reframed Kantian philosophy as a new system simply by removing the *Ding an sich*.

Since then, philosophers have continued to reject the *Ding an sich* in Kantian philosophy. Edmund Husserl's famous assertion in the *Logical Investigations* that we should and can "get back to things themselves" (2011, p. 168) is a prime example of this trend, in which the *Ding an sich*, the real, is not strictly critiqued but redefined or simply cast off as unnecessary and forgotten. The "thing itself" for Husserl is that which is presented to a perceiver. This is the root of Husserl's phenomenological methodology, which is precisely what Kant rejects in his conception of the *Ding an sich*, which is in itself not capable of being revealed *via representation*. Thus, Husserl's "reintroduction of the things themselves" is merely a perversion of the Kantian position on the concept.

Picking up this system of phenomenology, and attempting what can be considered a phenomenological approach to the very same topic that captured Kant's interest, was Husserl's student Martin Heidegger. In his major work *Being and Time*, Heidegger drafts a phenomenological analytic of *Dasein*, that way of Being which we are. Just as Kant attempted to provide an analytic of pure reason, that which he thought to be a primary aspect of our being the way we are, Heidegger gives the same analytic, but finds us as *Dasein* to *be* in a fundamentally different way than Kant held. This mode of *being-in* which he emphasizes is essentially one that is phenomenological, in that he treats *Dasein* as *in-der-Welt-sein*: a mode of being which necessitates an absence of the *Ding an sich* from his philosophical analytic, thus eliminating the metaphysics of *Dasein* whilst maintaining an ontology.[49]

---

[47] Previously, Jacobi also criticized the *Ding an sich*, however not extensively nor with as much of an impact. For more on Jacobi's criticisms of Kant see Friedrich Heinrich Jacobi (1976) *Friedrich Heinrich Jacobi Werke (1815), Vol. 2*.

[48] In this work Schulze criticizes not only Kant himself, but also Reinhold, who was a supporter of the Kantian system. For a great analysis of Schulze's work and its response to Reinhold, see James Messina's (2011) article "Answering Aenesidemus: Schulze's Attack on Reinholdian Representationalism and Its Importance for Fichte".

[49] This can be seen in Martin Heidegger (2011) *The Concept of Time*. For a great commentary on this see in Heidegger's thought, see Theodore Kisiel (2014) "Why the First Draft of Being and Time was Never Published".

In what way can it be possible to speak of an ontology of *Dasein* in the absence of a metaphysics of *Dasein*? We must distinguish here between ontology as such and the *metaphysics* of that ontology. In the former, we are concerned with the "what" of being, in the latter the "how" of it. This "how" is what stretches beyond the mere immanence of the ontological, and it is in the lack of a "beyondness" through which Heidegger can maintain his ontology without a metaphysics. That is to say, it is the singular focus on the finitude of *Dasein* that requires from Heidegger precisely this distinction. As I hope to show, this concern for the finitude of *Dasein* alone also limits Heidegger's ontological investigation as well, trapping him into an analytic of only the ontic, not truly of the ontological.

A recent push, however, and one that is growing in popularity, attempts to reexamine Heidegger's ontology, questioning its limitedness. Object-oriented ontologists, such as Graham Harman, suggest that the ontology of "world" which Heidegger grants to *Dasein* and keeps away from other beings, can and in fact *must* hold valid amongst beings in general and not be limited to *Dasein*.[50] This view suggests that the salvation of the *Ding an sich* is not only possible, but necessary. This being the case, not only are we to reinstate the *Ding an sich* for the possibility of a more comprehensive ontological system, but also for a metaphysics of *Dasein*. We must first, if we are to find a possible metaphysics of *Dasein*, find the very grounding for metaphysics. This is to ask the question: if a metaphysics of *Dasein* is possible, where are we to discover the grounding for this metaphysics within the Kantian system? We must return to the Kantian philosophy of the *Ding an sich*, but how can this lead to the ground of metaphysics? This chapter will focus on the search for this ground.

Insofar as metaphysics can be considered as the "science" dedicated to discovering first principles, as Aristotle (2002) suggested, the *Critique of Pure Reason* can be considered to be a treatise on establishing the groundwork of metaphysics. However, the metaphysics which Kant aimed at delimiting was not strictly limited to the discovery of first principles; the *Critique of Pure Reason* was not only an epistemological treatise, but rather was also an ontological one. Thus, the major question of the *Critique of Pure Reason* becomes in what form of ontology does a "critique" of pure reason take shape?

Ontology, as the study of "what-is", Being as such (ὄντος), must always be directed at something, even if that upon which it has been directed is ontology itself. Ontology is always an ontology of some "thing", or of that which is con-

---

50 Although many of his works outline the various arguments and reasoning for this, perhaps the most detailed is offered in Graham Harman (2011) *The Quadruple Object*.

trasted to nonbeing.⁵¹ There is always an object for which an ontology is considered.⁵² If we are then to suggest that Kant was setting forth an ontology, it seems clear that the Ontology which he sought to delimit was that of pure reason. Pure reason forms the foundation of his enquiry into the metaphysics of knowing, and as such, we may say, of the fundamentals of *Dasein*. Pure reason as *a priori* is the easy candidate for the cornerstone or grounding of a Kantian ontology. However, there are two problems with this claim that must be discussed.

First, any ontology which Kant may be said to have formulated within the confines of his *Critique of Pure Reason* is not a completed ontology.⁵³ Second, Pure Reason as such is not capable of possessing an ontology. There can be no ontology of pure reason, for pure reason is itself a faculty in the Kantian system. Thus, the question becomes: from what did Kant source an ontology? We will proceed to address the first of these; the second will be addressed later.

The Problem of a Complete Ontology

Kant reconsidered the source of knowledge as no longer being determined by the objects of knowledge, but rather by the very limits or constraints of the subject. This is why the *Critique of Pure Reason* is often mistaken for being only an epistemological masterpiece. Indeed, much of what Kant achieves from this so-called "Copernican revolution"⁵⁴ is a reversing of the primacy of epistemology, which dominated modern thought; it is a reversal that sparks a shift from epistemological concerns as primary to ontological ones. Therefore, although this claim may seem at first to be counter-intuitive to many, I will argue that the

---

51 Heidegger (2018) in *Was ist Metaphysik?* discusses what he terms the "Nothing" and its relation to a necessary ontology. For more on the treatment of ontology and nothingness in Heidegger, see Stephan Käufer (2005) "The Nothing and the Ontological Difference in Heidegger's What is Metaphysics?".
52 That is to say, the categories. In this work I will focus on Kant's categories. See also Aristotle's (1975) work on the categories for more on how the categories predicate ontology in *Categories and De Interpretione*.
53 Adrian Johnston (2008) writes in his work *Žižek's Ontology: A Transcendental Materialist Theory of Subjectivity* that "For *Kant*, phenomenal reality is *partial* and *incomplete*, a field of fragmentary experience constrained by the limits constitutive of the finite subject" (Johnson 2008, p. 178).
54 Kant considered his transcendental philosophy to be similar in its effect as Copernicus' heliocentric model of the solar system. For additional discussion on how what Kant did for philosophy is akin to what Copernicus did for science, see Ermanno Bencivenga (1987) *Kant's Copernican Revolution*.

first *Critique* should be read, also and perhaps primarily, as a metaphysics which emerges mainly out of a "critique of reason" and an epistemology itself.

Insofar as Kant aimed at reversing the primacy of the epistemological over the ontological, there is never a clear intention to draft a complete ontology. As Heidegger rightly points out, the *Critique of Pure Reason* serves as a "laying of the ground for metaphysics and thus of placing the problem of metaphysics before us as a fundamental ontology" (1997, p. 1). It is not so much the case, then, that Kant sought to establish an ontology rather than set forth its primacy and lay the ground for a "future metaphysics".[55] There are thus three questions that we find cast upon us here, all of which Heidegger addresses:
1. What is a fundamental ontology?
2. What is the process of this "laying-the-ground"?
3. How can Kant's *Critique of Pure Reason* be viewed as a *Grundlegung*?

It will now be necessary to provide answers to each of these questions before proceeding further. The answers can be best expressed by considering the following themes: fundamental ontology as a groundwork for a future metaphysics, and the *Critique of Pure Reason* as *Grundlegung*.

Fundamental Ontology as a Groundwork for a Future Metaphysics

In his *Prolegomena to Any Future Metaphysics*, Kant famously suggests that his dogmatic slumber was interrupted by the skepticism of David Hume (2004, p. 10). Hume, who had all but eliminated knowledge through his claim that there was no knowledge outside of empirical causal relationships (and even this was problematic), sparked in Kant a desire to save knowledge. But true knowledge, non-subjective knowledge, or non-causal knowledge is only possible through metaphysics. Metaphysics enquires into the very foundations of things, the hidden structures of being. An epistemological foundation thus requires a metaphysics; this metaphysics must be one capable of providing for such an epistemology. This is precisely why Hume's rejection of the possibility of metaphysics serving as grounding for epistemology brings knowledge itself into ques-

---

55 The title of his work *Prolegomena to Any Future Metaphysics* indicates as much and in it he aims to do precisely this.

tion, and as such, why Kant seeks to restore such a metaphysics he believes suitable for said task.[56]

To be clear, it is not that Kant sought metaphysical knowledge, which is impossible in his doctrine, but rather that real knowledge, that is, non-subjective knowledge, is knowledge that does not rely upon our empirical reality. That is to say, knowledge requires, as it were, metaphysical or *a priori* knowledge. Thus, Kant's desire to save knowledge requires a revival of metaphysics, and even puts him in the role of the metaphysician. How does Kant reverse the trend of the downfall of metaphysics and knowledge?

Kant portrays this shift as a similar experiment to that of Copernicus' model of the sun, and thus refers to it as a "Copernican Revolution." He writes in the preface to the second edition to the *Critique of Pure Reason*:

> [Hitherto] it has been assumed that all our knowledge must conform to objects. But all attempts to extend our knowledge of objects by establishing something in regard to them *a priori*, by means of concepts, have, on this assumption, ended in failure. We must therefore make trial whether we may not have more success in the tasks of metaphysics, if we suppose that objects must conform to our knowledge. This would agree better with what is desired, namely, that it should be possible to have knowledge of objects *a priori*, determining something in regard to them prior to their being given (Kant 2007, p. 22).

With this new focus on the individual, the preconditions of knowledge, or as Kant terms it, the *transcendental*, he believes there is a possibility that we can establish something *a priori* about the objects and thus result in the production of some firm knowledge previously thought impossible. Ultimately, this results in the discussion of *intuition* and Kantian epistemology.

However, this entire epistemology falls back on, relies on, and grounds itself in a metaphysics: or more precisely, an ontology. But even this requires grounding in something more primary, a "fundamental ontology" as Heidegger calls it. Heidegger provides us with a clear answer of what is meant by a fundamental ontology. It is "the metaphysics of human *Dasein* which is required for metaphysics to be made possible" (Heidegger 1997, p. 1) Making the connection of this need to recognize and treat carefully the necessary preconditions of knowledge and metaphysics, it becomes clear that this is, for Kant, a *transcendental ontology*.[57]

---

[56] For an excellent discussion on Humean epistemology see Robert E. Butts (1959) "Hume's Scepticism" and Donald C. Ainslie (2015) *Hume's True Scepticism*.

[57] This is my term for that ontology which is necessary in order that any ontology may be devised, a *metaontology*. For Peter Van Inwagen's (1998) discussion of *meta-ontology* see his article "Meta-ontology". For Markus Gabriel's (2015) project of a transcendental ontology see his greatly interesting work *Fields of Sense: A New Realist Ontology*.

Two questions remain before us here: the process of laying the ground, and – as we will discuss later – the problem of transcendental ontology. Laying the ground is a difficult task, particularly in the case of a fundamental ontology. To set forth and explicate the various preconditions of metaphysics requires penetration into the very primacy of things. Doing so requires the breaking down of *Dasein* to uncover those preconditions, the basic structure, through which metaphysics can be rendered possible. This breaking down of *Dasein* reveals the structural composition of this being to be finitude, infinitude, nonfinitude, and transcendental.

The problem of the source of Fundamental Ontology

If we are to read Kant, as Heidegger himself does, as laying the ground for a fundamental ontology, then the problem arises with the identification of the source of this groundwork in the Kantian system as formulated within the *Critique of Pure Reason*. Where is the source of fundamental ontology to be found? Heidegger finds the source within the interworking of *understanding* and *sensibility*. Let us evaluate this suggestion and see if the sought-for source can be located here, as has been claimed.

Why is it in *understanding* and *sensibility* that Heidegger finds the necessary groundwork? The grounding of fundamental ontology is directly connected to the experience of *Dasein*. That is to say, it is intricately directed by the finitude of knowledge and more specifically the means by which *Dasein* acquires this knowledge. It is out of this that "the dimension within which the task of laying the ground" takes place (Heidegger 1997, p. 24). But what exactly does this reveal about the grounding?

It is precisely the "necessary way in which understanding and sensibility belong together in the essential unity of finite knowledge" which is unveiled (ibid, p. 25). That which serves as necessity for the possibility of finite knowledge is also that which is necessary for fundamental ontology. Heidegger makes this clear when he writes:

> If finite knowledge, however, has its essence precisely in the original synthesis of the basic sources [*Grundquellen*] and if the laying of the ground for metaphysics must push ahead into the essential ground of finite knowledge, then it is inescapable that the naming which indicates the "'two basic sources [*Grundquellen*]'" already suggests an allusion to the ground of their source [*ihren Grundquellen*], i.e., to an original unity (ibid, p. 25).

Here then the question must be regarding the finitude of ontology, or rather how it is that something finite might render fundamental ontology possible? Heidegger turns towards an analytic of finite reason, the essence of the ground. The analytic prescribed reveals the ground of finite reason through the "letting-be-seen" of its origin and development. In this sense, it is called "freeing" and this freeing, "which an ontology essentially makes possible, brings metaphysics to ground and soil [Grund und Boden] in which it is rooted as a 'haunting' of human nature" (ibid, p. 29).

Thus, the problem of the source of a fundamental ontology lies in this hauntingness of the very finitude of *Dasein*. It is a question of how, in being finite, *Dasein* is ever to understand its relation to being as such. It is in finitude that the source of a fundamental ontology can be identified. Thus, it is clear that Heidegger finds the grounding of metaphysics in reason, particularly finite reason; finite "pure" reason, in fact, as Heidegger himself indicates.[58] Thus to answer the question of the source of fundamental ontology, that is, to address the problem of finitude in *Dasein*, it is also necessary to consider exactly in what way reason is finite, and note the difference between finite reason and finite pure reason.

However, it should be noted that it would be truer to Kant to assert finite reason as this "finitude" and pure reason as separate, extending its limitations beyond the finite. Yet, this too would be mistaken if we are seeking to address fundamental ontology. Pure reason is, itself, not enough to be the origin of the source of fundamental ontology. Instead, we must look to that which is transcendental, as Heidegger himself notes: "To make the possibility of ontology into a problem means: to inquire as to the possibility, i.e., as to the essence of this transcendence which characterizes the understanding of being, to philosophize transcendentally" (ibid, p. 10). That transcendental aspect of *Dasein* which can lead us to the source of fundamental ontology is, instead, what we must now uncover. In doing so it will be revealed that finitude is only one part of *Dasein* and to end at the transcendental, such that we may search out this grounding, we must first discover the nonfinitude and the infinitude of *Dasein* as well. Through exploring these, we will find the source for the grounding of a fundamental ontology. The search for humanness and its role in establishing an ontology rests on an exploration of the ontical and ontological modes of *Dasein* which can then propel us into a rethinking of the correlationism of Kant, along with its necessity.

---

58 "Analytic thus becomes a letting-be-seen [Sehenlassen] of the genesis of finite pure reason from its proper ground" (Heidegger 1997, p. 29)

Chapter Four
The Ontical Modes of Dasein

I have suggested that we are here to explore the finitude, nonfinitude, infinitude, and transcendental aspects of *Dasein*. Yet, it must first be shown that *Dasein* indeed consists of these four aspects. It may at first seem to be a misuse of Heidegger's *Dasein* to imply that there can be anything but the finitude of *Dasein*, since *Dasein* is necessarily in the world, which is itself finite.[59] It is perhaps most necessary to discuss the infinitude and nonfinitude of *Dasein*, since the finitude is fairly clear and in line with Heidegger's concept of *Dasein*, while *Dasein's* nonfinitude may sound more surprising. Additionally, there exists a transcendental aspect of *Dasein* that serves as the precondition of experience: namely in this case, the experience of Being as the being *Dasein*.[60]

Thus, we must ask ourselves to where we can trace the origin and the development of these four aspects of *Dasein*, and specifically the infinitude and the nonfinitude. Indeed, these cannot be found in Heidegger's analytic, and thus we must seek a justification for such a breakdown of *Dasein* elsewhere. If we are to find agreement with Heidegger that the Kantian system provides for the groundwork of a fundamental ontology, then this means that the Kantian system structures the necessary framework through which we may understand *Dasein* as an *ontical relation in the world:* that is, empirical *Dasein* rather than a purely ontological one.[61] In other words, any suggestion that Kant is not concerned in his work with the understanding of the fundamentals of being *Dasein*, as Heidegger understands it, is a misunderstanding of both Kant and *Dasein*.

Of course, this is not to suggest that Kant perfectly captures the essence of the being of *Dasein* in his system and that there is no point of contention between Kant and Heidegger. Nevertheless, Kant is first and foremost concerned with analyzing the very aspects that he finds to be essential to our being what we are.[62] In this way, Kant's system can be read as an analytic of *Dasein*, much in the same

---

59 World here refers to not the universe but rather only to the world of *Dasein*, the world of relationality.
60 In his Letter on Humanism, Heidegger writes: "The introductory definition, 'Being is the *transcendens* pure and simple', articulates in one simple sentence the way the essence of Being hitherto has been cleared for the human being" (Heidegger 1977, p. 217), reiterating the statement "Being is the *transcendens* pure and simple" from *Being and Time* (Heidegger 2010, p. 37)
61 That is to say, it provides an ontological ground for the ontic-relationality of *Dasein*.
62 This is nevertheless for Kant necessarily in the world – as for him it is our experiences that makes us what we are.

way as Heidegger's own work. Where, then, is the difference? Why does Heidegger move away from the transcendental system in his analytic, if he can suggest that the system is entirely centralized in the groundwork of a fundamental ontology?

Although it can be suggested that Kant expressed and laid the foundation for a fundamental ontology, there are many aspects of his system that were criticized and eliminated through the history and development of German philosophy up through Heidegger's own analytic of *Dasein*; concepts such as *noumena* were seen as contradictory and unnecessary for understanding our being and the world around us. The transcendental approach was not removed entirely, as the transcendental ego remained a consideration up until Heidegger noted that this brings *Dasein* out of pure finitude, a thing which did not align with his conception of *Dasein* as engulfed in its finitude.[63]

I would suggest, however, that it is in fact in the transcendental system that we may analyze *Dasein* entirely, and not just in its finitude. That is to say, if instead of the elimination of the transcendental ego, we imagine the re-addition of noumena into the analytic of our being, we find the finitude of *Dasein* to be just one mode of *Dasein*'s being-in. A brief discussion is necessary here, as Heidegger attempted to balance finitude with transcendence.

He asserted a *finite transcendence* in which "transcendence means the being in itself accessible to a finite creature" (Heidegger 1997, p. 114). This raises the question of the being in itself, which seems to suggest a thing-in-itself of *Dasein*. Heidegger does not dive deeper into the subject, though this is undoubtedly because it is Being itself which is the in-itself of *Dasein* for Heidegger. However, this falls short of a sufficient source of transcendence. Being is not a part of *Dasein*, but rather the reverse. *Dasein* is a part of Being. Thus, although Being *transcends Dasein*, it is neither the in-itself of *Dasein* nor some *thing*[64] accessible to *Dasein*. The relationship between *Dasein* and Being rests solely in the Being of the former: that is, existence. The way *Dasein* is, namely being-in-the-world, is the relationship between *Dasein* and itself. Thus, the being in itself of *Dasein* is that which makes its way of Being what it is: that is, its Being *Dasein*. In this way the transcendence of *Dasein* is transcendental.

Although what I seek to argue here shares the sentiment of Heidegger's conception of *being-in*, it also differs from it. To begin to show this, I will examine the articulation of *Dasein* and its various modes of being which can be found in

---

[63] We see this, for example, throughout Heidegger's work, and especially in *Being and Time* (Heidegger 2010).
[64] Thing here refers to an aspect or part of a being.

the first *Critique*. These are, as stated previously, finitude, infinitude, non-finitude, and the transcendental mode of being-in.

Finitude

Dasein is temporal, rooted and grounded in its finitude. It can be said that the most finite disposition is the very awareness of finitude, of mortality, as that which can be held as most certain, most knowable amongst the various possibilities of knowledge.[65] But how is it that we come to be made aware of this certainty? It is through the very limitedness of reason itself, that is, the finitude of reason. Let us examine this point.

Reason as the further unification of concepts into coherent patterns, which is called thought, is limited first and foremost by those concepts which it unifies. Thus, reason is dependent upon said concepts and is as such limited. It can only be applied to those concepts which are presented to it, and is itself not creative: namely, it does not form concepts.[66]

Reason is also limited in virtue of its procedure. The operation of the application of reason towards the unification of concepts is such that there is a "chain of logics" from which it springs.[67] That is to say, there is a structured order followed by reason so as to allow for its tasks to be fulfilled. As Kant suggested,[68] there is a chain of reasoning from an origin point, towards the instant of current reasoning such that any unification of concepts can be rendered possible. He writes:

---

[65] We are reminded of this by Aegisthus in *Clytemnestra:* "There's nothing certain in man's life but this: That he must lose it" (Lytton 1867, p. 89).
[66] Here I deny David Hume's articulation in *Treatise of Human Nature* (1896, pp. 106-117) of the first sense of imagination and accept only the second in which imagination is cast apart from the faculty of reason. Heidegger also holds this position suggesting that reason is not itself creative: "Finite knowledge is noncreative intuition. What has to be presented immediately in its particularity must already have been 'at hand' in advance". Later, "pure intuition", he writes, "must in a certain sense be creative" (see Heidegger 1997, p. 31). In the first of these we note that finite knowledge, which must come from impure reason or sensible reason, is noncreative and in the latter that pure intuition, which can correspond to pure reason insofar as pure intuitions can only be qualified through pure reason not sensible reason, is creative. We can therefore see how Heidegger's articulation expresses a similar attitude as Hume's.
[67] For more on the operation of reason and logic, see Matthieu Queloz's (2016) article "Wittgenstein on the Chain of Reasons".
[68] Susan Neiman reminds us of this position in her work *The Unity of Reason: Rereading Kant* when she writes "*Kant* holds *logic* to consist not of independent principles but of 'links in a chain of method' or ways of transforming and relating statements already given" (1997, p. 63).

> All possibility presupposes something actual in and through which all that can be thought is given. Accordingly, there is a certain reality, the cancellation of which would itself cancel all internal possibility whatever. But that, the cancellation of which eradicates all possibility, is absolutely necessary. Therefore, something exists absolutely necessarily (Kant 2003, p. 127).

Thus, logic and reason itself require a necessary existence in order to be able to render thought possible and the unification of concepts fulfilled.

It is the case that one cannot reason from a non-existent starting point.[69] In this case, there would be no way actually to unify concepts. As such, due to the requirement of the possibility of reason being that there exists an origin point, reason is immediately bound by its position within a limited set, that is, its finitude.[70]

Reason, as finite and impure, is also forever caught up in the experiential possibilities of *Dasein*. This is to say, (impure) intuitions – the basis of concept formation – are rooted in experience, and as such deal most intimately with phenomena: things as they appear, since this is how we form concepts about objects and reason about them.[71] *Impure reason,* or *sensible reason* is that reason which is most exemplified in *Dasein* as it is the reason we are immediately conscious of and with which we invest in or engage with the world. Let us consider how this engagement through finite reason occurs.

Two aspects here are of crucial importance: perception and receptivity. In order that reason may be put to the task of the unification of concepts, both per-

---

69 This was supposedly shown early in *On the Nonexistent* by Gorgias. Although lost, we get a glimpse of his thought from Sextus Empiricus: "Moreover, neither can the existent be generated. For if it has come into being, it has come either from the existent or the nonexistent. But it has not come from the existent. For if it is existent, it has not come to be, but already exists. Nor from the nonexistent. For the nonexistent cannot generate anything, because what is generative of something of necessity ought to partake of positive existence. It is not true either, therefore, that the existent is generated" (2000, p. 71).
70 The finite nature of reason is indicated also by Roger Bacon in *Opus Majus*, when he notes that "Reasoning draws a conclusion and makes us grant the conclusion, but does not make the conclusion certain, nor does it remove doubt so that the mind may rest on the intuition of truth, unless the mind discovers it by the path of experience" (1928, p. 583).
71 Susan Neiman again offers a great summary of this process. "This may be understood as follows. A state of affairs is presented in appearance. Reason is thereupon moved to ask for its conditions, that is, the premises upon which it appears in just this way at just this time. The regress thus prescribed is simply the attempt to describe the ordinary data of sense experience. A full explanation cannot rest content with the statement of the conditions of the initial state of affairs that demanded it. These conditions, in turn, must be explained, and their conditions, until we reach a point at which no further explanation is conceivable" (1997, p. 63).

ception and reception of an object is required so that through *intuition* one may derive concepts. Without perception, which is the primary encounter with an external object, intuitions cannot happen.[72] Perception occurs by means of sensation, yet it is through perception that we experience. This experience must be quantified for it to be intuited by *intuition*.

Receptivity is that faculty which quantifies perception, that is to say, the object of our perception is presented to our mind through the ability of receptivity.[73] Thus, insofar as we perceive an object external to us, to the extent that we intuit that object and form concepts from it, we do so only through the mediacy of receptivity, through the object being presented to us. Considering the role of perception and receptivity as necessary components of the faculty of reason, the immediate limitation of reason is clear.

Reason can only unify concepts based on those objects which have been presented to the mind *vis-à-vis* receptivity, which is itself only a functioning rooted in the perceptivity of objects.[74] As perception is dependent upon sensation, we may briefly outline the limited nature of sensation to explain reason as finite.

Many thinkers have articulated the concern of relying on our senses to produce knowledge that is well grounded.[75] Yet perceptions and sensations give to receptivity that which presents objects to us in an entirely indirect manner. For the object of sensation does not itself impress upon the mind as was once

---

[72] A point of clarification is needed here. Perception is the most primary encounter because while sensation is more direct and thus primary in terms of succession (it occurs prior to), sensation does not generate an experience until mediated through perception, that is, perceived. Nothing can replace perception as the most primary means of experience. We can here be reminded of Schopenhauer: "That books do not take the place of experience, and that learning is no substitute for genius, are two kindred phenomena; their common ground is that the abstract can never take the place of the perceptive" (1969, p. 74).

[73] "Our knowledge springs from two fundamental sources of the mind; the first is the capacity of receiving representations (receptivity for impressions), the second is the power of knowing an object through these representations (spontaneity [in the production] of concepts). Through the first an object is *given* to us, through the second the object is *thought* in relation to that [given] representation (which is a mere determination of the mind)" (Kant 2007, p. 92).

[74] We may for this reason be correct in thinking of reason as not a faculty in and of itself but a mere tool used by a different faculty; it is better thought of as a category of a faculty.

[75] Examples include René Descartes (2011) *Meditations on First Philosophy: With Selections from the Objections and Replies*, David Hume (1995) *An Enquiry concerning Human Understanding*, Gottfried Wilhelm Leibniz (1991) *Discourse on Metaphysics and Other Essays*, George Berkeley (1995) *A Treatise concerning the Principles of Human Knowledge, Wherein the Chief Causes of Error and Difficulty in the Sciences, with the Grounds of Skepticism, Atheism, and Irreligion, Are Inquired into*, Bertrand Russell (1997) *The Problems of Philosophy*. Note that some of these thinkers have nevertheless held to the claim that it is still via sense that we gain knowledge.

thought,[76] but rather the mental cognition of the object is what is presented: that is, the sensational qualities[77] of the object are perceptible and are what is received by the mind.

In this way, *Dasein* is constantly engulfed by existence as a phenomenon and "Phenomena are constantly folded back upon themselves" (Pike 1950, p. 42). Yet, this reveals a truth connected to the Being of *Dasein;* the engagement of *Dasein* with phenomena is that of a phenomenon with other phenomena, itself included.[78] *Dasein* has a *privilege*[79] insofar as it allows for the very possibility of recognizing its Being as an engagement with phenomena, a necessarily reflective position. It is this very recognition, regardless of how subtle it may be, that *Dasein* not only comes to regard its own status of Being, but also in which *Dasein* reflects and exemplifies its own existence as a phenomenon itself; *Dasein*, in this way, has the character of both engaging with phenomena as well as being engaged by phenomena, as a phenomenon. Thus, not only is *Dasein* finite in terms of reason, but also by virtue of its necessarily being a phenomenon as *in-der-Welt-sein*. Phenomena as objects are limited in several ways in Kant: magnitude, temporality, and perceptibility.[80]

Any object which entails, in virtue of its Being, the ability to be sensed (that is, affectability) must also have magnitude; it must have properties of both extension and shape with which it is extended. This shape is referred to as the figure of the object. Now, this figure can be external, in which case we discuss its extension, or internal, in which case it occupies our faculties through affections *vis-à-vis* sensation.[81] It is for this reason that Kant distinguishes between *extensive* and *intensive* magnitude.

---

76 For example, see Florian Cajori's (1899) *A History of Physics in Its Elementary Branches: Including the Evolution of Physical Laboratories* and John I. Beare's (1906) *Greek Theories of Elementary Cognition: From Alcmaeon to Aristotle*. Both works offer a great insight into the history of physics and cognition, and in particular how it was thought that we came to perceive the world around us.

77 Secondary qualities as termed by John Locke (1824) in *An Essay Concerning Human Understanding*. Also known as accidents. These are the non-essential qualities of a being.

78 As James Jeans writes in *Physics and Philosophy* "By performing observations on the world, we alter it" (2009, p. 172).

79 It must be noted that this does not belong solely to *Dasein* in virtue of its being itself. Rather this belongs most *innately* in *Dasein* due to its activity towards this position held.

80 Just to keep in mind we are specifically here speaking of phenomena and not the *Ding an sich* or of *noumena*, which are not bound by these.

81 For a great commentary on how the geometric figure was thought of and transformed in mathematical history, see Morris Kline's (1974) *Mathematical Thought from Ancient to Modern times*.

Of the former, Kant writes: "I entitle a magnitude extensive when the representation of the parts makes possible, and therefore necessarily precedes, the representation of the whole" and thus, since "the [element of] pure intuition in all appearances is either space or time, every appearance is as intuition an extensive magnitude" (2007, pp. 198–199). This is to say that insofar as we perceive an object, that object is necessarily intuited as holding space, time, or both, prior to the affection of the senses that occurs through sensation. It is through the *a priori* intuition of the object, the 'pure' form of *intuition*, such that the object has extensive magnitude – it is an appearance.

In connection with the *a priori* magnitude, *extensive magnitude*, which is present due to the initially *pure intuition* enabling the very ability to experience phenomena as external to oneself, there is the *a posteriori intensive* magnitude that establishes the degree of the magnitude of which it is an affection of the senses. "*Intensive magnitude*," Kant writes, is "a degree of influence on the sense" which "must be ascribed to all objects of perception" since it is "apprehended only as unity" and "does not involve a successive synthesis proceeding from parts to the whole" of the representation (ibid, pp. 202–203). To the extent, then, that an object affects the senses, it is in possession of *intensive* as well as *extensive* magnitude.

Dasein considered as a phenomenon is characteristic of both *extensive* and *intensive* magnitudes. In the case of the former, as with all phenomena, space and time as *pure* intuitions determine *Dasein* as *extensive*. *Dasein* exists for other beings, as well as to itself, as an appearance with extension in space and time. It is the manifestation of *intensive* magnitude that is of particular interest. It would seem that *intensive* magnitude could only apply to that which is in itself *external* to *Dasein* as it is the degree to which such objects affect the senses. However, *Dasein* itself presents *intensive* magnitude *to itself*, in part due to its self-positing and self-reflexivity. In other words, the very nature of *Dasein* as *in-der-Welt-sein*, that is to say, by the simple fact that *Dasein* has "world" it must also have *intensive* magnitude.[82]

---

[82] This is similar to the self-posited "I" present in Fichte or Hegel. For these see Hegel's (1977) *Phenomenology of Spirit*, and Fichte's (1994) *Introductions to the Wissenschaftslehre and Other Writings*. For commentary on intensive magnitude, the "I" in Hegel and Fichte, and the relationship between the two, any of the following works are a great starting point: Schaub's essays "Hegel's Criticisms of Fichte's Subjectivism. I" (1912) and "Hegel's Criticisms of Fichte's Subjectivism. II" (1913); John Lachs' (1990) essay "Human Natures", Robert Williams' (1985) article "Hegel and Transcendental Philosophy", and Mandt's (1997) article "Fichte, Kant's Legacy, and the Meaning of Modern Philosophy".

All phenomena exist not simply as extension, but also temporally. Time limits phenomena in two ways, depending on the being of their being in time. If alive, through death; if not alive, through erosion and decimation. A phenomenon that is not alive is limited by time through decimation, that is, through its decomposability. Although this is a physical limitation, it is also a temporal limitation as it occurs to an object, given sufficient time. Thus, no object in time can avoid eventual decimation within time; "you cannot conquer time," as Auden's poem goes (1940).[83] A phenomenon that is alive eventually meets death. *Dasein* has a specific mode of being-in which establishes a more intimate connection with this temporality of being *Dasein*, *sein-zum-Tode*, which will be discussed in more detail later on. The *Innerzeitigkeit* of *Dasein* is a main source of finitude, as time itself is limited.[84]

Phenomena are also limited by means of their perceptibility, or the mere fact that they must, by virtue of being a phenomenon, be perceived. In this way, as explained above, phenomena are limited insofar as they only appear in a certain way, and this appearance is all that can be perceived. That which lies beyond the appearance[85] cannot be perceived and thus, when encountered as a phenomenon, places upon anything (in this case, *Dasein*) a limitation.

Insofar as *Dasein* is itself a phenomenon, it is singular; that is to say that *Dasein* is also finite in terms of its incapability of being divisible. That which is infinite can be divided endlessly; an infinite substance is not limited in its own being "one", as *Dasein* is, due to its singularity.[86] As Blaise Pascal noted that the human being is finite and as such nothing when compared to the infinite nature of the universe.[87]

---

83 Indeed, it seems, even ideas decay. For example, John Locke in *An Essay Concerning Human Understanding* Book II, Chapter 10, writes: "There seems to be a constant decay of all our ideas; even of those which are struck deepest, and in minds the most retentive, so that if they be not sometimes renewed by repeated exercises of the senses, or reflection on those kinds of objects which at first occasioned them, the print wears out, and at last there remains nothing to be seen" (1846, p. 103).
84 H.L. Mencken in *Treatise on the Gods* writes: "In looking backward, as in looking forward, early man was quite unable to imagine endless time. Always he concluded that the animal creation, including his own kind, must have a beginning, and the earth he walked on with it" (1930, p. 200).
85 Beyond the appearance here refers to the *Ding an sich*.
86 As we are reminded by Aristotle, when he writes in *Physica*, "What is one is indivisible whatever it may be, e.g. a man is one man, not many" (2017, p. 71)
87 The full original passage from *Les Pensées* reads, "*Car enfin qu'est-ce que l'homme dans la nature? Un néant à l'égard de l'infini, un tout à l'égard du néant: un milieu entre rien et tout*" (Pascal 1858, p. 46).

Nonfinitude

There is also an aspect of *Dasein* insofar as *Dasein* is being-in-the-world that, although finite, remains free and unbound by its finitude and pushes *Dasein* towards its infinite potentiality. Namely, there is in Kant, a distinction between reason, in its practical sense, and pure reason.[88] The former represents the finite nature of *Dasein*; however, the latter does the same for what I may term the *nonfinitude* of *Dasein*. An analysis here will indicate that by leaving out pure reason, Heidegger fails to recognize the intermediary nonfinitude of reason alongside its finitude.[89]

First, we must recapitulate the Kantian expression of pure reason. As indicated in Chapter One, 'pure' in a Kantian sense refers to that which is independent of experience and has no ties to an external cause.[90] In distinguishing between reason as dependent upon experience, and pure reason as independent of it, Kant also reveals the nature of reason as bridging the gap between knowledge gained from experience and a more metaphysical knowledge.[91]

Reason, insofar as it serves the task of quantifying (that is, the unification of) concepts formed through experience and sensation, is limited as described in the previous section. However, what about pure reason, which is *purified* of this reliance upon experience? Is it too limited in similar fashion? If not, is it infinite? If so, how can it truly be "pure" and *a priori*?

It seems clear that pure reason as *a priori* is removed from experience entirely. Pure reason is transcendental, as it provides the foundation of knowledge and experience generally. As such, it can easily be said to be abstracted from experience altogether. Kant writes that "Mathematics presents the most splendid example of the successful extension of pure reason, without the help of experience" (2007, p. 576). While it can be argued that mathematics exists in the world

---

[88] Simpler terms to help illustrate the distinction would be *sensible* or *intuitive reason*.
[89] Although Heidegger discusses pure reason in *Kant and the Problem of Metaphysics*, pure reason as it is treated in Kant is removed and lacking from the existential analytic of *Dasein* in *Being and Time*. For Heidegger's treatment of pure reason refer back to *Kant and the Problem of Metaphysics* (Heidegger 1997).
[90] This is of course only *mostly* correct. *Pure reason* is the mode of reasoning which is done without reference to or being necessitated by experience. The act of reasoning itself (even if through *pure reason*) is nonetheless an experience and so *pure reason* is not entirely removed from experience. Thus, the opening words of Kant's introduction to the *Critique* state as much "There can be no doubt that all our knowledge begins with experience" (Kant 2007, p. 41).
[91] Kant himself would not appreciate the use of the term metaphysical here. I have chosen this term rather than *a priori* purposefully and it follows my interpretation of Kantian worlds. See chapter three of this work for a discussion of this.

around us and as such we experience it daily as an ontological entity, it is nevertheless present *a priori* or in a "pure" manner.⁹²

But if pure reason is not limited in the same ways as what we may call *intuitive* or *sensible* reason, then is it by this fact alone infinite? Does it lack limitation altogether? It might be easy to jump to this conclusion, for if something is unlimited then it appears infinite. But as all of Kant's philosophy suggests, appearances are singular perceptions and as the saying goes *"Frontis nulla fides"* (Juvenal 2004, p.148).⁹³

Indeed, pure reason does have limitations of its own, as shown in two sections of the *Critique:* the *paralogisms* and the *antinomies*. Beginning with the former, we will discuss these and articulate in what way *pure* reason may be said not to be infinite. The *paralogisms* are aimed at showing the fallacious application of *pure reason,* that is to say, the limitations of its application to concepts. Reason generally, whether *pure* or *intuitive,* is a unifier of the highest order. This means, however, that it can only be applied in a specific manner – the difference is the concepts to which it *can* be applied, either *a priori* or *a posteriori*.⁹⁴ In its application to these concepts, it must function as reason and cannot, in virtue of its being a category,⁹⁵ extend beyond this mode of application.

The *paralogisms* themselves deal with claims that can be made regarding the soul, its permanence, simplicity, status as a substance, and relation to the outside world of phenomena. With each of these, Kant shows the problem with applying (pure) reason to reach the stated conclusion of the various claims. In reviewing each of the four paralogisms of pure reason, the fallacies of thought can be identified.

To begin with, Kant challenges the claim that the soul is permanent, or more specifically, that it is a substance.⁹⁶ Rene Descartes' famous assertion of the *cogito,* an "I" which is indivisible, asserted the permanence of the soul as a substance in its articulation.⁹⁷ Insofar as the soul is a substance, Descartes suggest-

---

92 Hilary Putnam (1985), as one example, makes such a claim about the ontological status of mathematics in his wonderful work, *Mathematics, Matter, and Method. Philosophical Papers, vol. I.*
93 Translation: Trust not what appears.
94 The former consists of reason as applied to concepts devoid of the need for empirical data, the latter of reason applied towards the empirical data intuited.
95 As noted earlier, I here reject the usual assertion that reason is a faculty; instead, I treat it as a sub-faculty, a category.
96 In speaking of the soul, it is important to note that Kant necessarily is referring to the activity of thought; or more specifically, of that being which possesses thought. For more on this see Kant (2007, p. 332-333)
97 A phenomenological account of the Cartesian soul is given in excellence by Michel Henry (1993) in his chapter "The Soul According to Descartes".

ed that it could be known through the application of reason – *ego cogito, ergo sum*.[98] However, Kant vehemently opposed this position, suggesting contrarily that if the soul is to be considered a substance, then as a *Ding an sich* it cannot be known.[99]

In concluding his criticism of this notion that the "I" is a substance, he writes that the articulation that "The soul is substance" can be considered as valid

> if only it be recognised that this concept [of the soul and of substance] does not carry us a single step further, and so cannot yield us any of the usual deductions of the pseudo-rational doctrine of the soul, as, for instance, the everlasting duration of the human soul in all changes and even in death – if, that is to say, we recognise that this concept signifies a substance only in idea, not in reality (Kant 2007, p. 334).

In other words, even if the soul is a substance, it is an unknown substance; *Ignoratur enim, quæ sit natura animai* (Lucretius 2008, p. 214).[100] This is because it is simply the *a priori* basis of representations, that is, of *intuitions*. It is thus a part of every intuition, though it is itself not intuited, and is as such indistinguishable from intuitions themselves.

Kant next proceeds to critique the claim that the soul is simple. What Kant is criticizing here is, more fully, the claim that the soul is a thing such that it is not "regarded as the concurrence of several things acting" (2007, p. 335). That is to

---

98 Earlier in the *Discourse on Method*, Descartes expressed his position as "Et remarquant que cette vérité, *je pense, donc je suis*, était si ferme et si assurée, que toutes les plus extravagantes suppositions des Sceptiques n'étoient pas capables de l'ébranler, je jugeai que je pouvais la recevoir sans scrupule pour le premier principe de la Philosophie que je cherchais" (Descartes 1908, p. 102).

99 That the soul is a thing-in-itself for Kant is well noted. "Kant tells us that if matter were a thing-in-itself, then as a composite being it would be completely distinguished from the soul as a simple being because he is not even entertaining the possibility that the soul could be a mere appearance rather than a thing-in-itself" writes Julian Wuerth (2014, p. 180). The assertion that the soul may be a mere appearance is an interesting thought to consider, though only briefly here. It requires no deep penetration to recognize that appearances are such due to the procedure of experience, one which includes perception. Insofar as perception enables a representation to the mind, the basis of an appearance, we cannot include the soul as among appearances. The soul, if we are to consider it as the transcendental ego, then with any representation, it is itself represented vis-à-vis representation itself, it is that to which representation occurs, and as such does not require perception. Thus, it is not an appearance.

100 The whole saying reads in translation: "For they know not what is the nature of the soul, whether it is born or else finds its way into them at their birth, and again whether it is torn apart by death and perishes with us, or goes to see the shades of Orcus and his waste pools, or by the gods' will implants itself in other breasts" (Lucretius 1948, p. 30).

say, that it is a singular acting thing rather than a multiple. In holding that the soul is indivisible, Descartes suggested that the underlying substance of thought was a singular whole; a thinking whole rather than thinking parts.[101] Kant suggests that this overlooks the unification of parts for a singularity. In particular, Kant's answer is apperception, and more specifically the unification of apperception.

Apperception itself, Kant defines as the faculty which unifies, or synthesizes, representations and affections of the senses (ibid, p. 141). Put more simply, it considers various *representations* and finds the mode of connection which relates them into a unified whole. As such, it is perhaps more appropriate to consider it a faculty of the discovery of interrelatedness of representations, rather than of unification, as apperception is itself not a faculty of unification, but rather presents that which can unify representations.

Kant furthers the notion of apperception by also presenting it a transcendental status. He writes that "This transcendental unity of apperception forms out of all possible appearances, which can stand alongside one another in one experience, a connection of all these representations according to laws" (ibid, p. 136). Thus the distinction, that is, what is added to transcendental apperception, is that it unifies experience, whereas apperception is directly involved with the empirical status of representations of sensible intuitions. In this way, the soul cannot be known as an indivisible substance, but rather as a plurality unified *vis-à-vis* the faculty of apperception. Instead, the *cogito* presumes, and therefore is preconditioned by, thought itself; as such, it cannot give proof of the claim that the soul is simple.

The third paralogism calls into question the claim that the soul requires an eternal and unchanging "I" at its core in order that it remain constant and consistent, enabling shifting thoughts; otherwise, thoughts would also remain constant, which is evidently not the case. Kant here argues that insofar as the "I" is only experienced subjectively, there is no ground for holding that it is permanent and unchanging. This is related to the above criticism offered by Kant: for since the concept of "I" is present, transcendentally, as a condition of thought itself, it cannot be known in and of itself. This leads directly to the fourth paralogism, which seeks to provide a proof that the soul is entirely distinct from the world of experience.

The same issue is at work here, as pure reason attempts to extend itself beyond its limits. Just as we cannot know the "I" in itself, we cannot know objects

---

[101] Steven J. Wagner notes that Descartes was "committed to the indivisibility of any substance" in his article "Descartes on the Parts of the Soul" (1984, p. 64).

(that is, the external world) in themselves, apart from our intuitions of them. It is in this sense, then, that the world of experience is nothing more to us than an *internal* representation, a world of appearances.[102] Thus the "I" representing, and which is itself present in representing, is also always connected to the external world, insofar as both are "within" us as mental projections. The fourth and final paralogism thus seeks to refute the assertion of traditional idealism, which holds that there is no proof of or knowledge about the external world to be gained.

The paralogisms show then that reason, including *pure reason*, can only be applied in a particular way, and as such has certain limits that cannot be bypassed. Limitation that comes from "worldliness" itself is unavoidable, even by the likes of Kantian *pure* reason. Not only, however, can *pure reason* only be applied in a specific manner, it also has limitations as to that to which it can precisely be applied. While the paralogisms show the former, the latter is articulated through a series of what Kant calls *antinomies*.

This section from his *Critique of Pure Reason* aims specifically at showing the impossibility of using reason to come to conclusions about certain questions that we often raise. Kant sets up antinomies, showing arguments for both the thesis and antithesis and concludes that neither is more persuasive than the other. Through examining the antinomies and showing how one of the proofs is indeed more accurate than the other in consideration with the phenomena/noumena distinction.

The first antinomy we will examine is the very first addressed by Kant himself. The thesis for this antinomy is that the world is limited by space and is temporally finite; that is, it has a beginning and will also have an end. Kant gives proofs of this claim suggesting "If we assume that the world has no beginning in time, then up to every given moment eternity has elapsed, and there has passed away in the world an infinite series of successive states of things" (Kant 2007, p. 397). What this means is that, if the world is eternal, then every moment which is subsequent is also eternal. Thus, an infinite number of events will have taken place in each moment.

In addition, something which is infinite can never have a complete set of instances; that is, cannot have a complete series.[103] This is because the very nature of an infinite series is that it cannot have a first or a last, something which is a necessary precondition of a notion of completeness, and so cannot in any way

---

102 As Sartre once wrote in his excellent play *Nausea:* "Things are entirely what they appear to be – and behind them...there is nothing" (1964, p. 96).
103 In *Physica* Aristotle writes as much: "Nothing is complete (τέλειον) which has no end (τέλος); and the end is a limit" (2017, p. 70).

ever be completed, only continuous. Thus, this thesis concludes that it must be impossible for the world to be infinite, since one of its preconditions would be to have a traceable series of successive events, which as stated would not be possible if the world were considered infinite. There is, however, another proof which is necessary in order to show that the world is not (as it is according to this thesis) infinite, but rather finite.

Another aspect of the thesis presented is that the world is limited by space, that is, it is not boundless but instead has established boundaries. In order to form this proof Kant assumes the opposite: that the world is infinite in space. However, if this were true then "the successive synthesis of the parts of an infinite world must be viewed as completed, that is, an infinite time must be viewed as having elapsed in the enumeration of all coexisting things" (ibid, p. 398). Of course, this cannot be the case as Kant claims, since it was shown in the first proof that the world cannot be infinite in time and still have a series of successive events.[104]

Since there cannot be successive events, how then can the world be limited by space? Space must then be seen as infinite; there can be no way that the world is temporally infinite yet limited by space, nor the other way around. This is because infinitude requires, and can only maintain more infinitude and not anything finite, as it has been shown that this is impossible. Instead, the world must be confined within a set space that has boundaries and limits, as it has been proved that the world is limited temporally, and so then (as just explained) this requires the world to also be limited as regards its spatiality.

The antithesis to this antinomy argues that the world is infinite in time without beginning or end, and in space is not confined within boundaries. Kant addresses this claim through the same technique employed in proving the thesis of this antinomy. First, assuming the opposite (namely, that the world has a beginning in time), Kant recognizes that this means there was a time prior to the beginning of the world that was "empty".[105] This would indeed have to be the case, since if there were a time prior to the world, it would have to be an empty time in which there was essentially nothing. However, this does not make sense, according to Kant, since "no coming to be of a thing is possible in an empty time,

---

104 This dates to Aristotle, who noted in his work on physics that "A quantity is infinite if it is such that we can always take a part [or piece] outside what has been already taken. On the other hand, what has nothing outside it is complete and whole" (2017, p. 70).

105 Modern science has much to add here, though it remains beyond the scope of this work. Nevertheless, it should be noted that this very concern Andrei Linde called "the most intractable problem of modern cosmology" as cited in the essay "What the Big Bang Explains—What It Doesn't!" (1996).

because no part of such a time possesses, as compared with any other, a distinguishing condition of existence rather than non-existence" (ibid, p. 397). In other words, if there is this so-called "empty" time, in which no world exists, then there is no distinguishing factor, or moment, between the existence or non-existence of the world. That is, nothing would ever come to be in the world, nor would the world itself ever have come to be; nothing begets nothing. *"De nihilo nihil, in nihilum nil posse reverti,"* as Persius once noted (1987, p. 83).[106] Therefore, it seems like the world must be infinite as regards time; that it does not have a beginning or an end, but simply is.

Once again, to assert the infinite spatiality of the world, the proof for this second part assumes that the world is finite. That is to say, it is limited by its own spatiality. This also must mean, however, that it exists within a limitless empty space, which contains the limited world; things are thus in relation within space but now also to the space itself. For how else would it be possible to be limited, since it would not even be existence unless there were a limitless space beyond it? We know however that this could not be the case, since as Kant suggests "the world is an absolute whole beyond which there is no object of intuition, and therefore no correlate with which the world stands in relation, the relation of the world to empty space would be a relation of it to no object" (Kant 2007, p. 398). Clearly, as I do not presume anyone should find a problem with this, there cannot be a relation to what would be nothing, since the very notion of a relation is that something which is being is related to another thing which is also being. That is to say, relation is between beings, and does not and could not involve nothing.[107] So it seems that, if all the above is true, the world cannot be limited in space but can only be infinite, specifically infinite in time and in space.

These two proofs establish the reasoning behind the thesis of this first antinomy. However, if we evaluate these proofs carefully enough, it becomes evident that there is an immediate problem with the mode of reasoning. Kant's proof explains eternal temporality as having the act of elapsing. However, can we truly

---

106 Translation: Nothing can be born of nothing, nothing can be resolved into nothing. Previously, Parmenides offered a similar notion in *About Nature:* "τί δ' ἄν μιν καὶ χρέος ὦρσεν ὕστερον ἢ πρόσθεν, τοῦ μηδενὸς ἀρξάμενον, φῦν; οὕτως ἢ πάμπαν πελέναι χρεών ἐστιν ἢ οὐχί" (Parmenides, Fr. 8) (Burnett 1920, p 175).
107 This is not to say that all relationality is relational. There can be a nonrelational relationality.

conceive of an infinity of time in terms of elapsing? [108] Elapsing is always in reference to a past succession of time, that is, time which has or is currently passing; a mere succession of events is not an elapsing of time and does not require time. Rather, time if infinite could still allow for successive events. How can this be so?

One must remember what is meant by "infinite". Infinite means without beginning and end. It thus requires a continuous stream; there is neither a beginning nor an end to time, but this would also require a singular time; since if there were more than one time there must necessarily be an elapsing of time from one to the next. If this were true, time could not be infinite, since an initial time would then be required which was then also the first time to elapse into another time. Time always is, but does not necessarily elapse in itself; rather, the succession of events which take place within time – time as an infinite source – then establishes the appearance of elapsing. To recapitulate, time does not and cannot elapse if time is infinite. Yet this does not mean that there cannot be a succession of events within time. Thus, when the proof extends to the claim that there cannot be a complete series of events in an infinite time, this is not the case, since time is not necessary for events to pass; rather, the succession of events is what enables a perception of time, not the other way around.

If we are then to look at Kant's explanation of why successive events cannot occur in a singular time, are there any problems with this claim, such that we might prove the assertion here that there could be such succession? Kant deals with this, if we recall the first proof, by suggesting that if there were a singular time, and an infinitude of time, then there would be an infinite number of events in each moment of time, such that there would be an eternity of time with each passing moment. Although at first Kant's argument seemed to be strong in arguing against the possibility of an infinite time, after the aforementioned considerations it appears to have lost its veracity. If we contemplate a bit on the topic, and recall words such as "passing" and "moment", these words do not belong to one claiming an infinitude of time. For as we have said, if time is infinite, there must only be one singular time. If this is the case, then there is no "moment" except for the moment which is eternal and infinite as the entirety of the infinitude of time.

If we consider, for example, the number of events which occur in a "moment", it is impossible to calculate, but it is much more than a small few. If

---

108 Juan Ramón Jiménez offers us the following: "Transition is a complete present which unites the past and the future in momentary progressive ecstasy, a progressive eternity, a true eternity of eternities, eternal moments" (1957, p. 231).

we can then agree (and I see no reason not to) that if there is an infinity of time, and so one singular time which is stretched *ad infinitum,* we can also agree that the number of possible events in this singular time would increase *ad infinitum.* The problem, then, is the tendency to view time in regards to "moments" when there could be only one moment stretching into infinity, such that it enables an infinitude of successive events. Each of these proofs seems to be lacking in a fundamental way; neither is sufficient.

After examining the proofs for both the thesis and the antithesis on the infinity of the world, Kant moves forward into what he calls "observations"; this is where he outlines the problems which he finds coming out of reasoning this way about the world, and continues to provide explanations of the proofs. To begin, Kant asserts the true meaning of infinity as being something incapable of being complete; a completed thing is finite in that it is started and finished, whereas infinity can never be. Kant states that the successive "true transcendental concept of infinitude synthesis of units required for the enumeration of a quantum can never be completed" (2007, p. 401). Therefore, the world cannot possibly have a beginning in time, since this notion runs contrary to the very conception of infinitude.

There are also additional comments which Kant makes in regards to the support of the antithesis that the world must be infinite and not, as the thesis argues, finite. The major aspect of this proof lies in the treatment of the concept of empty space, which if the world were finite, would in fact exist. Although Kant shows that this is absurd, since then things would be in relation to space itself, which would be empty and thus be nothing, not an object, he also criticizes the proof insofar as it treats space as a determinant of appearances, when in actuality it is appearances which are determinants of spatiality.

> Space, it further follows, whether full or empty, may be limited by appearances, but appearances cannot be limited by an empty space outside them. This is likewise true of time. But while all this may be granted, it yet cannot be denied that these two non-entities, empty space outside the world and empty time prior to it, have to be assumed if we are to assume a limit to the world in space and time" (Kant 2007, p. 400).

In other words, if the world is finite and so then is limited, empty space and time must be assumed. In addition, empty space and time, though not determinants of appearances, would also have to lie in an infinite part of the world, outside the one in which we experience and encounter appearances. This leads again to the same problem that things would then be related to empty space, which Kant claims cannot be the case. So, the claim can be made that the world must indeed be infinite.

In the second of the antinomies, the topic is the very composition of the world of experience, namely, whether it be comprised of that which is singular and simple, or rather entirely of composites. The thesis of this antinomy holds that the former is the case; that the world is composed of simple, indivisible parts. Immediately this thesis seems to ring true – for there could be no composite without the simple parts from which it is to be composed.[109] Indeed, any composite must *ex vi terminorum* be a compound of simpler components.

Taking the opposite position, assuming that nothing exists which is not already composite, it can be shown why this thesis must be true. If it were indeed the case that all that exists is of a compound nature, then composition itself "as applied to substances, is only an accidental relation in independence of which they must still persist as self-subsistent Beings" (Kant 2007, p. 403). This is, however, contradictory to the very thesis for which it attempts to provide a proof. It can thus be said that all things are composed of that which is simple, out of which composites are formed.

Yet this mode of argumentation is not without flaws itself. For, to think that "although we can never so isolate these elementary substances as to take them out of this state of composition, reason must think them as the primary subjects of all composition, and therefore, as simple beings, prior to all composition" is to mistakenly think that we can know that which lies outside of direct experience – a thing which Kant is adamant that we cannot (ibid). Without a doubt, all that appears to us through *intuition* is composite. The simple is never represented to our faculties, and insofar as this is the case, it is never known directly to us. Thus, to hold that the simple represents all that exists, and objects of appearance are only of a composite nature, is no more than mere speculation and not something known through *pure reason*.

Postulating the antithesis, that everything exists as a composite, can be asserted and proved in the following manner according to Kant. That which exists external to a subject must also occupy a space; further, it must occupy a space equal to the parts of the composite. Following this to its logical extreme, it must also be the case that "the simple would be a composite of substances" (ibid). This follows given that everything simple, insofar as it necessarily is *in a space*, would also itself be composed of "a manifold of constituents external to one another, and is therefore composite" (ibid).

---

[109] We see this in modern science, which continues to break down particles into smaller subparticles. Though it appears thus far that the quantum particles (such as quarks) cannot be broken down further.

Not only is this contradictory, thus showing that all is truly composite and proving the antithesis, it also establishes an infinite feedback loop in which all composites, composed of that which is simple, which in turn are themselves composed of a multitude of parts and are thus composites in and of themselves, are in fact composed of composites. In this way, the antithesis is proved in two fashions: first due to the contradiction of assuming the thesis, and second due to the regress problem that arises when the thesis is supposed.

There is, however, a second aspect to the claim made by the antithesis: namely, that there cannot exist anything that is indeed simple, but *only that* which is composite. In other words, due to the problem identified in the articulation of the thesis, that we do not directly perceive anything simple but only composites, it cannot thus be said that anything simple exists based on our perception and relation to the world of objects. Therefore, "the absolutely simple is therefore a mere idea, the objective reality of which can never be shown in any possible experience" (ibid).

In order to suggest that anything which exists, exists as simple, what would be required is an empirically-based *intuition* which does not consist of a manifold, but rather is already *intuited* only in something singular, a unity.[110] However, "An absolutely simple object can never be given in any possible experience", and as such it can be claimed that "nothing simple is to be found anywhere" in the world of sense, from which *intuition* arises (ibid, p. 404). Since no *intuition* of that which is simple *itself* can be formed, it must then be the case that all is composite and nothing is simple.

There are likewise problems which arise in the proof provided here for the antithesis. Regarding the first claim of the antithesis, that no composite is made of that which is itself simple, which leads to the stated regress problem, it is logically necessary that a simple entity be postulated. Even if a simple is made of a composite, there arises a logical necessity to assume a simple substance at the very base level. Barring this assumption, one is left with a circular argument. Thus, at some level, a simple composed of composites must also be composed of that which is simple. In other words, the argument in favor of the antithesis proves nothing, as it can also be used in favor of the thesis, with the same force behind it.

The second claim of the antithesis is much more problematic regarding the simple, insofar as it "excludes it from the whole of nature" rather than just "from the intuition of the composite" as does the first (ibid). The very problem articulated with reference to the first claim is merely emphasized and more prominent

---

[110] In Kantian terms this would mean intuiting *noumena*.

with the second claim as presented here. There exists a *chain of reasoning* that presupposes a simple substance such that any composite must be composed of simple-composites.[111] Thus, even if the simple can be removed from the possibility of being *intuited*, insofar as they do not appear to us in the world of sense, the simple is nevertheless always presupposed *a priori*.

Commenting further on the thesis, Kant argues that space must be treated as a whole of which there are parts (*totality*), rather than as a whole made up of parts (*composite*). This is directly related to his earlier discussion of space as *pure intuition*, space as a singular rather than "one among many" (spaces). However, in conflict with this, "Since space is not a composite made up of substances (nor even of real accidents), if I remove all compositeness from it, nothing remains", Kant writes; not even a single point, as that would be to limit space and individuate a singular space amongst others (ibid, p. 405). Insofar as that which is simple is substance, rather than a part, it is akin to Leibniz's *monad*. Indeed, we are immediately reminded of the statement he makes in his *Monadology*: "*c'est dans la substance simple, et non dans le composé, ou dans la machine qu'il la faut chercher*" (Leibniz 1886, p. 51). A simple taken as part of a composite is, Kant suggests, *atomus*.[112] The simple can fall victim to overextension as it is applied to more than what it actually is. In this case, a simple can "be made to apply to everything composite" and thus a single simple can become thought of as the whole of a composite (Kant 2007, p. 406).

The question becomes, though, at which point of the breakdown of substances is a simple or composite identified? For everything to be composed of simple parts, there is required a constant reference to a simpler thing, *ad infinitum*. The so-called "proof" for the thesis that all things are reducible to simple parts is thus one which is mathematical in nature, entailing the problem that mathematics is closer to things in themselves than to appearances,[113] and "when philosophy here plays with mathematics, it does so because it forgets that in this discussion we are concerned only with *appearances* and their condition" (ibid).[114] The composite cannot then be understood in terms of the simple; the composite can-

---

111 This refers to the same chain of logics or reasoning mentioned earlier.
112 He writes in the *Critique of Pure Reason* in response to Leibniz's conception of a *monad*: "The word *monas*...should refer only to the simple which is *immediately* given as simple substance" (Kant 2007, p. 406).
113 The integration of mathematics into nature has been suggested since the time of Pythagoras. For an excellent modern treatment of this see Marcus du Sautoy's (2008) *Symmetry: A Journey Into the Patterns of Nature* and Heinz R. Pagels' (1982) *The Cosmic Code: Quantum Physics As The Language Of Nature*.
114 Italics from the original.

not itself be said to be an intuition, but rather requires the simple in order that, insofar as appearances are composites, it can be intuited as composite.

Clearly this is problematic, not only for proving the antithesis, but also in virtue of its being impossible via sensible intuition. According to Kant, there is a specific way in which we must conceive of a composite whole, as the following passage suggests:

> Though it may be true that when a whole, made up of substances, is thought by the pure understanding alone, we must, prior to all composition of it, have the simple, this does not hold of the *totum substantiale phaenomenon*[115] which, as empirical intuition in space, carries with it the necessary characteristic that no part of it is simple, because no part of space is simple (ibid, pp. 406–407).

Due to space as *pure intuition* being responsible for *appearances* insofar as we can experience objects in space as represented to us, space is not simple and is itself the precondition of *outer sense;* that is, it is that which makes up the *worldliness* of *Dasein*.[116] To say this in simpler terms, it is because the objects of sense, of the world of *Dasein*, are not encountered as things in themselves.

Here, Kant argues once more against the thesis that the "I" might be the singular simple substance. As he did earlier, Kant claims that "Self-consciousness is of such a nature that since the subject which thinks at the same time its own object, it cannot divide itself" and it must as such always be recognized in terms of compositeness (ibid, p. 408). The question here becomes whether or not the "I" of "I think" necessarily always contains itself within the object of its thought; does the "I" always appear to us as a composite? Certainly, Kant thought this was the case, though we will later consider this notion further.

Kant continues his antinomies by dealing with the notion of freedom, a concept heatedly debated over the centuries. The thesis provided for this antinomy is that it is necessary to assume the causality of freedom. In order to show the proof for this thesis, it is assumed that the only form of causality is natural causality; that is, the laws of nature. Therefore, every event has a preceding event, or cause, out of which it comes to be the case.

If this be granted, that this is the way which natural causality functions, then it too must be universally agreed that each and every cause itself must have a cause of its own, and so forth *ad infinitum*. "But the law of nature is just this,

---

115 Translation: entire substantiality of the phenomenon.
116 As Stephen Frederick Schneck so clearly puts this in his work *Acting Persons: New Perspectives:* "Heidegger construes worldliness, it bears iterating, as an existential, that is to say, as a way in which *Dasein* exists; so construed, worldliness is an essential part of 'being in the world'" (2002, p. 76).

that nothing takes place without a cause significantly determined *a priori*. The proposition that no causality is possible save in accordance with nature, when taken in unlimited universality, is therefore self-contradictory" (ibid, p. 410). There must be another form of causality which we could assume, a causality which has itself as a cause and is thus spontaneous: the causality that is freedom. Without the causality of freedom, even cause and effect, natural causality, is not a complete form of causality. Thus, there is freedom in the form of this spontaneous causality.

Is there any evident problem with the initial arguments used in the proof? If we recognize the major claim in the above proof, then there arises the question of spontaneity. The first question one should ask is whether or not what we call freedom can truly be understood in terms of spontaneity? Is being spontaneous enough to call it free? This, however, is a concern easily put to rest, since the proof is attempting to establish freedom as a causality, and spontaneity is necessary for the cause to be free. In other words, causality by virtue of the term itself cannot be equated with a conception of freedom. However, it *could* be free if it is a cause itself and thus is spontaneous as Kant claims.[117]

But what should be asked is a more fundamental question. That is, what can be spontaneous? Something which is spontaneous is that which is uncaused, or caused out of its own self[118]; in a world governed by causality and nature, there can be no such spontaneous event, since every event has a cause which preceded it. The only possible event which could be left uncaused, and therefore unaccounted for, would be the first cause.[119] Even if it would be possible to know the first cause and determine whether or not it itself had a cause or was spontaneous, is this enough for real freedom? The freedom awarded by this proof is simply a spontaneous first cause which begins a series of effects. Nothing more can or will be spontaneous as now everything, every event, has a cause and thus is not free. We can therefore deem this spontaneity as merely that, not as a freedom from causation.[120]

---

117 Note here that there is the deeper problem posed by hard incompatiblists who hold that regardless of the reality of causal determinism, freedom does not exist. One example of such a position can be found in Derk Pereboom's (2005) article "Defending Hard Incompatibilism".
118 Self-causality is itself problematic. Is something self-caused not simply spontaneous? It would seem that anything arising out of its own causality, meaning uncaused by anything other than itself, is indeed spontaneous.
119 Such as Aristotle's Unmoved Mover mentioned in *Metaphysics* (2002). For good commentary on the Unmoved Mover in Aristotle's work, see R. Michael Olson's (2013) essay "Aristotle on God: Divine *Nous* as Unmoved Mover" and H. J. Easterling's (1976) article "The Unmoved Mover in Early Aristotle".
120 It is unclear however, how such an event could actually impact us at all.

The antithesis for this antinomy, namely that there can be no freedom and that everything goes in accordance with nature, is proved once again through *reductio ad absurdum*. Assuming that there is a transcendental, spontaneous freedom, where does this lead us? The following selection provides for an overall summarization of the proof for this anti-thesis:

> But every beginning of action presupposes a state of the not yet acting cause; and a dynamical beginning of the action, if it is also a first beginning, presupposes a state which has no causal connection with the preceding state of the cause, that is to say, in nowise follows from it. Transcendental freedom thus stands opposed to the law of causality; and the kind of connection which it assumes as holding between the successive states of the active causes renders all unity of experience impossible. It is not met with in any experience, and is therefore an empty thought-entity (Kant 2007, p. 410).

In other words, all events, effects, *et cetera,* have a cause. A spontaneous cause would presuppose a state in time in which there was no causality, that this first cause was uncaused and yet brought with it the establishment of a causal nature. This seems unfathomable to Kant, and so the antithesis stands, with its claim that there cannot be any freedom.

Analyzing the antithesis for this antinomy, are there any problems in the proofs given in support of it? While the proof seems to hold tightly, there is an obvious overstepping when we evaluate the claim "Transcendental freedom thus stands opposed to the law of causality." Is this a valid claim? Does transcendental freedom really stand in opposition to the law of causality? Or rather, is it an entirely separate entity? If we understand transcendental freedom to be that causality which is spontaneous and is thus uncaused, there is no reason that this runs counter to the law of causality. The law of causality explains that all events have a cause, and thus are not free[121]; transcendental freedom is not an event, however, and is not in opposition to causality but its very source.

However, the question persists: whence did the law of causality get placed in motion or action? Does the law of causality extend *ad infinitum?* Simple reasoning can explain this possibility away, since if there be a chain of causality, the chain must have a first link, otherwise no chain would be possible at all; even if there will be no way to understand this first cause, there must be one which is the source of all that has occurred *a posteriori*. Thus, it can be determined that there is necessarily a first cause, which itself must be uncaused and thus

---

[121] It is important to note however, as Heisenberg did in *Physics and Philosophy: The Revolution in Modern Science*, that "causality can only explain later events by earlier events, but it can never explain the beginning" (2000, p. 32).

spontaneous. This could be called transcendental causality; whether or not it is appropriate to call it "freedom" is another question altogether. Overall, it appears that there is a fundamental error in this proof in its assumption that the conception of a spontaneous cause is contrary to the law of causality.

Kant continues to examine the antinomy of freedom in both aspects: transcendental causality or the lack thereof. In regards to the thesis of this antinomy, namely, that there must exist a transcendental spontaneous causality that is freedom, Kant sheds light upon the problematic nature of positing an uncaused cause. The curiosity then becomes, can we assert spontaneity upon a cause such that it begins a chain of causality? But it cannot be determined how the spontaneity of a cause is even possible[122]; what can be determined, however, is that this type of causality is required for there to be any nature and causality, not to mention any experience at all. "The necessity of a first beginning, due to freedom, of a series of appearances we have demonstrated only insofar as it is required to make an origin of the world conceivable; for all the later following states can be taken as resulting according to purely natural laws" (Kant 2007, p. 413).

What is argued for here, then, is the necessity of spontaneity in an original cause, though it gives rise to causation from nature, such that experience can be made possible; that is, so that we may conceive of a possible beginning of the world. Though this reverts back to a posing of the question of whether or not there is an origin of the world, this is not of concern here, as what is of importance is that it gives rise to a conceivable (that is, possible) origin of the world.

Kant also provides a further explanation of the antithesis of the freedom antinomy as well. He asserts that proponents of this claim, that there is no spontaneous causality that is freedom but only the causality of nature, suggest that there is no necessity of an original cause. Instead, they propose that proponents of the thesis, which assert a freedom of causality, do not have the authority to insist on a spontaneous first cause, but rather that it is merely a product of imagination. In addition to there being no validity to the claim, they also suggest it is not necessary to have a primordial cause.

> Since the substances in the world have always existed – at least the unity of experience renders such a supposition – there is no difficulty in assuming that change of their states, that is, a series of their alterations, has likewise always existed, and therefore that a first beginning, whether mathematical or dynamical, is not to be looked for (Kant 2007, pp. 412– 413).

---

[122] Avi Sion (2014) gives a good description of spontaneity and even argues that everything can be deemed spontaneous in *Logical Philosophy*.

In other words, the apparent eternality of the substances which compose the world thus also mean that that which is composed of those substances (namely, the changes and alterations of those substances) must also be eternal; there is, then, no need to search nor to ponder the possibility of a spontaneous beginning, since the necessity of this causal freedom has been shown to be moot. Instead the world, and thus the law of causality, can be shown to be eternal.

The final antinomy of pure reason concerns the positing of the existence of a necessary being. The exchange between necessity and contingency is, in this antinomy, thoroughly discussed. The thesis of the antinomy asserts the necessity of a necessary being as the cause of the world. The proof of this thesis rests, in no small way, upon the Kantian understanding of time. Insofar as the world consists of a series of events, that is, since there is a constant alteration across time of such events and occurrences in the world, it is indeed plausible to assume the logical necessity of a necessary being as the primary cause of *succession*.

This is, in fact, the same series of causation as articulated in the previous antinomy. Every event or condition of the series is subsequent to an additional or previous condition. "Alteration thus existing as a consequence of the absolutely necessary, the existence of something absolutely necessary must be granted", Kant writes (ibid, p. 416). Due to the very fact of alteration, then, it can be posited that there exists something necessary upon which all else is predicated, or conditioned. Being conditioned is a state of succession from that which is itself original, or unconditioned.

As being predicated upon or conditioned by that which is necessary, each and every entity which is so must be existent *in the world*.[123] So too, however, must that which conditions be present *in the world* rather than external to it; that which is absolutely necessary must necessarily be in the sensible world as well. As Kant indicates, "if it existed outside of that world, the series of altercations in the world would derive its beginning from a necessary cause which would not itself belong to the sensible world", and this is not a possible relation "since the beginning of a series in time can be determined only by that which precedes it in time" (ibid). This would indeed not be possible if the necessary being existed external to the world of sense. In order to be the necessary cause of an existent condition, it must be in the same time as the series in which the condition is shared, but before the series is itself born; that is to say, it must be the very first instance of time in the series, yet nevertheless in time.[124]

---

[123] *World* here means specifically the "world of sense".
[124] "For a beginning is an existence preceded by a time in which the thing that begins did not yet exist." (Kant 2007, p. 416)

Under the presumption that a necessary being exists in the world, then, "Either there is a beginning in the series of alterations which is absolutely necessary, and therefore is without a cause, or the series itself is without any beginning, and although contingent and conditioned in all its parts, none the less, as a whole is absolutely necessary and unconditioned" (ibid, p. 415–416). It is the latter position which holds more interest here, as it posits the whole as being unconditioned and necessary, rather than a beginning point which itself would be necessary and unconditioned. [125] This suggests that, even without a designated beginning, the totality of the world is absolutely necessary and not contingent upon anything else, which means then that the world must itself exist in this manner.[126] Kant however asserts that this alternative is likewise impossible. His argument here, though, is unimpressive. The alternative contradicts itself, he writes, "since the existence of a series cannot be necessary if no single member of it is necessary" (ibid, p. 416).

The antithesis of this antinomy claims, in a twofold manner, that a necessary being does not exist. This is broken into the claims that a necessary being does not exist in this world, nor outside it acting upon it as a cause. In this way, the antithesis holds that not only is a necessary being nonexistent *in the world*, but likewise, directly attacking the latter part of the claim of the thesis, a necessary being does not exist outside the world serving as the cause of the sensible world.

While the first part of this antithesis (namely, that a necessary being does not exist *within the world*) has been discussed in the above critique of the thesis, as well as by many since the earliest mythological conceptions –as Bultmann noted[127]–the latter claim, that a necessary being does not exist *outside* the world and act as its cause, is a more intriguing argument. Again, his defense of this, the apparent contradiction between *cause* and *externality*, is not a suitable reason for the dispelling of the claim itself. He suggests that "this cause must itself begin to act, and its causality would therefore be in time, and so would belong

---

125 Indeed, as Kant iterates the former is impossible and non-sensical. "The former alternative, however, conflicts with the dynamical law of the determination of all appearances in time" (2007, p. 416)
126 We can recall the following from *Queen Mab:* "Spirit of nature! all-sufficing power, Necessity! thou mother of the world!" (Shelley 1813, p. 82)
127 "God has his domicile in heaven. What is the meaning of this statement? The meaning is quite clear. In a crude manner it expresses the idea that God is beyond the world, that He is transcendent. The thinking which is not yet capable of forming the abstract idea of transcendence expresses its intention in the category of space" (Bultmann 1991, p. 294). This is reminiscent of Augustine's praise in *The City of God* that the "Heavenly City outshines Rome, beyond comparison. There, instead of victory, is truth; instead of high rank, holiness; instead of peace, felicity; instead of life, eternity" (2003, p. 157).

to the sum of appearances, that is, to the world (ibid). This, however, assumes two claims about causality: first, that a cause must always itself be caused, and second, that an external cause cannot be caused by something which is external as well. Additionally, it holds that any external cause must still be in time, a characteristic of the sensible world. Therefore, the conclusion of the proof of this antithesis, namely that "the cause, would not be outside the world" does not follow (ibid).

As Kant continues to discuss this antinomy he suggests that it is only the cosmological proof of a supreme being which can be used to formulate the stated thesis.[128] This is because of the logical reasoning used to arrive at the necessity of a supreme or necessary being or cause. "Anything taken as condition must be viewed in precisely the same manner in which we viewed the relation of the conditioned to its condition in the series which is supposed to carry us by continuous advance to the supreme condition" (ibid, p. 418). This *chain of reasoning*, which constitutes the *cosmological argument* that leads us to an original cause, to necessity itself, is – Kant argues – the only mode available to form the proof required by the thesis.

This is problematic within the limits of *pure reason*, since the positing of necessity is only inferred from the concept of contingency which is present empirically in the sensible world; necessity cannot be shown through any appearance of the sensible world. Drawing seemingly from Aristotle's argument for the *unmoved mover*, Kant illustrates the problems with reasoning about the necessity of a primary motion, uncaused cause, or supreme being. The opposite of motion is rest, and that which is in motion must have at one point been in rest.[129] However "to obtain such a contrary opposite" that is, to conceive of it, "we require to conceive, that in the same time in which the proceeding state was, its opposite could have existed in its place" and so thus, it would have to be the case that "in place of motion, and at the same time at which it occurred, there could have

---

128 The cosmological argument refers to an attempt to prove a necessary being through facts and logics relating to causation. For this reason, Leibniz's Principle of Sufficient Reason can be made into a cosmological argument, as has been done so. Thomas Aquinas (2012) in *Summa Theologiae* also used such an argument for the proof of God. For more contemporaneous positions see William Lane Craig's (1979) *The Kalām Cosmological Argument*, Robert C Koons' (1997) article "A New Look at the Cosmological Argument", Graham Oppy's (2001) article "Time, Successive Addition, and Kalam Cosmological Arguments", W. David Beck's (2002) article "The Cosmological Argument: A Current Bibliographical Appraisal" and Andrew Loke's (2014) article "A Modified Philosophical Argument For A Beginning of The Universe".
129 "A motion has for its contrary in the strict sense of the term another motion, but it also has for an opposite a state of rest" Aristotle writes in *Physica* (2017, p. 133).

been rest" and this "can never be inferred from [the fact of] the alteration" of things in the sensible world (ibid, p. 420–421).

Indeed, the reasoning which leads to this conclusion (that of the necessity of a necessary being) is fallacious. Likewise, though, the antithesis proof falls short of applying *pure reason* appropriately. It is hardly even a task of reason, since to show the unnecessity of a necessary being, one must prove that the continuous regress of reasoning which is the cornerstone of the cosmological argument, "can never terminate in an empirically unconditioned condition" (ibid, p. 418). To do so would not only be impossible, but indeed, logical reasoning always assumes this very unconditioned condition to be the source; without this assumption, reasoning is groundless.

So far as the limits of reasoning is concerned, here specifically *pure reason*, there are the two stated theses in every antinomy: a thesis and an antithesis. To recall the one most recently discussed (namely, that a necessary being exists, and that a necessary being does not exist), the limitation of *pure reason* is clear, as shown through the fallacious arguments provided by Kant.[130] In fact, both these claims (in all the antinomies), fall victim to the same problematic reasoning that regular, *impure*, or *sensible* reason, is itself always subjected to. Kant indicates as much, stating that "the method of argument in both cases is entirely in conformity with ordinary human reason, which frequently falls into conflict with itself through considering its object from two different points of view" (ibid, p. 419). Thus the application of reason, *pure* or *sensible*, approaches the thesis and the antithesis in a logical but different manner, leading to the problem of both being logically valid forms of reasoning.[131]

The following questions arise:
1. Why does reason have these limits? What grounds these limits?
2. How does *Pure Reason* constitute a *nonfinite nature*?
3. In what manner may this affect *Dasein* as *in-der-Welt-sein*? That is, in what way is the 'world' of *Dasein* impacted by these limits of *pure reason*?

---

[130] W.T Harris also noted Kant's fallacious arguments, particularly in regards to the first antinomy. For his criticism of Kant see Harris' (1894) article "Kant's Third Antinomy and His Fallacy Regarding the First Cause".

[131] In other words, both can be valid or critiqued by the same set standards. There are many who have critiqued Kant's antinomies, but a good, though Hegelian, critique can be found in Graham Schuster's (2014) article "Is Reason Contradictory When Applied to Metaphysical Questions?". Also, a most excellent in-depth review of the antinomies can be found in Victoria S. Wike's (1982) *Kant's Antinomies of Reason: Their Origin and Their Resolution*.

The last of these can only briefly be touched upon here, and will be discussed more prominently in the next chapter, following commentary on the previous two. The first may also only be introduced here, as any discussion of it would necessitate a complete revision after commentary on the final one. Thus, our focus will be on the non-finite nature of pure reason. While it would be easy enough to state that the ground of the limits of reason is the empirical, sensible world, and the very relation of *Dasein* to this world, this does not satisfy the former part of the first set of questions. Therefore, it is best suited for our purposes to evaluate this ground of the limits of reason, so as to be posed to best address why, in fact, these limits exist.

A Commentary on the Limits of Pure Reason as Opposed to Sensible Reason and the Nonfinite Nature of Pure Reason

As previously discussed regarding the limits of sensible reason, reasoning reaches beyond its limits due to the function of synthesis which it provides to the conceptualization of the understanding as applied to sensation and sensible data. As such, its limitations are entirely due to the issue of perception and appearance described earlier. *Pure reason*, however, reaches beyond its limits in an entirely different manner. Pure reason does not have limitations insofar as it is grounded *in* empirical analysis, but rather due to *a priori* limitations on this very analysis.[132] It is important here to note that Kant highly praises *pure reason* and its overextension to the extent that these abstract ideals of pure reason are fundamental to humanity as a whole and are, as such, of the highest order of science.

> Whether the world has a beginning [in time] and any limit to its extension in space; whether there is anywhere, and perhaps in my thinking self, an indivisible and indestructible unity, or nothing but what is divisible and transitory; whether I am free in my actions or, like other beings, am led by the hand of nature and of fate; whether finally there is a supreme cause of the world, or whether the things of nature and their order must as the ultimate object terminate thought an object that even in our speculations can never be transcended: these are questions for the solution of which the mathematician would gladly exchange the whole of his science. For mathematics can yield no satisfaction in regard to those highest ends that most closely concern humanity (Kant 2007, p. 422–423).

---

132 In referencing the antinomies of pure reason Kant writes that there are "just four series of synthetic presuppositions which impose *a priori* limitations on the empirical synthesis" (2007, p. 422).

Thus, despite the fact that *pure reason* extends beyond its limits when reaching towards these questions and concerns articulated by means of the antinomies, the topics addressed are no less than the very root of human science, and for that reason should not be so easily discarded, even if not relied upon as a sure source of knowledge.

The limits of pure reason, then, are rooted in the attempted application of *a priori* principles to empirical data with the intention to then reason about *a priori* concepts not grounded in the sensible world, such as freedom. It is this circularity of reasoning that presents itself as the problematic use of pure reason and which will be discussed at greater length in the following chapter. Nevertheless, this limitation of pure reason also indicates precisely the status of pure reason as being *nonfinite* as opposed to the finitude of sensible reason.

Sensible reason is strictly finite, insofar as it is limited to the quantification and unification of sense data and empirical representations. Pure reason, insofar as it is not limited itself via the sensible, finite, world, is not simply finite, as it extends beyond this through *a priori* principles. Yet these principles, while not bound by the finitude of the sensible world and therefore not finite, are nevertheless bound by the finitude of reason itself such that the *a priori* nature of *pure reason* is limited by reason as a category and its procedural application.[133] Therefore, despite not being merely finite and extending beyond the finitude of the sensible world to which it is applied, it is nonetheless limited and so cannot be infinite. We must therefore consider pure reason as the mediator between the finitude and infinitude of *Dasein*. Thus, as I have termed it, it is *nonfinitude*.

---

[133] Reason as a category functions in and as part of a procedural manner leading to an experience. This cannot be escaped, which is the problem articulated through the presentation of the antinomies.

Chapter Five
The Ontological Modes of Dasein

Infinitude

Reason as finite is itself a phenomenon. Pure reason as unbounded is no longer a pure phenomenon, but rather positions itself as able to conceptualize noumenal notions, such as freedom. Insofar as *Dasein* can conceptualize noumena, as Kant is clear that this is distinct from knowledge of noumena, then it is only by relating these notions to that which he finds within himself.[134] The only way to conceptualize that which is unknowable is if it bears relation to that which can be known, as Meno himself learned.[135] When Kant confers freedom as noumenal, is it freedom generally, or one's own personal freedom? Indeed, he speaks of both, but it is only through recognizing freedom in one's self that they can recognize freedom external to them. Freedom as a noumenon must then be present within *Dasein*. How can this be known and what does it tell us about *Dasein*?

In the first instance, it must be determined what precisely is meant by noumena. In many readings of the Kantian system, a noumenon is considered to be simply a non-sensible entity, making it often seem synonymous with the *Ding an sich*.[136] Yet insofar as noumena are contrasted with phenomena, which are themselves a base or grounding of knowledge, then so too must noumena hold this status as well, with the obvious distinction that the phenomenon is sensible knowledge, whereas the noumenon is non-sensible knowledge, which also recalls us to Walt Whitman's poem *Of the Terrible Doubt of Appearances*.[137]

---

134 "What our understanding acquires through this concept of a noumenon, is a negative extension; that is to say, understanding is not limited through sensibility; on the contrary, it itself limits sensibility by applying the term noumena to things in themselves (things not regarded as appearances" (Kant 2007, p. 273).
135 Since "man cannot search either for what he knows or for what he does not know. He cannot search for what he knows—since he knows it, there is no need to search—nor for what he does not know, for he does not know what to look for" (Plato 2002, p. 70).
136 This is the most popular view and has been so since Friedrich Paulsen's (1963) work *Immanuel Kant: His Life and Doctrine* popularized it when it was first published in 1902. Others, such as Graham Bird (2006) in *The Revolutionary Kant: A Commentary on the Critique of Pure Reason*, have held such a view along with the majority of Kantian scholars.
137 "May-be the things I perceive, the animals, plants, men, hills, shining and flowing waters, The skies of day and night, colors, densities, forms, may-be these are (as doubtless they are) only apparitions, and the real something has yet to be known" (Walt Whitman 1882, p. 101).

Here, then, a point must be made clear. The *Ding an sich* and the noumena serve different roles in Kant.[138] The latter fulfill a claim of knowledge while the former acts as the underlying unknowable, "that which makes a thing what it is." To that end, these being two separate concepts, we must distinguish further between them as well as clarify the roles filled by each and how they best fit into the Kantian system. To do so, we begin with the *Ding an sich*.

The Kantian *Ding an sich* represents the underlying essence of the appearance of the object perceived by sensation. Thus, it is that which is left unsensed by sensation and is, in fact, lacking in sensibility. As Kant writes in the *Prolegomena*:

> if we view the objects of the senses as mere appearances, as is fitting, then we thereby admit at the very same time that a thing in itself underlies them, although we are not acquainted with this thing as it may be constituted in itself, but only with its appearance, i.e., with the way in which our senses are affected by this unknown something (Kant 2004, p. 66).

The *Ding an sich* then affects our senses in such a way so as to cause the appearance of a thing, of an object of sensation. Nonetheless, this "thing itself", which is the root of affection on sensation, the basis of perception – for to perceive is to perceive some object – is in itself, always left unsensed, and insofar as it remains unsensed, it is never represented to us, lingering only as unknown. This is because it is in fact not a thing at all.[139] Kant noted the logical necessity of the *Ding an sich*, writing that it follows:

> from the concept of an appearance in general; namely, that something which is not in itself appearance must correspond to it. For appearance can be nothing by itself, outside our mode of representation. Unless, therefore, we are to move constantly in a circle, the word appearance must be recognised as already indicating a relation to something, the immediate representation of which is, indeed, sensible, but which, even apart from the constitution of our sensibility...must be something in itself, that is, an object independent of sensibility (Kant 2007, pp. 269–270).

---

138 For examples of scholars who treat the *Ding an sich* and, at least, positive noumena as the same see, Donald Gotterbarn's (2009) article "Kant, Hume and Analyticity" and Teodor I. Oizerman's (1981) article "Kant's Doctrine of the 'Things in Themselves' and Noumena".

139 Richard F. Grabau explains this in his article "Kant's Concept of the Thing-in-itself: An Interpretation" when he writes that "The thing-in-itself cannot strictly be a thing at all because in Kant's thought "thing" always refers to a phenomenal object, i.e., to a determinate object structured by the categories of understanding and forms of intuition. Nor can the referent of thing-in-itself be reality in the sense of being wholly outside of experience" (1963, p. 770).

Yet this indicates more than simply the *Ding an sich*, since it also introduces the noumena as opposed to the phenomena. For the *Ding an sich*, which Kant has shown to be logically necessary, must also (insofar as it is an object of any kind) produce a non-sensible intuition: that is to say, *intellectual intuition*, which is by necessity *pure* and thus introduces the noumena.[140]

In briefly introducing the noumena, Kant indicates that if "I postulate things that are mere objects of understanding, and which, nevertheless, can be given to an intuition, although not to one that is sensible – given therefore *coram intuiti intellectuali*[141], – such things would be entitled *noumena (intelligibilia)*" (ibid, pp. 265–266). Thus, the noumena are a target of *pure intuition* that is already always-present in the understanding, therefore being strictly intellectual and not sensible, unlike other intuition.[142]

Kant distinguishes, however, between positive and negative noumena, in the revised "B" edition of the text, the former strictly relating to the notion of pure intellectual intuition, the latter relating to something entirely different. He writes that "If by 'noumenon' we mean a thing so far as it is *not an object of our sensible intuition*, and so abstract from our mode of intuiting it, this is a noumenon in the negative sense of the term" (ibid, p. 268). In other words, the *negative* noumenon is one which is an "object" abstracted from *intuition* yet nevertheless present as *intuition*, insofar as it is *intellectual intuition*.

In what way, then, does *Dasein* relate to noumena? That is to say, how exactly are we to relate *Dasein* to the Kantian concept of noumena? It is fairly clear that, since noumena are distinguished from phenomena, everything which is a *phenomenon* is also a noumenon. Insofar as *Dasein* is itself a phenomenon, such that it is *in-der-Welt-sein*, so too must it be a noumenon in and of itself. The so-called "I" of identity (that is, a self-consciousness) must always precede as well as accompany any and all *sensible intuitions*, as a form of immediate *intellectual intuition*. As such, this is what presents to us the noumena of *Dasein*. Precisely what this means for *Dasein* will be a topic of discussion later. However, suffice it here to state the necessity of the noumena in order for an object to be a phenomenon.

Yet we must also distinguish *Dasein* as noumenal from *Dasein* as *Ding an sich*. The question of whether *Dasein* itself is a "thing-in-itself" raises a further question as to the way in which *Dasein* intuits itself. If in its *intuition* of itself *Dasein* abstracts from *intuition* itself, then *Dasein* is a *negative* noumenon. If on the

---

140 Gram (1981) provides a great analysis of intellectual intuition, tracing its development after Kant through German Idealism in his article "Intellectual Intuition: The Continuity Thesis".
141 Translation: Through intellectual intuition.
142 To clarify, space and time are still considered sensible intuition despite being *a priori*.

other hand *Dasein intuits* itself as an already present *intuition* of the understanding – an *intellectual intuition*[143] which, as a part of the understanding, unifies intuitions – then *Dasein* is a *positive* noumenon.

The question thus becomes whether *Dasein* intuits itself in the manner of intuition – that is, *intellectual intuition,* or whether it does so through abstracting from the manner of intuition, i.e., *sensible intuition.* Kant himself did not think we could represent to ourselves a noumenon in the *positive* sense, stating that "Since, however, such a type of intuition, intellectual intuition, forms no part whatsoever of our faculty of knowledge, it follows that the employment of the categories can never extend further than to the objects of experience", though he suggested that "there are intelligible entities corresponding to the sensible entities. There may also be intelligible entities to which our sensible faculty of intuition has no relation whatsoever", however, "our concepts of understanding, being mere forms of thought for our sensible intuition, could not in the least apply to them. That, therefore, which we entitle 'noumenon' must be understood as being such only in a negative sense" (Kant 2007, p. 270). If Kant is right about this, then *Dasein* must be a *negative* noumenon.

Indeed, it seems certain that *Dasein* insofar as it recognizes itself as *Dasein* is a *negative* noumenon. However, the immediate cognition that facilitates this recognition of *Dasein* as *Dasein* is always preceded by a subconscious reflection, an ever veiled-presence. That is to say that this recognition is simply an unveiling of that which is already there, already *intuited* though not brought into representation as it lacks affection of the senses. Instead, it is a purely *intellectual intuition*, an already-present *intuition*, not of sensation, but of the understanding itself. This is necessary, as without this the very concept of "I" such that *Dasein* could recognize itself in its being-what-it-is, is not a unified concept. It is, then, not contrary to Kant, but a step beyond his position, to say that the *positive* noumenon (of *Dasein*) is that which is itself responsible for the unification of the concepts of understanding, but is itself not applied to sensible intuition.

It must now be asked, then, what kind of object is a *positive* noumenon? The answer to this is an indication of the "what" of *Dasein* rather than the "how." That is not to suggest that it is indeed that *what* of *Dasein*, inasmuch as it is the *what* of the *how* that *is itself* represented in being *Dasein*. In other words, that which represents the positive noumena of *Dasein* is that which is *transcendental* to *Dasein*; namely, I argue, the *transcendental ego.*

---

[143] It should be noted that Kant does not think we possess *intellectual intuition* and thus makes no claim regarding the existence of positive noumena. See below.

Transcendental

In chapter one of book two of the *Critique of Pure Reason,* Immanuel Kant discusses the paralogisms of the mind. In particular, Kant seeks to break away from the prominent argument of the day: the Cartesian *cogito.* Thus, Kant is – though without a complete expression of it– pushing for a new conception of self, a new way to understand identity formation: indeed, a new, *transcendental* ego.[144] Through a close reading, we can see that the transcendental ego is indirectly hinted at in a footnote, whether or not Kant consciously realized this discovery. The main footnote in which I believe Kant introduces what can genuinely be called the transcendental ego, or "I" (insofar as he makes the "I" transcendental as a necessary precondition of the "I think" and it is in this way distinct from his notion of transcendental apperception) is the following passage:

> The 'I think' is, as already stated, an empirical proposition, and contains within itself the proposition 'I exist.' But I cannot say 'Everything which thinks, exists'. For in that case the property of thought would render all beings which possess it necessary beings. My existence cannot, therefore, be regarded as an inference from the proposition 'I think,' as Descartes sought to contend – for it would then have to be preceded by the major premiss [premise] 'Everything which thinks, exists' – but is identical with it. The 'I think' expresses an indeterminate empirical intuition, i.e. perception (and thus shows sensation, which as such belongs to sensibility, lies at the basis of this existential proposition) But the 'I think' precedes the experience which is required to determine the object of perception through the category in respect of time; and the existence here [referred to] is not a category. The category as such does not apply to an indeterminately given object but only to one of which we have a concept and about which we seek to know whether it does or does not exist outside the concept. An indeterminate perception here signifies only something real that is given, given indeed to thought in general, and so not as appearance, nor as thing-in-itself (*noumenon*), but as something which actually exists, and which in the proposition 'I think', is denoted as such. For it must be observed, that when I have called the proposition, 'I think', an empirical proposition, I do not mean to say thereby, that the 'I' in this proposition is an empirical representation. On the contrary it is purely intellectual, because belonging to thought in general. Without some empirical representation, to supply the material for thought, the *actus* 'I think', would not, indeed, take place; but the empirical is only the condition of the application, or of the employment, of the pure intellectual faculty (Kant 2007, p. 378).

---

[144] For clarification, it is important to note that Kant himself never argues explicitly for a transcendental ego, nor uses this language. Fichte claimed a pure ego, Hegel an absolute ego and Husserl (and later Sartre) a transcendental ego. For a great commentary on the transcendental ego and how it gets developed from Kant through German Idealism and into Hegel's work, see Frederick C. Beiser's (2002) *German Idealism: The Struggle against Subjectivism, 1781-1801.*

The depth of the problem raised by positing a transcendental ego must first be addressed. What is a transcendental ego? What does it transcend? Let us consider these questions first.

Prior to the aforementioned footnote, Kant discusses self-consciousness at length. Self-consciousness, we might say, is what constitutes an ego, or at least a great deal of it. Self-consciousness is then an awareness of one's own existence, being, and more importantly thought; it is a certainty.[145] Kant sees the Cartesian reliance on thought for the understanding of self-consciousness to be misguided. For self-consciousness is not in thought, but in perception. As Kant writes:

> I cannot have any representation whatsoever of a thinking being, through any outer experience, but only through self-consciousness. Objects of this kind are, therefore, nothing more than the transference of this consciousness of mine to other things, which in this way alone can be represented as thinking beings" (ibid, p. 332).

Here, self-consciousness is transferable from something internal to us into the object external to us that we perceive – it is in this way that we recognize the consciousness of others, the "thinking" category of being of the other.[146] As such, our self-consciousness is understood by means of our perception of objects.

In discussing this aspect of consciousness and thought in subjects, Kant slips in the following footnote:

> 'Thought' is taken in the two premisses in totally different senses: in the major premiss, as relating to an object in general and therefore to an object as it may be given in intuition; in the minor premiss, only as it consists in relation to self-consciousness. In this latter sense, no object whatsoever is being thought; all that is being represented is simply their relation to self as subject (as the form of thought) (ibid, p. 371).

In this footnote, while the noumenal and phenomenal distinction is still prominent, it is not the focus. Instead, we have a distinction between the consciousness which relates to objects as subjects, and the consciousness abstracted away

---

[145] Sam Harris also states as much in what is perhaps his best known work *Waking Up: A Guide To Spirituality Without Religion* when he writes that "Consciousness is the one thing in this universe that cannot be an illusion" (2014, p. 54).

[146] For discussions and critiques of this notion see Pierre Keller's (1999) *Kant and the Demands of Self-Consciousness*, Thomas Sturm's and Falk Wunderlich's (2010) article "Kant and the Scientific Study of Consciousness", and Yibin Liang's (2017) article "Kant on Consciousness, Obscure Representations and Cognitive Availability".

from objects as subjects. This latter articulation is what can be called consciousness *qua* consciousness, or what has been called the *transcendental ego* or *transcendental apperception*. However, this is not enough, since consciousness is only ever consciousness, regardless of its relations to objects.

It is necessary (most of the time), in order to acknowledge that we have any sort of capacity to know anything about the world around us, that we first believe the knowledge that we can know or understand ourselves as such. That is, we must have knowledge of the fact that we are selves, entities capable of positing objects outside of ourselves and having intuitions of them.[147] Surely we are unique in this regard, since every other being posits itself insofar as it exists around objects outside itself as those external objects stand in relation to their own selves, without any knowledge that they are "selves."[148]

This is what we call self-reflexivity. This ability to reflect upon one's own self is something unique to us, and must be *a priori* with respect to any other ability of the categories to understand and qualify the sensible world. Kant, fittingly, posits a unity of self. The common example is that of hearing a melody, not as a scrambled manifold of singular notes, but as a harmonious comprehensive whole.[149] So too, when we have a conversation with someone, it is not simply that we recognize singular words which we then combine into a structured sentence, but rather that we understand the sentence as a whole; we take it collectively.

This is an automatic process that requires nothing from us. We do not need to contemplate the words used in order to experience the whole of the compound sentence.[150] For Kant, this means that in order for this to be possible (that is, in order that we can have unified experiences spread out across time) we must have a self which is removed from the self of experience. In other words, there must be

---

[147] Matthew Boyle in his article "Two Kinds of Self-Knowledge" (2009) argues that there are two distinct types of self-knowledge: one based on sensations and the other rooted in judgements.

[148] This holds no bearing on the ontological priority or status of the being but merely is a mode of being-in as manifested ontically.

[149] We see this example used for instance in Ramakrishna Rao's (2002) Consciousness Studies: Cross-Cultural Perspectives, Georges Dicker's (2011) Berkeley's Idealism: A Critical Examination, and Lawrence Kaye's (2015) Kant's Transcendental Deduction of the Categories: Unity, Representation, and Apperception.

[150] Although we may understand in its totality, it may be necessary to do so through reflection on its composition. "To understand a sentence we must know more than the analysis of this sentence on each linguistic level. We must also know the reference and meaning of the morphemes or words of which it is composed; naturally, grammar cannot be expected to be of much help here" (Chomsky 1957, pp. 103–104).

a unifying self, holding together all the experiences of the conscious empirical self, which is itself established by and through *transcendental apperception*. Yet we experience this empirical self, along with the transcendental self, only as a phenomenon; it only ever appears to us, and we can posit its being-there, but there can be no knowledge of its existence or of what it means for it to be existing, since this transcendental self is in fact a noumenon.

This raises serious questions regarding the ability to actually posit the *transcendental ego* or transcendental self. For example, we do not only experience things as a whole. Surely, we experience singulars over time, which we then unify.[151] Why, then, is it necessary to have a unifying self, beyond a unifying aspect of the categories? In addition, what does it mean that this transcendental self is a noumenal self? Since all objects are things-in-themselves and we can only experience them as they appear to us, and I myself, my own "self" is a thing-in-itself that I cannot know, how is it that it appears to me and leaves only an appearance as a phenomenon?

According to Kant, objects around us are only appearances and we can recognize that they are phenomena and not things-in-themselves if we put in the footwork necessary to point this out, as he himself has done. But it becomes much more complex and difficult to then suggest that I myself am only an appearance, not insofar as I relate to others, but insofar as I relate to my own self. Thus, what this comes down to is the fact that it becomes difficult to assert that we know that this transcendental ego is necessary, so that we can experience things as a collective whole (such as melodies, etc.). Yet we cannot know things as they are in themselves, even our own selves, but only through their appearances, but nonetheless that they also exist beyond the way they appear to us, as things-in-themselves. This is an extremely difficult proposition to make, since Kant himself has said that we cannot know such noumena, but can only know that they are there because it is necessary that they be.[152]

To better understand this, we must consider the distinction, which ultimately rests on the transcendental ego, between phenomena and noumena. As articulated before, Kant's attempt to save knowledge – that is, to refute Hume's devastating claim that we cannot know anything since we only know how we perceive things – makes an epistemological distinction between the things that we can know (appearances) as per Hume's argument, and the things we cannot or do not have access to, namely the things-in-themselves. Having discussed this dis-

---

[151] For a great discussion of this aspect in Kantian thought see H. J. Paton's (1937) classic article "Kant's Metaphysic of Experience".
[152] Henry E. Allison (1978) offers a good treatment of this as it is articulated in Kant in his article "Things in Themselves, Noumena, and the Transcendental Object".

tinction earlier, it will only be necessary here to note in what precise way this distinction is drawn from the transcendental ego.

This distinction between phenomena and noumena allows Kant to claim that we do have genuine knowledge of the things which we experience, the phenomena of everyday life, thus avoiding the skepticism of the Humean tradition.[153] Instead, what we do not have knowledge of is the way in which things really are. One might wonder in what sense Kant is offering us knowledge at all. Whereas Hume might suggest that the only genuine knowledge is knowledge of things-in-themselves, this is not the case for Kant. Due to the distinction he draws, genuine knowledge *may be* of things in themselves, which we just cannot access, but also knowledge of things as they appear to us is considered to be knowledge. Thus, what Hume may call a false form of knowledge Kant sees as a genuine kind, just not of things as they really are.[154]

From this epistemological distinction between noumena and phenomena, between things-in-themselves and things as they appear to us, Kant indirectly derives what we may call the notion of a transcendental ego. As previously noted, this is posited in a footnote which raises a plethora of questions. However, before we even begin to posit answers to those questions, we must first elaborate on what a transcendental ego might be. Most often viewed as synonymous with the transcendental unity of apperception, which was discussed in a previous section, and traced through German Idealism where it transforms into Hegelian *Geist*, the transcendental ego is the aspect of the "I think" which is necessary such that experience is possible.[155] This immediately recalls *transcendental apperception*, though the two are not the same.[156]

---

[153] For more on Hume's skepticism and, in particular, the relation between the skepticism of Hume and Kant's ultimate rejection of it, see Michael N. Forster's (2009) chapter "Humean Skepticism" in *Kant and Skepticism*.

[154] Harold Langsam (1994) offers a good account of the difference to be found in Kant between genuine knowledge and knowledge of things as they really are, in his article "Kant, Hume, and Our Ordinary Concept of Causation".

[155] For a discussion of how the basic articulations of what might be called a transcendental ego, in Kant, wound up leading to Hegel's conception of *Geist*, see Robert Williams' (1985) article "Hegel and Transcendental Philosophy".

[156] For the differences between the transcendental ego and apperception, see Henry Somers-Hall (2012) *Hegel, Deleuze, and the Critique of Representation: Dialectics of Negation and Difference*. Most, as stated, take these to be one and the same. Consider, in this regard, E.G. Ballard, et. al. (1962) *Studies in Social Philosophy*, and Aron Gurwitsch (1966) *Studies in Phenomenology and Psychology*. For commentary on transcendentality, apperception, and the "I" in Kant, see Joseph Evans (1984) *The Metaphysics of Transcendental Subjectivity: Descartes, Kant, and W. Sellars* and Siyaves Azeri's (2010) article "Transcendental Subject vs Empirical Self: On Kant's Account of Subjectivity".

Transcendental apperception, as mentioned above, is indeed that which makes experience possible, and so the confusion of the two is well-found. *Transcendental apperception* unifies and qualifies experiences into *qualia,* that is, into conscious experience.[157] Though the *transcendental ego* also unifies experience, there is a distinction which must be made. Apperception arises out of the "I think" as the "I" must have experience in order for apperception to unify this into *qualia,* such that the "I" becomes "I think". We must consider here what Kant says of the "I think".

Kant writes that:

> The thought that the representations given in intuition one and all belong to me, is therefore equivalent to the thought that I unite them in one self-consciousness, or can at least so unite them...For otherwise I should have as many-coloured and diverse a self as I have representations of which I am conscious to myself (Kant 2007, p. 154).

It is *apperception* that is responsible for the unification into self-consciousness, such that the "I" is always "I think". However, there is required an "I" prior to the self-consciousness of the "I" as "I think". The question arises, then: is the Cartesian *cogito* indeed necessary?[158]

One may recall the all-too familiar example, in which a person has been wearing colored lenses through which they perceive the world since they were born. To the individual, the world appears blue, pink, etc., which is not the way the world really is. However, since that is the only way the individual has experienced it, it is their genuine world of experience. This is indeed how the transcendental ego has been described; it is the unifying factor through which all separate parts of an individual are amalgamated into a singular.[159] Thus it can be said that the transcendental ego functions as do the lenses in the example above. The transcendental ego, then, is the unifying factor behind these experiences. In a sense it is like the lenses themselves, allowing us to make sense of the way things appear to us; it is a noumenal self, which we experience only insofar as it appears to us, or only insofar as it is a phenomenon. However, this assumption of the distinction between noumena and phenomena seems to come

---

[157] A word used to designate individual experiences of conscious activity. For more on the term and its defining characteristics see Daniel Dennett's (1988) "Quining Qualia".

[158] A good work to read on the subject is Richard E. Aquila (1998) "Self-consciousness, self-determination, and imagination in Kant". In it, Aquila reads the paralogisms keeping the *cogito* in mind. What follows is an excellent analysis.

[159] Kant (2007) explains this process in the *Critique of Pure Reason* (pp. 440-441). Also see David Carr's (1987) chapter "The Problem of the Non-Empirical Ego: Husserl and Kant," in *Interpreting Husserl*.

from nowhere, and is supplemented only by the positing of the *transcendental ego*.

Without the transcendental ego, it seems that the assumption of a noumenal/phenomenal distinction is presumed on a very loose grounding and is taken as a given; that is, I experience the world only ever as a subject, or subjectively.[160] This is also to say that objects do not exist in the world (which is my world) objectively, but only ever as a representation to me. While this is a pleasant thought, there is no reason to believe it, unless one says of self-consciousness that the way I am conscious of these objects being subjective is because I exist at the same time both subjectively and objectively; that is, I exist objectively to myself, but can only understand myself subjectively. I must think about my objective self, it is not self-evident. It never occurs to me that I am an objective self, since anytime I consider what I am, what the "self" is, I am always doing so through self-reflexivity, which is of course subjective and occurs through the faculty of *transcendental apperception*. However, I believe such interpretation of the transcendental ego to be misguided, as this does not distinguish sufficiently between the *transcendental ego* and *transcendental apperception*.

For well indeed, while the lenses in the analogy reveal the way in which we come to experience the world and understand ourselves through our perception of it, they do not bridge the gap between the worlds of appearances and of things-in-themselves. Such a task should in fact be the most primary function of the *transcendental ego*. So, while *transcendental apperception* unifies *qualia* into *self-consciousness*, it is the *transcendental ego* which unifies into the singular as with the lens example above. The question to be asked here is, is it not the *transcendental ego* that unifies our being not only insofar as we appear in the world, but also insofar as we are *in the world?* Let us consider this more deeply.

The footnote mentioned at the onset of this section, articulates an "I" that operates transcendentally, differs from Descartes' *cogito*, and is not itself a faculty – which transcendental apperception is a faculty, and so the two must in fact be distinct. A crucial point to note here is that it is not a "thing-in-itself" according to Kant. I would argue that the only reason he suggests this is because he has committed himself to stating that the *Ding an sich* is not known to us, whereas this "I" is known insofar as it is always present, though not empirically, as stated in the footnote: which for Kant suggests it cannot actually be known, as

---

160 This has been the major criticism leveled against Kant regarding the subject. For a discussion of this and other claimed contradictions in Kant, see Derk Pereboom's (1991) noted article, "Is Kant's Transcendental Philosophy Inconsistent?".

it is not empirical. As such, it reads as if it were a thing-in-itself, and yet Kant denies this is the case.

The sentence *"was in der Tat existiert und in dem Satze: Ich denke, als ein solches bezeichnet wird"* along with the claims that it is *"nicht als Erscheinung, auch nicht als Sache an sich selbst* (Noumena)" poses the truly interesting conundrum, since the question then becomes: what is it? (Kant 1889, p. 342). If it is an appearance, then it does in fact depend on sense experience; if not – if it is a thing-in-itself – then it would not necessarily depend on an individual's experience. The reason it seems to be neither is that Kant articulates it as transcendental; it is a precondition of both – in which case, it is not dependent upon experience but rather is the precondition of it.

The last part of this footnote, *"Allein ohne irgend eine empirische Vorstellung, die den Stoff zum Denken abgiebt, würde der Actus: Ich denke, doch nicht stattfinden, und das Empirische ist nur die Bedingung der Anwendung oder des Gebrauchs des reinen intellectuellen Vermögens,"* appears to work against this by suggesting that without experience, the "I" of "I think", this transcendental "I" which serves as a precondition is also not present (ibid). This would, however, in such an interpretation, conflict with pure intuitions, i.e, space and time as preconditions of experience. For even these intuitions, though not empirical, presuppose an "I think," which was indicated when Kant wrote, as earlier cited:

> The thought that the representations given in intuition one and all belong to me, is therefore equivalent to the thought that I unite them in one self-consciousness, or can at least so unite them...For otherwise I should have as many-coloured and diverse a self as I have representations of which I am conscious to myself (Kant 2007, p. 154).

If pure intuitions presuppose an "I think," then that "I" cannot be rooted entirely in sense experience. That is to suggest that one must be primary and the other secondary.

I believe this can be addressed by a distinction between noumena and *Ding an sich*. Kant distinguishes between positive and negative noumena. The *Ding an sich* represents noumena as negative noumena, while Kant seems to doubt the very existence of positive noumena. By positive noumena Kant refers to non-sensible intuition, which requires intellectual intuition as a faculty – precisely the source of Kant's doubt, as he suggests that we do not have such a faculty. This would mean that to think of a thing is to have that thing represented (representation by means of the categories, though, only applies to sensible objects for Kant, which gives rise to the problem). But what of the "I" in the "I think"? It must necessarily be represented within thinking, and yet is itself non-sensible:

never an object of thought, but the subject of it, though it is nevertheless applied to sensible objects – if "I think" of a hammer, I am thinking of the relation between "I" and "hammer". If this is indeed the case, then the "I" would be a positive noumenon, and in fact the only one necessary to posit.

The issue raised earlier regarding the final sentence of the footnote is only there because Kant did not note the relation between his discussion of the "I" as presented, and the positive noumena. Instead, he reverted back to the grounding that empirical data gives for intuition, and thus for knowledge generally.

Thus, in order to make this distinction seem plausible, the transcendental ego is necessary for Kant, but the ramifications of positing a transcendental ego extends well beyond Kant. It has sparked a huge debate in Western philosophy that continues to this day. What is the transcendental ego, and how does it fit into both Kant's philosophy and philosophy as a whole? I will end my thoughts on this point by saying that the transcendental ego for Kant, being the unifying factor of subjective experience, is thus our objective self. However, because I must reflect upon the subjective self, I can only know *subjectively* that I am an objective self, at least in Kant's understanding. This makes me wonder whether Kant missed something in his understanding of the transcendental ego. Perhaps he did. If we take for granted that there is a transcendental ego which we can know exists, as Kant presumes, and that he missed something which allows one to know that it is objective, beyond mere subjective ponderings and musings, then perhaps there is something or some way through which we can know our objective, transcendental self, in an objective, transcendental way.

If it is true that there is a distinction between the noumenal and the phenomenal, then this cannot simply be a distinction that is formed in the mind; that is, it cannot simply be an *a priori* category of the mind, but must be more foundational than this would suppose. Ultimately, such a distinction must be ontological and not merely epistemological. That is to say, it cannot just be a division between things as they appear and things in themselves, but must also make a statement about the way in which things *are*. Kant's notion of noumena versus phenomena appears to be only an epistemological consideration – it distinguishes between what we have access to, or knowledge of, and that which we cannot have knowledge of.[161]

---

[161] This is indeed how it has been treated by a vast majority of scholars, including Patricia Kitcher (1999) in her article "Kant's Epistemological Problem and Its Coherent Solution", Nicholas F. Stang (2014) in his article "The Non-Identity of Appearances and Things in Themselves", Michael Oberst's (2015) article "Two Worlds and Two Aspects: on Kant's Distinction between Things in Themselves and Appearances" and Reed Winegar's (2017) "Kant on Intuitive Understanding and Things in Themselves".

Is it possible that Kant wanted to see such a distinction as ontological as well? If so, he does nothing to clarify or denote that this is the case; the entirety of his *Critique* is focused on identifying what we can have knowledge of, and how we get that knowledge; indeed, he sets this discussion up against that which we cannot know. However, there is nothing that emphasizes the ontological implications of holding such an epistemological view.

Robert Greenberg's book *Kant's Theory of A Priori Knowledge* reveals the problem of a Kantian ontology, noting:

> an ontology of any theory of a priori representations or knowledge would consist of particular and contingent existences, any such theory that has an ontology would confront this general problem, of keeping the representations or knowledge a priori while making its own commitment to existing objects (Greenberg 2001, p. 19).

But if one is to assert such an epistemological position, it must stem from an ontology that allows for an explanation that is fitting for the case. Indeed, things in themselves versus how they appear is an ontological distinction, though this itself is left undiscussed in the *Critique*.

If Kant did indeed intend to posit this distinction ontologically as well, then it becomes all the more curious as to where this ontological distinction can truly be found. It is here that we return to the question of fundamental ontology. We must briefly reconsider Heidegger's claim that Kant's *Critique* moves us towards such an ontology.

To recapitulate, fundamental ontology is that which seeks to understand the Being of beings and in this way is the only means by which we can "disclose the ontological truth of the human being" (Rae 2010, p. 28). Thus, although Heidegger's primary goal is to evaluate being, it must be done through the way in which we have the most access, fundamental ontology, or, the inquiry into the being of our being. By analyzing the relationship between being and our being a being (that is, the ontological difference), Heidegger believes we can gain better access to being as such.[162]

This is the famous Heideggarian distinction between the ontological (being as such) and the ontic. The latter represents the relationality of beings. This *ex-*

---

[162] The ontological difference is the term applied to Heidegger's distinction between beings and being as such. It has been discussed in length by many. See Martin Heidegger (1982) "The Problem of the Ontological Difference" in *The Basic Problems of Phenomenology,* Graeme Nicholson (1996) "The Ontological Difference", Slavoj Žižek (2017) "The Persistence of Ontological Difference," in *Heidegger's Black Notebooks: Responses to Anti-Semitism*, and Daniel Dahlstrom (2017) "Rethinking Difference" in *Heidegger's Question of Being*.

istential, as Heidegger termed it, is the everydayness of our being *Dasein*. In other words, everyday *Dasein* is necessarily ontic-existentiell, not ontological. The ontological-existential is always the framework of being that underlies the being, in this case *Dasein*. Heidegger's notion of *das Man*, the "they-sel'" which consumes *Dasein* and plunges it into inauthenticity, recalls Spinoza's conception of united speciesism or sociality of species. Jason Almog writes on this that for Spinoza "without other humans, I have no existence and acting power" and therefore that, in a very-much Heideggerian sense, "there is no other way for me but the human-species way" (2014, p. 123). The analytic of *Dasein* is therefore an ontic analysis, not an ontological one. In what way, then, can Heidegger's analytic of Dasein provide for anything but an ontic evaluation of our being? Indeed, *Sorge* is most representative of our ontic *being-in-the-world*.[163] In focusing on the worldliness of *Dasein*, Heidegger – and the phenomenological method generally – can never root out *Dasein* in the ontological sense. This is because insofar as *Dasein* is *being-in-the-world*, we are necessarily speaking of *Dasein* referentially, that is, in relation to some*thing*. *Dasein* always stands in relation to some other being and is in constant engagement with this relationality and this engagement is rooted in *Sorge*. In Heidegger, it is the modes of being-in, namely, *Zuhandenheit und Vorhandenheit*, which together account for the relationality of the world of *Dasein*.[164] That is to say, *Zuhandenheit* and *Vorhandenheit* are the modes through which *Dasein* engages with its world and this engagement takes the form of a relation. Insofar as *Dasein* engages with its world, it stands in relation to that world.[165]

What we are left with is an incomplete analysis of our own being, much less Being itself. That is to say, Heidegger does not present a fundamental ontology but merely a phenomenological description of our way of being insofar as *Dasein* is ontically relational and *in the world*. Instead, if we are to seek a fundamental ontology, then we must look to *Dasein* in an ontological sense.

Heidegger thought the *Critique of Pure Reason* offered the groundwork for this. If indeed it does, then it must be in the distinction between the noumenon and phenomenon, as well as in the related transcendental ego, which posits a different kind of world. It is in this that we may find the grounding of a fundamental ontology, and the necessity for a critique of humanness.

---

163 Wu Shiu-Ching (2016) offers an excellent analysis of the concept in "On the Priority of Relational Ontology: The Complementarity of Heidegger's Being-With and Ethics of Care".
164 The present-at-hand and ready-to-hand distinction has been discussed widely. See, for examples of different treatments, David Weinberger (1980) "Three Types of 'Vorhandenheit'" and Graham Harman (2010) "Technology, Objects and Things in Heidegger".
165 A more detailed account of this will be found in Chapter Five.

Chapter Six
Metaphysics of *Dasein*

The Worlds of *Dasein*

The various modes of *Dasein* as read through the Kantian system, and the *transcendental ego* in particular, make clear the necessity of a delimitation of the concept of "world". The *transcendental ego,* insofar as it is the necessary precondition of experience, also then serves as the ground of a fundamental ontology. If we are to conceive of a fundamental ontology (as Heidegger does) as one that directly addresses the metaphysics of *Dasein* and which, furthermore, makes all metaphysics possible, then where else would we be able to locate this fundamental ontology, which Heidegger himself suggests can be found in Kant?

Indeed, it must be out of the *transcendental ego* that we derive a fundamental ontology. There are two reasons we can be sure of this claim. First and foremost, two of the modes of *Dasein* discussed so far, *reason and pure reason,* are non-metaphysical aspects of *Dasein's being-in*. The other mode(s), the noumenon and the *transcendental ego,* are metaphysical and thus represent the metaphysics of *Dasein*.[166] In this way, the first condition of a fundamental ontology is satisfied. However, the *transcendental ego* satisfies the second condition as well.

The second condition, namely that it is what makes metaphysics possible, is fulfilled by the *transcendental ego* in a number of ways. There is only one way that must really be articulated here, as it is sufficient to demonstrate the case. The *transcendental* in Kant is that which is the condition upon which other qualities are conditioned. As such, the *transcendental ego* is indeed fitting as it is *transcendental* and necessarily, then, a precondition. But beyond this it is not only a precondition of experience, but a precondition of *being,* and thus of metaphysics – at the very least, of the metaphysics of *Dasein* and of the ability of *Dasein* to experience or to conceptualize metaphysics.

The question that now needs to be addressed is this: what, in fact, is the metaphysics of *Dasein*? Indeed, the *transcendental ego* is a metaphysical mode of the being-in of *Dasein,* and so, as transcendental, is the precondition of the metaphysics of *Dasein*.[167] However, we must now ask ourselves: does the *tran-*

---

[166] This, in fact, refers to only one aspect, as the *noumenon* of *Dasein* is the *transcendental ego*. For further discussion of the relationship between the *noumenon* of *Dasein* and the transcendental ego, see Colin Marshall's (2010) article "Kant's Metaphysics of the Self".
[167] Metaphysical here meaning beyond our direct experience.

scendental ego in fact account for the metaphysics of *Dasein?* In particular, we must be interested in the ontological foundations of *Dasein*. Insofar as this is the real question at hand, then focus should be placed on understanding the "world" of *Dasein* and what it means precisely for *Dasein* to have "world".

World in Kant

Worldliness is a crucial concept in Heidegger's analytic of *Dasein*.[168] With it comes the articulation of *Dasein's "throwness"*[169] *and* "fallenness". Yet the concept of "world" is also central to the Kantian system, though this is not always made evidently clear by his writing style. Nevertheless, Kant's presumptive reliance on the concept of "world", that is, with a particular conceptualization of world, can be noted quite easily when thinking through his discussions of sensation, the *Ding an sich,* and other such concepts. Here I will consider the concept of "world" as it is articulated throughout the Kantian doctrine.

To provide only a short answer, one may state simply that "world" in Kant refers to the world of sense.[170] While this is correct, it is no doubt a simplification which runs the risk, if interpreted strictly, of misunderstanding the importance of this concept for the whole of his systematic philosophy. In a systematic philosophy, every single concept is vital to the whole since, building off each other, the whole of the system can be pieced together into something coherent.[171] Indeed, then, it is important to elaborate on the concept of world as the *world of sense*;

---

168 It is discussed at length in Heidegger's (2010) *Being and Time*. Also see, for additional commentary on the concept, Alejandro A. Vallega (2003) *Heidegger and the Issue of Space: Thinking on Exilic Grounds,* and Svetlana Boym's (2009) article "From Love to Worldliness: Hannah Arendt and Martin Heidegger".
169 *Geworfenheit.*
170 Of course, Kant distinguishes between the world of sense (*mundus sensibilis)* and the intelligible world (*mundus intelligibilis*) however, as will be discussed later, when Kant uses the term "world" on its own, he is referring to the sensible world. For more on the discussion of world in Kant's work and the different between the sensible and intellectual world in Kant, see Catherine Wilson's (1988) chapter "Sensible and Intelligible Worlds in Leibniz and Kant," in *Metaphysics and Philosophy of Science in the Seventeenth and Eighteenth Centuries,* and Arthur Melnick's (1989) work *Space, Time, and Thought in Kant*. Also, a general reader interested in the development of the concept of world after Kant should see Sean Gaston (2013) *The Concept of World from Kant to Derrida*.
171 Perhaps the best work on systematic philosophy generally and on what makes a philosophical position systematic is Walter Taylor Marvin's (1903) classic *An Introduction to Systematic Philosophy*.

doing so requires much of what can be called a recapitulation of what has been discussed in relation now to the concept of world.

The epistemological discussion in the *Critique of Pure Reason* surely indicates that world is directly concerned with the world of sense, or as Kant himself often calls it, the sensible world. Certainly, it is the sensible world which takes up much of the conversation regarding knowledge as it is the world of sense which gives rise to the appearances which then enables experience. For without the world of sense, without appearances, what "world" could there be in the Kantian system? In fact, the sensible world *is* the world – at least, it is our experience of it and as such it is *our* world, it is the *world* of *Dasein*,[172] the world of objects as they appear or present themselves to us.

Regardless of the necessity of the sensible world for there to be a "world" at all – for what kind of world cannot be experienced?[173] – this world of sense can only be a single part of a much more complex "world". Consider for example Kant's discussion of space and time, a topic of lengthy discussion earlier in this text as well. In his dissertation, *On the Form of the Principles of the Sensible and Intelligible World*, Kant states that the sensible world is formed by space and time as *pure intuitions*, and that space and time are ideal rather than real objective qualities.[174] Thus, the world of sense is formed by something external to it, and as such by something more primary: an *intelligible world*.[175]

---

[172] This world of *Dasein* is notably Heidegger's. However, it is easy to see it articulated in Kant as well.
[173] Many have posited a world which cannot be experienced. One point of comparison here that is often articulated is between Kant and Plato on an inexperienceable world; see, for example, their treatment as the same position in Sandra A. Wawrytko's (2013) chapter "The Buddhist Challenge to the Noumenal: Analyzing Epistemological Deconstruction," *in Constructive Engagement of Analytic and Continental Approaches in Philosophy*. For Kant, this takes the form of the *Noumenal* world. For Plato, the world of forms was not itself experienced, but merely recalled. Liu Piyong (2013) in *On Plato's Theory of Forms*, offers a good discussion on Plato's forms and the inability to experience them directly. I, however, do not think Plato's and Kant's "intelligible world" are the same. One reason for this is that Plato's intelligible world of forms articulates any given being's perfection – a form of an object is the most perfect version of that object or entity. Under Kant's position, the intelligible world, or *noumenal* world of things-in-themselves, consists not in perfection but, as I will argue in clarity later in this book, in potency and possibility.
[174] Kant (1992) makes this clear in his dissertation "On the form and principles of the sensible and the intelligible world [inaugural dissertation]," in *The Cambridge Edition of the Works of Immanuel Kant, Theoretical Philosophy*.
[175] We are here reminded of Plato's world of ideas which were ὑπερουράνιος τόπος. See Plato (1956) *Plato's Phaedrus*, to best grasp Plato's intelligible world.

Thus, any discussion of world in the Kantian system must also pay attention to this *intelligible* counterpart to the world of sense. That is to say, "world" for Kant is both. Of the *intelligible world,* Kant states "The mundus intelligibilis [intelligible world] is nothing but the general concept of a world in general, in which abstraction is made from all conditions of its intuition, and inference to which, therefore, no synthetic proposition, either affirmative or negative, can possibly be asserted" (2007, pp. 401–402).[176] Whether or not there is more to the *intelligible world* is a conversation for later; however, it can nevertheless be said that it is necessary for the world of sense, for "appearances cannot be limited *by an empty space* outside them" (ibid, p. 400).

The *mundus intelligibilis* is noumenal, and though Kant in the *Critique of Pure Reason* stresses the unknowability of noumena, and thus of the intelligible world as a whole, it is still worthy of examination. In particular, the question must be raised regarding the relationship between the world of sense and the intelligible world. Nowhere in Kant's *oeuvre* can this relationship be better understood than in the antinomies, the very clash between phenomena and noumena, as discussed above. It must be shown, then, how the antinomies, and the thesis and antithesis articulated in each of them, lend themselves to an understanding of the relationship between these "worlds".

The Worlds of Kantian Thought as Articulated through the Antinomies

Having previously completed a thorough examination of the antinomies, the next stage in an analysis of Kant's treatment of them is to understand the purpose they serve, in particular in their relation to this discussion of world. So then, we must ask, why set up antinomies and show the proofs of both the thesis and antithesis? The antinomies are, in general, claims made from two distinct angles or perspectives, set up so that neither assertion can claim or show dominance or superiority over another. Stated more simply, the primary goal was to further express and provide evidence for the limits of our ability to reason; that is, to show that there are certain things we cannot reason about though we seek explanations for them nevertheless.[177] This is due to the nature of reason, which aims not only to reason about experience but also about that which is beyond

---

[176] In other words, it cannot be known, other than its existence as a nonrelational abstraction.
[177] For both a description of why they capture our attention, an examination of the antinomies themselves, and a possible offering of a solution, see Paul Carus' (1915) article "Kant's Antinomies and their Solution".

our experience, and as such, that which is impossible for reason to know or understand.

What we are then left with is a grasping at unknowable knowledge, in opposition to Camus' focal concern when he writes that "I do not want to found anything on the incomprehensible. I want to know whether I can live with what I know and with that alone" (1991, p. 40). And since it is beyond our capability to reason about such things, reason can reason about anything and leave an opening for the correctness or infallibility of that which comes out of its reasoning; once we open the door to the path of knowledge, we must walk it.[178] Kant puts this best when he writes that "Each of them is not only in itself free from contradiction, but finds contradictions of its necessity in the very nature of reason – only that, unfortunately, the assertion of the opposite has, on its side, grounds that are just as valid and necessary" (2007, p. 394).

From here, then, after having examined the antinomies and recognizing the problems that are inherent in the proofs that were used, we turn to a question which arises as the most crucial of all possible ponderings rising from the antinomies: do they work in the way in which Kant hopes? That is, do they truly show that reason cannot give explanations of certain things? If we are to make a claim, whether it is to confirm that the antinomies do work, or if it is to deny that they fail in the goal at hand, we must first analyze how it is that they are meant to succeed in the task at which they are aimed. The antinomies are supposed to show that neither the thesis nor the antithesis is more valid or more provable through reasoning. Over the course of our examination of the antinomies in the previous chapter, we have shown that there are a few crucial problems in the arguments which are supposed to make the thesis and the antithesis equally valid.

Consider again the antinomy of the infinitude of the world. The arguments about time miss out on key aspects of the problem: most notably, that time if infinite would give rise to unlimited amounts of successive events in each moment that elapses. Kant states that the successive "true transcendental concept of infinitude synthesis of units required for the enumeration of a quantum can never be completed" (ibid, p. 401). Therefore, the world cannot possibly have a beginning in time, since this notion runs contrary to the very conception of infinitude. Time does not need to elapse, or have specific moments, in order to give rise to these successive events in the world; rather, these events would be infinite as well, even in a singular time, which is what it would be if it were infinite.

---

178 Recall here James Boswell's note in *The Life of Samuel Johnson:* "He who has provoked the lash of wit, cannot complain that he smarts from it" (1831, p. 88).

Likewise, as shown earlier in the antinomy of freedom, there arise problems with the conception of spontaneity, which of course is the cornerstone of the argument for transcendental freedom. "The necessity of a first beginning, due to freedom, of a series of appearances we have demonstrated only insofar as it is required to make an origin of the world conceivable; for all the later following states can be taken as resulting according to purely natural laws" (ibid, p. 413). What is argued for here, then, is the necessity of spontaneity in an original cause, though it gives rise to causation from nature, such that experience can be made possible; that is, so that we may conceive of a possible beginning of the world. But how we can assert spontaneity for a cause such that it begins a chain of causality is completely unclear.[179] Is there a way in which we can examine the extent to which the antinomies truly show the capabilities of reason?

Similar problems were addressed previously regarding the other two antinomies, and so do not need to be restated here. More important is that, while Kant believed he had shown the impossibility of reason accessing answers to that which is not rooted in experience, there remains the question of whether or not he truly succeeded. The answer to such a question is twofold. On the one hand, it is obvious that reason, by its very nature, reaches towards these "unknowable truths."[180] But are they really unknowable? Indeed, reasoning does provide valid argumentation for both the thesis and the antithesis for each of the stated claims. Kant takes this to mean that reason cannot give a true account, but rather creates these theories out of a more imaginative process.[181] So instead of the ability to reason being that which gives rise to sound arguments, pure reason can only provide valid arguments in certain cases: that is, in cases in which there is no direct experience of that which is being reasoned about.[182]

Thus, for Kant, since reason can prove both the thesis and the antithesis for each of the antinomies equally valid, pure reason is limited in its ability to rea-

---

[179] There is much scholarship on the concept of spontaneity in Kant. For some great examples see Michael Gass' (1994) article "Kant's Causal Conception of Autonomy", Stanley Rosen's (2001) chapter "Is Thinking Spontaneous?", in *Kant's Legacy: Essays in Honor of Lewis White Beck*, and Thomas Land's (2006) article "Kant's Spontaneity Thesis".

[180] We can see this for example in Richard Routley's (2010) article "Necessary Limits to Knowledge: Unknowable Truths".

[181] For a discussion on the role of imagination in the antinomies see Guelfo Carbone (2016) "Kant's Antinomies Concerning the World Problem Starting from Cassirer-Heidegger's Debate in Davos (1929)". For comments on imagination in Kant generally see Jane Kneller (2007) *Kant and the Power of Imagination*, and T. Ayas (2015) "Reflections on Kant's View of the Imagination".

[182] Graham Bird (2006) suggested this as well in The Revolutionary Kant: A Commentary on the Critique of Pure Reason.

son about certain things. The meaning of this is that reason cannot truly prove either side more vividly, and thus that there is no way to know certain things – namely, those which are not experienced – through reasoning.[183] But could there be another explanation as to why reasoning has the capability to account for both the thesis and antithesis of the antinomies? That is, does this fact necessarily mean that reason cannot give us real answers to these postulations? Or rather, could it mean something more fundamental about the nature of reasoning? In order to answer this question, we must consider further this notion of world in Kant, and as such, the distinction between the noumena and phenomena that is established.

Kantian Worlds Overview

There has been much discussion regarding the "Kantian worlds"[184] and how they need to be interpreted in order to make sense of the philosophy of Kant. In the *Critique of Pure Reason*, Kant often discusses the existence of both the phenomenal and noumenal worlds (that is, the world of sense and the intelligible world) as if they were distinct, and yet at the same time refers to some things as appearing and existing not strictly as phenomena but also as noumena, though the *Ding an sich* is unknowable. As stated before, 'world' for Kant, and likewise the influence it holds over his philosophical system, must include both the noumenal and phenomenal worlds and not prefer one over the other.

What must be discussed here, then, are the two major interpretations of the Kantian system regarding the relationship between these two worlds. Are they two separate worlds? Or on the contrary, are they one and the same "world"? These are the two most common interpretations and are usually referred to as the "Two Worlds Interpretation"[185] and the "Two Aspects Interpretation"[186] and deal with the nature not only of the world of sense and the intelligible world, but also the nature of the objects within them. Through further analyzing these interpretations, it will become clear where they fail to account for all of

---

183 For a great discussion on this see Henry E. Allison's (2004) chapter "The Antinomy of Pure Reason," in *Kant's Transcendental Idealism: An Interpretation and Defense*.
184 This is my term to designate the phenomena/noumena distinction. For a great general description and evaluation of the problem of Kantian worlds see Ralph C. S. Walker's (2010) article "Kant on the Number of Worlds".
185 For just one example, see James Van Cleve (1999) *Problems from Kant*.
186 See, for some examples, Lucy Allais (2004) "Kant's one world: Interpreting 'transcendental idealism', and Richard McCarty (2009) *Kant's Theory of Action*.

Kant's philosophical positions, and that we require a new interpretation of Kantian worlds in order to have a complete philosophical perspective.

The Two Worlds Interpretation

Of the two major interpretations of Kant, the two worlds interpretation is the more *ontological.* It holds that there are two ontologically distinct worlds of existence, the world which we experience and have knowledge about (that is, the sensible or the phenomenal world) and the world consisting only of things in themselves, termed the intelligible or noumenal world. Thus, those who hold this interpretation claim that Kant's distinction articulates an ontological separation between the phenomenal and noumenal; in other words, both the world of sense and the intelligible world are objective and real, not ideal. Let us consider how this interpretation fits within the Kantian system.

Many times in the *Critique*, when Kant discusses the noumenal/phenomenal distinction, he treats these as two ontologically distinct modes of existence: things exist in one fashion in the way we perceive them or the way they appear to us, and additionally in an objective real way, which we cannot have access to, as a thing-in-itself. *Esse quam videri*[187] expresses the difference. We see, for example, colors, shapes, and patterns; however, because of the very nature of experience being subjective, everything we perceive through sensation is simply the way in which the object appears to us; it is not the way the thing really is, in its essence. That objective reality, however, must be there, since we cannot think of an object without its being objectively real in and of itself.

Strawson, who is associated with this interpretation of Kantian worlds, suggests that things that appear to us must also have an objective existence as things-in-themselves. He writes:

> It may be conceded that each one of us can perfectly well imagine a stretch of his own experience as being such as the sense-datum theorist describes...But of course it is not enough that, equipped with the conceptual resources we are equipped with, we can form such a picture. What has to be shown is that the picture contains in itself the materials for the conception of itself as experience. What has been shown is that it does not (Strawson 2007, p. 109).

This is true because things-in-themselves must be present to impress in the perceiver's mind the representation that one may have. Thus, it should be noted

---

[187] Translation: to be rather than to seem.

here that everything is reduced to the inner, to subjective experience and mental apparatuses. The only things which exist objectively are things-in-themselves, which must be the case if they are to allow for perception and appearances. Jonathan Bennett, however, is unconvinced by Strawson's criticisms of Kant, noting that "Strawson inevitably implies many conclusions about how particular Kantian passages should be construed or revised, but defends few of them" (1968, p. 2).

The issue here becomes this: can we have knowledge of things in themselves? It seems as though Kant himself was confused as he often contradicted himself on this topic.[188] However, I believe that Kant thinks we have some knowledge regarding things-in-themselves, though perhaps not a complete knowledge of them. I agree with James Van Cleve when he writes: "what is denied to us is not any access whatever to these things, but only knowledge of their intrinsic or non-relational features...the phrase 'knowledge of things as they appear' contrasts not with 'knowledge of things as they really are' but with 'knowledge of things as they intrinsically are'" (1999, p. 150).

The assertion here is clear: Kant gives us knowledge of appearances and of things as they are, but limits our ability to know things as they are *intrinsically*, or in their essence. While I do concede the later part of Van Cleve's assessment, there is a major problem with this claim. Things-in-themselves are what things really are, and they are essences; thus, we cannot have knowledge either of things-in-themselves or of essences. Van Cleve's claim works only if an element of uncertainty is included and used to articulate a possibility of knowledge by an act of swaying one to a side, as in the claim of the great Roman playwright Terence.[189] Thus, we may say that we have knowledge of appearances, which could be things as they really are (which makes sense in Kant's understanding of experience), and as such we have knowledge of things as they really are, insofar as they are available to us. While such an interpretation includes Kant's semi-skepticism of reason,[190] it does not seem to fit into his larger project more generally.[191]

---

[188] For consideration on some of the contradictions in Kant see Ronald Glass (1971) "The Contradictions in Kant's Examples" and Pauline Kleingeld (2017) "Contradiction and Kant's Formula of Universal Law".

[189] Terrance wrote: "*Dum in dubio est animus, paulo momento huc illuc impellitur*" (1810, p. 435).

[190] For an excellent resource on Kant's concern with skepticism, see Michael N. Forster (2009) *Kant and Skepticism*.

[191] Kant's larger project, beyond even proving the possibility of knowledge, lies in the formulation of a systematic philosophy. That is to say, his work pushes towards such an end, whether

Van Cleve's claim holds that there is a distinction between how things *really* are and how they *intrinsically* are. Indeed, Kant does not deny that we know things as they really are, but rather only insofar as each is a *Ding an sich*. A more accurate reading of Kant shows that, in his philosophical system, both things as they appear and as they are in themselves are how a thing *really* is, with the qualifications, respectively, of insofar as they appear and insofar as they are in and of themselves. However, neither appearance nor *Ding an sich* are less than what the thing is *really* and both can be said to be precisely this. Thus, the main problem with Van Cleve's position is this: the *Ding an sich* is that aspect of how a thing *really* is *intrinsically*, whereas an appearance is how a thing *really* is insofar as we can experience and interact with it.

The absolute necessity of understanding the *Ding an sich* in this way is clear when considering the entire Kantian project or agenda. Keeping this in mind, it does not befit such a project to state that we cannot have knowledge of the *Ding an sich*, and yet the *Ding an sich* is that which things are *really*. This would instead further the notion that genuine knowledge cannot be accessed by us through reason, so that we are left only with a subjective experiential knowledge. But Kant does indeed hold an objectivity.[192] Although Kant shares this sentiment regarding our ability to only access and gain knowledge that is empirically rooted in experience, he asserts vehemently that this is genuine knowledge; indeed, this means knowledge of things as they *really* are.[193]

As such, we remain bound to this interpretation of the *Ding an sich* as being – as Van Cleve suggests – how a thing *really is*, but with the added qualification, *intrinsically* how a thing really is. Van Cleve seems to think that we cannot know things as they *intrinsically* are, as he criticizes Kant who he claims "believes there are some objects, the things in themselves, that resist phenomenalist reduction" (Van Cleve 2003, p. 11).[194] Thus, it can be said that he does not hold a true two worlds view of the Kantian system. The dual-objects or two worlds view must

---

or not his philosophy may be called systematic. For more on this, see Paul Guyer (2005) *Kant's System of Nature and Freedom: Selected Essays*.
192 For more on this objectivity of Kant, see J. Michael Young (2009) "Kant's Notion of Objectivity".
193 For Kant, things really are as they appear as well as how they are in themselves. The former we have access to, the latter we do not. Nonetheless, for Kant, appearances are how things really are insofar as they are an appearance. Thus the expression "really are" can be confusing.
194 It is also good to note this is a poor reading of Kant. For Kant *things in themselves* do not resist phenomenalist reduction, they are themselves not phenomena and so would indeed be how a thing *intrinsically* is; that is to say, Kant would not see the need for this distinction.

fully lend itself to an interpretation that asserts the *actual* existence of both appearances (mind-dependent) and things in themselves (mind-independent).

Ultimately, then, things-in-themselves exist regardless of our ability to perceive them. They hold an objective reality unto themselves. Our perceptions, which are due to the existence of things-in-themselves, are mental states or projections of the things in themselves, though quantified and qualified through our faculties and *pure intuitions* of space and time as well. Yet Kant holds that things-in-themselves do not simply affect our senses, but rather claims that they are themselves outside space and time, and not within it.[195] Space and time, for Kant, are *pure intuitions* of the mind, and as such, if things in themselves truly lacked temporality or a spatiality to them, it would mean that they could not affect our senses, since space and time enable sensation and experience to be possible at all.

The problem here is that rather than giving appearances and things-in-themselves different forms of *actuality* – one subjective, the other objective – both become subjective mental affections. In other words, this view appears to force the Kantian system onto the edge of pure idealism,[196] as found in Berkeley.[197] However, there is a solution to this problem within the Kantian system. Kant suggests that there is indeed noumenal *affection*. Things-in-themselves affect our senses, which sparks the appearances that are represented to us.[198] However, the Kant-

---

[195] Henry E. Allison (1976) notes this as well in his article "The Non-spatiality of Things in Themselves for Kant".

[196] Philipp Mainländer finds this contradiction to be worth applauding as he writes in *Die Philosophie der Erlösung*: "Er that es, weil er Nichts mehr fürchtete als den Vorwurf, seine Philosophie sei der reine Idealismus, welcher die ganze objektive Welt zu Schein macht und ihr jede Realität nimmt" (1894, p. 438).

[197] For a discussion on Kant's philosophy and its relationship to idealism see Margaret Dauler Wilson (1971) "Kant and 'The Dogmatic Idealism of Berkeley'", Henry E. Allison (1973) "Kant's critique of Berkeley", Ralph C. S. Walker's (1985) chapter "Idealism, Kant and Berkeley," in *Essays on Berkeley: A Tercentennial Celebration*, Vance G. Morgan (1993) "Kant and dogmatic idealism: a defense of Kant's refutation of Berkeley", and Frederick C Beiser (2002) *German Idealism: The Struggle against Subjectivism, 1781-1801*. Colin Turbayne (1955) argues that Kant and Berkeley are more similar than is typically claimed in his article "Kant's refutation of dogmatic idealism". A similar claim is held by G.D Justin (1977) in "Re-Relating Kant and Berkeley". A more curious and middle approach is taken by George Miller (1973) in "Kant and Berkeley: The Alternative Theories". Additionally, for a great commentary on the distinction between Kant's and Berkeley's treatment of space in particular, see Ralph Schumacher's (2001) essay "Kant und Berkeley über die Idealität des Raumes" in *Kant Und Die Berliner Aufklärung: Akten des Ix. Internationalen Kant-Kongresses*.

[198] For a great discussion of affection in Kant see, Claude Piché (2004) "Kant and the Problem of Affection".

ian system as *transcendental* seems to suggest something quite different from this. Rather than things in themselves *affecting* our senses, which is to make an empirical claim out of something not empirical, a better reading would be to assert that things in themselves produce the ability, for lack of clearer terminology, of *affection* within the object. That is to say, noumenal *affection* is best interpreted through *transcendental affectionability*.[199]

Transcendental affectionability can be considered to be the necessary precondition of an object to affect another. It is an attribute of an object that renders it capable of affection. Affection itself occurs as an empirical phenomenon. However, the *thing-in-itself* can spark affection through noumenal *affection*, which is simply the empirical affection of the senses caused by the object in question. This arises not strictly from the empiricality of the object, but through its very ability to cause affection, its *transcendental affectionability*, which is itself present not in the experienced appearance of an object but rather in the *thing-in-itself*.[200]

The Two Aspects Interpretation

Unlike the two worlds interpretation, the two aspects interpretation simply seeks to identify the noumenal and phenomenal as characteristics of objects, rather than as two independently existing objects. That is to say that these are not distinct worlds of objects, but traits, or aspects of the same world or object. The world is both phenomenal and noumenal in different senses; in the first instance we have knowledge about certain things insofar as they appear to us, and in the second we lack knowledge of things in themselves. This interpretation is perhaps easier to recognize in Kant but more difficult to grasp intellectually, though it is the predominant reading of contemporary scholarship.

According to this interpretation of Kant, things-in-themselves do not exist independently of the object that appears to us. Thus, there's not a world of appearances *and* a world containing things-in-themselves, meaning that these do not exist separate from each other. Instead, these are simply two aspects of

---

[199] A good commentary on the "problem of affection" in Kant can be found in Anna Tomaszewska (2007) "The transcendental object and the 'problem of affection'. Remarks on some difficulties of Kant's theory of empirical cognition".
[200] This is quite clear since the appearance of the object is simply an appearance, which is *in the mind* and is not the *object itself* in Kant. Thus, that which makes an object able to make an affection on another object cannot be in the individual mind, but in the object itself, such that an appearance may in fact appear at all.

the same object. Such an interpretation "makes it possible to avoid saddling Kant with the excess baggage of an ontologically distinct, yet cognitively inaccessible, Noumenal realm" (Allison 2009, p. 112). Appearances are not reduced to purely mental projections of things that exist in themselves, but rather simply represent an aspect of an object which exists independently as a thing-in-itself, and which appears to us in a certain way, namely as an appearance of a thing itself.

According to Henry E. Allison, this one world interpretation of Kant eliminates the need to posit things in themselves as entities existing independent of the object and our mental perception of the object. He writes:

> Kant indicates that the identification of appearances with mere representations should be taken to mean that things as we represent them, that is, as spatiotemporal entities and events, have no mind-independent existence, not that the things we represent as spatiotemporal have no such existence at all (Allison 2009, p. 112).

Allison's view on this interpretation claims that it articulates mainly an epistemological distinction, not an ontological one; that is, the two aspects through which objects can be known, only one of which we can access, namely, the way in which the object appears.

Although this interpretation is certainly appealing, it is difficult to divest Kant from an ontological claim, as Heidegger suggests.[201] Kant was certainly focused on the ability of a system that could enable us to grasp genuine knowledge, but it would be a major devastation of his work to assume that this is his only concern in the *Critique*. Indeed, many of his epistemological claims are rooted in no small way on the underlying ontology of *transcendental idealism*.[202] This ontology cannot be read accurately as devoid of an ontological undertone. As such, even if one is to claim that the two aspects interpretation is more appropriate, it must be an interpretation that nevertheless reads the noumenal/phenomenal distinction in the *Critique* as primarily ontological. Indeed, there is in fact a version of the two aspects interpretation which suggests precisely this.

Rae Langton holds such a view and articulates it in her work *Kantian Humility: Our Ignorance of Things in Themselves*. Langton rejects Allison's interpretation calling it "ingenious" but problematic and suggests that "it is inconceivable

---

[201] For more on Heidegger's interpretation of Kant as primarily concerned with ontology, see Camilla Serck-Hanssen (2015) "Towards fundamental ontology: Heidegger's phenomenological reading of Kant".
[202] For more on Kantian ontology, see Chong-Fuk Lau (2010) "Kant's Epistemological Reorientation of Ontology".

that we could have an 'inextinguishable desire' to consider things abstractly without considering things abstractly" stating that this "is reason enough to reject Allison's anodyne interpretation" (1998, p. 10). Langton argues instead that the distinction is one between epistemic properties of objects, which can be known if they are *relational*, or cannot be known if they are *intrinsic*.

Her position stems from reading Kant as primarily claiming that reason is limited due to some level of accessibility to things-in-themselves. This may well be a fair reading of Kant's first *Critique*, but would require reading it outside the context of the Kantian system as a whole.[203] Further, on Langton's interpretation, things-in-themselves still need to be spatial and temporal in order that the "relational" properties, to use her terminology, can be represented to us while the intrinsic properties are left inaccessible to our reason. This, however, goes directly against Kant's very own strict words.

Therefore, if we want to adequately interpret the issue of Kantian worlds, we must read the first *Critique* while always bearing in mind the context of *transcendental idealism* not only as it is articulated in the *Critique* but also throughout his system. Of the system, Kant writes:

> everything intuited or perceived in space and time, and therefore all objects of a possible experience, are nothing but phenomenal appearances, that is, mere representations, which in the way in which they are represented to us, as extended beings, or as series of changes, have no independent, self-subsistent existence apart from our thoughts. This doctrine I entitle *transcendental idealism* (Kant 2007, p. 439).

This suggests that the ideality of things (that is, things in themselves) are the necessary precondition of appearances. This can only mean that things-in-themselves are outside of and independent of the mind and as such are not spatial or temporal.[204] Thus, a view which holds the contrary, while perhaps useful, cannot be accurate to Kant's systematic philosophy of *transcendental idealism*.

Although Allison's interpretation, as Langton also illustrates, is problematic in multiple ways, Langton's own interpretation does not eliminate these problems. The appearance and thing-in-itself distinction cannot be said to be two-aspects in the sense of Allison's epistemological emphasis, nor Langton's semi-

---

[203] Indeed, one may argue that there is no choice but to do so, considering the difficulties of reconciling many of the concepts in the later *Critiques* (*Critique of Practical Reason*, *Critique of Judgement*) as well as other later works by Kant with the first *Critique*. I would argue however, that these difficulties arise from a misunderstanding of Kant, rather than from inconsistencies of his thought.

[204] Again, it is good to keep in mind the possible contradiction since Kant says spatiality and temporality are necessary preconditions of affectionability.

ontological "relational" and intrinsic argument. Nevertheless, Langton's suggestion, though problematic as pointed out above, is correct to articulate a distinction between relational and intrinsic aspects; however, the application of these in her interpretation is misguided. Drawing on her novel idea, I propose a new interpretation.

The Two Relations Interpretation

Having discussed the two major interpretations of Kantian worlds, and examining the reasons why neither of these grant a complete view of the Kantian philosophical system, we must now consider positing a new interpretation that will not only solve this issue, but will be able to permeate contemporary philosophy. The way I propose to solve the problem of the antinomies is indeed by means of a separation of worlds, though not in the ontological sense of the two worlds or two aspects interpretations discussed previously. The noumenon and phenomenon are not two distinct objects, nor are they two aspects of one and the same object. In fact, it has little to do with the object, but is directly concerned with our *experience* of objects.[205]

For certain, Kant's primary focus (if we are to suggest that one focus predominates) is a *fundamental ontology:* or to merge Kantian and Heideggarian terminology, a *transcendental ontology.* But this ontology is located *within us.* Indeed, as Kant suggests, our *experience* of the world is purely a subjective one. Thus, we ourselves are at the center of our experience.[206] Insofar as a fundamental or transcendental ontology is that metaphysics of *Dasein* which gives rise to the very possibility of ontology, *Dasein* must possess a faculty responsible for the *ontology of appearances*. This faculty would be that which makes things appear to us in a particular way. One would be right to point here to a major push away from

---

[205] As will hopefully become clear later, this is not to suggest that this interpretation does not lend anything to our understanding of objects, but merely aims at indicating the fact that an object is what it is rather than how it appears to be as a phenomenon, as well as rather than being something in and of itself which is not accessible to us, a noumenon. This distinction only refers to our relation to objects, but does not speak to the objects themselves. Nonetheless, as will be shown later, the two-relation interpretation has much it could say about objects, though that is beyond the scope of the problem at hand. Essentially, I believe this to be the best way to read Kant, as his primary concern is with the manner in which we experience.
[206] My intention here is not to propose a *Dasein-centric* philosophical position. In fact, it is the opposite of that. I hope to make this clear in what follows.

Kant as he understands the things-in-themselves to be responsible for this: that is, for making things appear to us as they do.

However, I do not here wish to claim that *Dasein* has a faculty which takes over this task from things-in-themselves, nor do I wish to eliminate things-in-themselves. Still, in order for there to be a fundamental ontology at work in Kantian philosophy, a point on which I tend to agree with Heidegger, *Dasein* must possess such a faculty that would be responsible for the way in which things appear. Such a claim has been argued before by the likes of Henri Bergson in his *Creative Evolution,* a text which, as Harman points out, is largely underappreciated but can point us in the right direction to the investigation of relationality between non-human beings.[207] Bergson writes that:

> as it is indeed necessary to perceive a thing somehow in order to symbolize it, there would be an intuition of the psychical, and more generally of the vital, which the intellect would transpose and translate, no doubt, but which would none the less transcend the intellect. There would be, in other words, a supra-intellectual intuition. If this intuition exists, a taking possession of the spirit by itself is possible and no longer only a knowledge that is external and phenomenal (Bergson 1911, p. 360).

Where does this leave things-in-themselves?

I suggest that we understand things-in-themselves and appearances in Kant as ways in which we, *Dasein, relate* to objects *in the world*. I will here explain this position and then later articulate a defense. When we encounter objects, we always do so *in the world,* through some kind of *relationality.* This is very evident insofar as things appear to us. A cup of coffee on the table next to me appears to me as such in virtue of its relation to me.[208] What is less clear is the way in which things-in-themselves relate to me, a thing which Kant would seemingly suggest is not the case.

However, consider the cup of coffee on the table next to me. As an appearance, it relates to me as I experience it in its spatiality and temporality. The *Ding an sich* of the cup of coffee does not appear to me. I cannot see it, hear it, or sense it in any way, and therefore it does not appear to me, is not represented to me. Thus the question becomes: do we experience objects only insofar as they appear to us?

According to Kant, the answer is very clearly yes. He nevertheless insists upon an existence of the object beyond this appearance, which he terms a

---

207 "[T]he reader is referred to Bergson's strangely neglected *Creative Evolution* as a model for what it would take for philosophy to seize this bull by the horns" (Harman 2002, p. 71).
208 "Cup", "Table", "Next to", and even "me" all indicate some form of relationality in the world.

thing-in-itself, and thus proposes the two objects interpretation. Those who are critics of the thing-in-itself still answer yes, hence the two aspects interpretation. If, on the other hand, the answer to this question is no, then we are introduced to an entirely different outcome. I therefore propose a new way to interpret the Kantian system, which will also connect contemporary continental philosophical ideas back to this system.

If we are to suggest that we experience objects beyond the manner in which they appear to us, then we must outline how this can be possible. I have suggested above that the transcendental ego is itself a noumenon. As a noumenon, we have experiences of other noumena, things in themselves, insofar as they relate to us as phenomena, as appearances. However, we are nonetheless experiencing a thing-in-itself, even if it becomes cognized only as a phenomenon. Thus, the noumenal self, the thing-in-itself version of ourselves (that is, the "I", or transcendental ego) recognizes in appearances the thing-in-itself. How does this happen?

Coming back to the faculty responsible for *transcendental ontology*, Dasein must be *responsible* for the way in which things appear in some manner. Indeed, recalling that *pure intuitions* of space and time, which enable the experience of objects as appearances, are rooted in the mind (that is, *internally* to Dasein) this is a less specious claim. Thus, the way in which things appear to us is due in large part to our faculties as *Dasein*. Appearances as experienced are thus, as suggested in the two worlds interpretations, mental projections of things-in-themselves. This faculty of *Dasein,* then, is responsible for converting things-in-themselves (which are experienced immediately) into an appearance that can be cognized and represented to us in a qualified experience: one that appears to us as immediate, though it is in truth indirect – hence the example of the pink lenses as an articulation of the transcendental ego. The *thing-in-itself* of an object is then simply the way in which we experience an object prior to its being represented to us; the appearance of a thing is the qualified experience processed through sense.

Now, two objections might arise here that are worth dealing with immediately. These are the claims:
1. How can we experience a thing prior to its being represented to us (prior, that is, to our experience of it)?
2. How can we experience a thing without sensation?

Through dealing with the latter, I believe the former will become more clear. Kant does in fact suggest that we cannot experience that which is not empirical, due in fact to its thus not being able to be sensed. I agree with Kant on this point; however, I suggest that the thing-in-itself is in fact *empirical* since, as

I mentioned, we do experience it. However, this experience is not rooted in sense but rather in *transcendental affectability*. As mentioned above, though not fully discussed, *transcendental affectability* is the faculty through which we can be affected by that which ultimately becomes sensed. Insofar as the thing-in-itself can affect us through the faculty of *transcendental affectability*, it is sensed. To consider this more closely, let us consider how we come to have objects represented to us in Kantian philosophy.

In the first instance, an object affects our senses, i.e., we see the object. The sensation of the object is intuited in a particular way and ultimately is represented to us in the way that it appears. While this is an obvious oversimplification, it will suffice for the purpose here. When *transcendental affectability* enters the equation it alters the "what" of our objects of sense, though not the way in which we sense those objects. In other words, things-in-themselves would be enabled to affect our senses, though we would not have it represented to us. This is due to *intuition*, in particular the *pure intuitions* of space and time. Prior to an object being represented to us, it must be intuited, requiring the faculty of intuition. This faculty, *subjected* to space and time, intuits objects as spatial and temporal. Herein lies the problem for Kant: things-in-themselves are neither temporal nor spatial, and thus cannot be intuited, nor represented or known to us, and not even experienced.[209]

If we are to make the claim that things-in-themselves can affect our senses, then it must be in such a manner that they are not intuited (since they cannot be). Things in themselves as outside space and time can never be intuited, and therefore cannot be represented to us.[210] Thus, if things in themselves are nevertheless sensed in some fashion, without being *able* to be intuited as things-in-themselves, then there must be a faculty that Kant has overlooked in the process prior to the concepts of understanding, yet after the initiation of affection of the senses: a *transcendental* faculty which serves the purpose of qualifying the object of receptivity. I propose that we term this faculty the *transcendental modality of representation*.

---

209 Henry E. Allison (1976) offers a discussion of the inability to experience the thing-in-itself and its lack of spatiality in "The Non-spatiality of Things in Themselves for Kant" as does Desmond Hogan (2009a) in "Three Kinds of Rationalism and the Non-Spatiality of Things in Themselves".
210 Hoke Robinson's (1994) article "Two perspectives on Kant's appearances and things in themselves" offers a lot here regarding the relationship between representation and the thing-in-itself. He examines the reasons why the latter can never "appear" to us, even as a result of the former.

Transcendental modality as a faculty, I suggest, establishes a conversion process of sense-data and governs the procedure of transition from perception to representation. As the name suggests, *transcendental modality of representation* is that which makes it possible for an object to be represented to us, akin to Bergson's transcriber intuition.[211] Some points of further clarification are necessary here. It is specifically the *pure intuition* of space and time that makes the reception of the object representable to us as an appearance. In order to be represented to us, an object must be presented as in space and time by means of *pure intuition*.[212] However, if things-in-themselves are what give rise to the object as being able to be represented, then things-in-themselves must also have spatiality and temporality – an issue discussed previously in regards to leading interpretations of Kant, since he himself claimed that this is not possible.

If we are then to hold, as Kant does, that things-in-themselves do not possess spatiality or temporality, yet nevertheless give rise to the ability of appearance, then the question becomes: how is this possible? We are either to note this as a contradiction in Kant, assuming he did not notice this, or reconsider whether Kant did not articulate properly the process of noumenal affection. This problem is solved by the *transcendental modality of representation*. While *pure intuition* is responsible for the process which makes an object intuitable and thereby representable to us, through qualifying the object with the addition of space and time to its properties, this does not account for how it is that things-in-themselves *can at all* be given spatiality or temporality in the mind, when no such property of things in themselves exists.

Here, then, there enters the responsibility of the *transcendental modality of representation* which lends itself to the making possible of the addition of space and time as properties of things-in-themselves such that *pure intuition* may in fact make the object representable. That is to say, this faculty "converts" the sense-data which is perceived *via* receptivity into sense-data which contains *within it* the possibility of being intuited: namely, the possibility of the addition of space and time to its set of properties such that, ultimately, the object can be represented to us.

Thus, Kant was correct in many assertions regarding our experience, or lack thereof, of things in themselves: in particular, his claim that we do not experience things-in-themselves. To recapitulate his argument, we cannot experience things-in-themselves, since they are not intuitable due to their lacking spatiality

---

[211] We may also call it a schematism before the schematism articulated by Kant.
[212] Desmond Hogan (2009b) notes this in "How to Know Unknowable Things in Themselves," before going on in an attempt to uncover the possibility of knowing things-in-themselves.

and temporality; thus, we must indirectly experience objects as appearances rather than how they are *in themselves, which is also due in so small part to the finitude of reason noted earlier.*[213] What Kant does not account for, however, is the fact that while we only have access to appearances as they are represented to us, we are not "cut off" entirely from things-in-themselves, a point Langton asserted correctly, though we saw that her claim as to how and what we can know about them was problematic.

What do we have access to regarding the thing-in-itself? With the inclusion of the *transcendental modality of representation*, we "experience" things in themselves *a priori* to their being represented to us, but *a posteriori* insofar as things-in-themselves impress upon us. They are not "sensed" properly, but nevertheless they activate receptivity; after *pure intuition*, they become properly sensed as they become represented to us. We recall Bergson again, when he notes regarding his supra-intellectual intuition that:

> if we have an intuition of this kind…then sensuous intuition is likely to be in continuity with it through certain intermediaries[214]…Sensuous intuition itself, therefore, is promoted…It will no longer attain only the phantom of an unattainable thing-in-itself. It is…into the absolute itself that it will introduce us (Bergson 1911, p. 360).

Thus, things-in-themselves can best be understood as being experienced *transcendentally*, or what we *might* term *transcendental sensation*, a sensation prior to a realized, or actualized, sense – which can only occur post-representation. In other words, there is not simply *double affection* as Kant suggests, but this also requires and conditions a *double sense* as well: a *transcendental sense* of things in themselves which rouses receptivity and sparks the process of representation beginning, and *sensation proper* which occurs after representation and which accounts for our standard senses.

This leaves us with a new way of interpreting this distinction. Rather than be focused on the object, it is focused on the subject. Thus, it is not the way in which the objects exist, whether as two separate objects, nor two aspects of the same object but rather the way in which the "I" or transcendental ego relates

---

[213] This conception of "lacking", particularly regarding the faculty of reason "lacking" in its finitude, calls to mind Gehlen's anthropology which describes human beings primarily as *Mängelwesen*. For more commentary on Gehlen's work see Andrea Borsari (2009) "Notes on 'Philosophical Anthropology' in Germany. An Introduction".
[214] Such as *transcendental affectability*, as noted above.

to the objects, or more generally to the world around them.²¹⁵ Specifically, we relate to the world in two ways. First, we relate to the world insofar as it appears to us. This is the world of relations, interconnectedness, and the world in which we have direct experiences, a world of *Dasein*. As such, I term it simply the *world*, as it is that which Heidegger and Kant refer to as world, and additionally that which we are directly experiencing. Let us here consider more deeply the world of *Dasein* in Heidegger.

---

215 The claim here is not that the distinction says nothing about objects, since they too exist in a nonrelational way, but simply that, in Kant, the distinction serves to articulate something about the *manner* of *our experience*.

Chapter Seven
Heidegger's Being-in-the-World

Heidegger brought about a change in view, a break away from the Western tradition's ontological perspective; yet, in the process of this 'break', Heidegger brought with his philosophy the tenaciousness that comes with dogmatism, even if it aimed at truth since such truth clings only to the circle's edge.[216] I mean to suggest that Heidegger's perspective, which draws us away from the narrowness of the Western tradition's ontology, also carries with it the very same tenacity of the most primordial aspects of the old ontology which is problematic; that is, the unquestionable presuppositions from which ontology must begin. I propose here to explicate Heidegger's thought on *Dasein* and the World.

In *Being and Time*, Heidegger sets forth an existential analysis of *Dasein*. *Dasein*, or literally "there-being," is Heidegger's conception of the human being insofar as this being finds itself primordially in the *world*. Yet the world, in Heidegger's understanding, is not the way in which we often think of it. It is not that which encompasses everything in totality, but rather it is the totality of the web of relations between all beings; that is, the inter-relatedness of beings that are in the world, or relationality. To further address Heidegger's conception of *Dasein,* it is necessary to recognize the reason why he makes an attempt to depart from the modern perceptions, as well as to understand the manifold aspects of *world*. Through a better understanding of *world,* as Heidegger views it, a better grasp of the concept of *Dasein* can be achieved, and with it an increase of the awareness of the problematic nature of Heidegger's thought on world.

Dasein finds itself, first and foremost, *in the world*. But what does it mean to be *in the world?* In order that we may better understand *being-in-the-world,* we must first understand the primacy of it within the being of *Dasein*. To do this, we must quantify the meaning of the phrase *being-in;* that is, what does it mean to *be in* something? This could mean, in one sense, a relationship between two beings such that prepositions are required to make meaning out of them. Heidegger explicates this "categorical" form of relationship, writing that "By this 'in' we mean the relation of being that two beings extended 'in' space have to each other with regard to their location in that space" (2010, p. 54). For example, one might say "the rock is in the garden." This would represent the relationship between beings insofar as they are within space.

---

216 "The mind petrifies if a circle be drawn around it, and it can hardly be denied that dogma draws a circle round the mind" writes George Moore (1923, p. 198) in *Hail and Farewell!*

However, *Dasein* is not *in* the world in such a way that it is in a spatial relationship to the world. This makes clearer sense if one thinks of what a spatial relationship is. When one makes the statement "the rock is in the garden," both of the beings which are in relation to each other necessarily exist already within the world. But Heidegger claims that *Dasein* cannot be *in the world* in the same fashion as the rock can be in the garden, since the world does not have a being within space.[217] Therefore the relationship between *Dasein* and the world is not spatial, and by the same virtue, this relationship cannot be the same as the rock in the garden.

Then what sort of relationship is there between *Dasein* and the world? It is not *categorical*, but rather *existential*, according to Heidegger. This means that it is directly concerned with the very existence and experience of *Dasein* itself. Thus, being-in is "*the formal existential expression of the being of Dasein which has the essential constitution of being-in-the-world*" (ibid, p. 55).[218] In other words, *being in* is the mode of expression of the being of *Dasein* insofar as it has as its mode of being *being-in-the-world*. Yet it remains not entirely clear what the mode of *being-in-the-world* means for *Dasein*. In order to grasp *being-in-the-world* we must understand the concept of *being-together-with*, a most important mode of *being-in*.

Being together with does not mean to be present with another being; that is, it is not the same as suggesting "the fireplace is near the wall" or "the cup is on the table." For Heidegger, these denote an objectively present *being with* which places upon beings a relation to each other that is subsequent to *Dasein's being-in*. This is evident since:

> A being [*Seiendes*] can only touch a being present within the world if that first being fundamentally has the kind of being of being in – only if with its Dasein something like world is already discovered in terms of what beings can reveal themselves through touch and thus become accessible in their being present (Heidegger 2010, p. 55).

In other words, the first being, the one whose being present within the world is being touched, must be fundamentally *in the world*. Thus, the two beings cannot be in the relationship of *being together with*, unless the first being is *in the world* primordially.

---

217 He does so in both *Being and Time and* earlier since this stems from his concept of world and the indication that only *Dasein* has a world. For a discussion of the origin and development of the concept of world in Heidegger's early work, see Theodore Kisiel (1992) "Das Kriegsnotsemester 1919: Heideggers Durchbruch zur hermeneutischen Phànomenologie".
218 Italics from text.

Being together with is rather more accurately understood as "being absorbed in the world, which must be further interpreted, is an existential which is grounded in *being-in*" (ibid). Thus, since *being together with* is an existential of *being in, Dasein* has then as part of its being, *being together with*. This then means that *being-in-the-world* is for *Dasein, insofar* as *Dasein* is in the world, an aspect of being absorbed in the world. But what does it mean to be absorbed in the world? To be absorbed means, in one way, to be engulfed by, that is, to be surrounded by. *Dasein* is consistently surrounded by the world.

However, absorbed also implies an internal aspect to the act of being surrounded by, such that it can be best described as a *being engaged with* the world;[219] that is, *Dasein* in its *being-in* is engaged in the world, not simply surrounded by or resting within the world. To be engaged in the world is the way in which *Dasein* is actively involved in its *being-in-the-world*. Overall, *Dasein* takes an active role in its being; that is, *Dasein* is concerned with and about its *being in the world*. In what ways is *Dasein* concerned with its being? *Dasein's* concern is centered on the fact that it is always attuned, as Heidegger puts it.

Attunement and Care

Dasein, in its being, is always in attunement; that is, it is subjected to various moods. Attunement, or moods, become expressed in different ways and are commonly susceptible to conditional modes of change. This ever-changing nature of moods leads Heidegger directly to the conclusion that *Dasein* must always remain constantly attuned, though the expression of this fluctuates. What must be clarified, before any further examination of the world of *Dasein*, is whether or not *Dasein* is always attuned and if it is only the expression of this that changes, or rather the moods themselves.

At first glance, the notion of a possible lack of attunement seems preposterous, since this would mean that it is possible to feel nothing. Of course, it is not feasible to feel nothing, for what would it mean to do so? To feel nothing would be to have a complete lack of response to the world, which renders the experience or the feeling of nothing for *Dasein* implausible: for *Dasein* is always in its most fundamental state *in the world*, and thus in relation to it.[220] Heidegger

---

219 Glen L. Sherman (2009) examines and explains Heidegger's conception of authenticity in "Martin Heidegger's Concept of Authenticity: A Philosophical Contribution to Student Affairs Theory".
220 However, a particular mood, namely dread, "reveals" the nothing to *Dasein*, Heidegger writes in *Was ist Metaphysik?* "*In diesem durch die Angst enthüll-ten Nichts entgleiten wir uns*

recognizes the fact that *Dasein* must be attuned, suggesting that "The fact that moods can be spoiled and change only means that Dasein is always already in a mood" (Heidegger 2010, p. 131). One cannot be sad unless one was previously in a mood other than sad. Therefore, for Heidegger, the mode of being attuned is fundamental for *Dasein*, meaning that *Dasein* is always in attunement.

The expression of this attunement does change, however. As is evident from experience, moods are good, bad, neutral, or otherwise content. Through always being attuned and having a mood, *Dasein* is disclosed as the being which it must be. That is, it is disclosed as what it is: *Dasein* itself as what *Dasein* is. It is through moods that the character of *Dasein* is revealed.[221] But what exactly is this character which *Dasein* reveals itself as having as its Being through being always in attunement? Heidegger identifies this character of *Dasein* as *Geworfenheit*, or thrownness. He clarifies this notion, writing that "The expression thrownness is meant to suggest the facticity of its being delivered over *[Überantwortung]*" (ibid, pp. 131–132). However, what does it mean to be delivered over? Delivered over to what? The answer is: to the world.

Thrownness is the mode of being of this being, *Dasein*, insofar as it is handed over or dealt to the world; that is, insofar as *Dasein* is cast into the world, left to its fate and conditions, and must now accept these conditions as its own and press on. "*Le sort fait les parents, le choix fait les amis* " (Delille 1833, p. 75).[222] But being attuned, *Dasein* is directed both towards and away from its being thrown. While the latter of these is obvious through experience, since certain moods affect our perceptions – both what we are willing to perceive and the way in which we perceive it – the former is more elusive. What do moods direct *Dasein* towards? Before this question can be thought through, it is first necessary to better understand the way *Dasein* is thrown into the world, since it is thrown in such a way that it is directed towards something.

Dasein being primordially *in the world*, and so thus being always attuned, finds itself thrown into the world, and:

> as thrown, *Dasein* is thrown into the mode of being of projecting. Projecting has nothing to do with being related to a plan thought out, according to which *Dasein* arranges its being,

---

selbst. Das Nichts offenbart sich und umdrängt uns" (Heidegger 2018, p. 739). For a discussion furthering this as well as in general the connection between mood and nothing in Heidegger, see Lucilla Guidi (2017) "Moods as Groundlessness of the Human Experience. Heidegger and Wittgenstein on *Stimmung*". For a general discussion of affectivity and moods, see A. Elpidorou, and L. Freeman (2015) "Affectivity in Heidegger I: Moods and Emotions in Being and Time".
221 For more on the revealing of *Dasein* through *moods*, see David Weberman (1996) "Heidegger and the Disclosive Character of the Emotions".
222 Translation: Fate determines our relatives, choice determines our friends.

but, as *Dasein*, it has always already projected itself and is, as long as it is, projecting. As long as it is, *Dasein* always has understood itself and will understand itself in terms of possibilities (Heidegger 2010, p. 141).

This means that the world in which *Dasein* finds itself thrown also comes to be recognized as having possibilities: that is, there is something that can be done with the world and in the world. Due to our moods, the various relations within the world are meaningful;[223] in other words, they matter to us and we are concerned with them. In general, *Dasein* finds itself cast into a world of meaning that matters to *Dasein*. Thus, there is a fundamental characteristic of *Dasein* which has as its mode of being a genuine concern with its being.[224] This characteristic is none other than *Sorge*, or *Care*.

Dasein cares about its world and its being. The everyday existence of *Dasein*, that is, its everydayness, is characterized by *care* insofar as *Dasein* is concerned with its being and is engaged in its world. Yet because it is engaged in its world, care is not aimed specifically only at *Dasein's* being, but also the being of others as well. Heidegger points this out, writing that "The *average everydayness of Dasein can thus be determined as entangled-disclosed, thrown-projecting being-in-the-world, which is concerned with its ownmost potentiality in its being together with the 'world' and in being-with with others*" (ibid, pp. 175–176). Insofar as we care about being in general, and the world, we are always engaged in them.

Care is therefore a mode of being concerned with being as it unfolds through time. Thus, when Heidegger suggests that attunement lends itself to directing-towards, he is arguing that *Dasein*, through the mode of care, is directed towards its future. However, before he can truly make this claim, he must first introduce a fundamental characteristic of *Dasein* which directs this being (insofar as it is in its being always attuned) towards the future. This *being directed towards the future* is further evaluated by Heidegger insofar as it establishes a mode of being of *Dasein*, as *Sein-zum-Tode* or being-toward-death.

Being-toward-death is *Dasein* as it is *being directed towards* the future.[225] *Dasein* is always aimed at its own being, and therefore aimed at its own nonbeing

---

[223] For more on the relationship between moods, meaning, and authenticity in Heidegger and in general see A. Krebs, and A. Ben-Ze'ev (2017) "Preface to the Meaning of Moods".

[224] There are many who make the claim that there is no meaning of life. However, I think Kurt Baier's articulation in *The Meaning of Life* that those who do, "mistakenly conclude that there can be no purpose *in* life because there is no purpose *of* life" is accurate in its dismissal of such a proposition (2008, pp. 101-102).

[225] For Anthony Bartlett (2003), this indicates *Dasein* as a victim of sacrifice, though I think this reads too strongly into Heidegger's biblical references.

as well, since nonbeing is an aspect of being itself. That said, it must be kept in mind that *Dasein falls prey* to the "they."[226] That is, *Dasein* remains always under the influence of the "they," *das Man*, and that this distracts *Dasein* from being authentically in the world. This victimization of *Dasein* is reminiscent of Buber's claim that *"Das aber ist die erhabene Schwermut unseres Loses, daß jedes Du in unsrer Welt zum Es werden muß"* (1997, p. 22). This also distracts *Dasein* from its *being-toward-death;* that is, as *Dasein falls prey,* and thus is in an inauthentic mode of being, *Dasein* does not recognize that its primary mode of being is as a *being-toward-death*.

So, despite *Dasein* being a *being-toward-death*, this is not a continuous thought of mortality, or a state of fearing death, but is rather a mode of being futural which is fundamental to the being of *Dasein*. In addition to the lack of authenticity in the everydayness of *Dasein*, there are fleeting occasions which enable *Dasein* to draw back from the "they," and instead truly become aware of its own being insofar as it is a *being-toward-death*. Heidegger writes on this subject, suggesting that though always falling prey, "Resolute, *Dasein* has brought itself back out of falling prey in order to be all the more authentically 'there' for the disclosed situation in the 'moment' ['*Augenblick*']" (Heidegger 2010, p. 313). This "moment" is to be understood as fleeting; that is, *Dasein* does not, and for Heidegger rather *cannot*, remain in a constant authentic mode of being. Instead, *Dasein* will always revert back to falling prey to the "they."

All of what has been discussed thus far articulates *how Dasein is in the world*, according to Heidegger. We have an obligation as *in-der-Welt-sein* to act; it is our condition, as Maurice Blondel wrote.[227] But we must now consider: what is *world* in Heidegger? That is to ask, what composes the world of *Dasein*? We will here proceed to address this question.

The Way Which We Relate to the World: Ready-to-Hand vs. Present-at-Hand

Heidegger recognizes that *Dasein* has what we may think of as a utilitarian attitude towards the world as a fundamental part of its nature, and that this is the

---

[226] For what is perhaps the best analysis on *Das Man* in Heidegger see Hubert L. Dreyfus (2008) "Interpreting Heidegger on *Das Man*".
[227] "Impossibility of abstaining and of holding myself in reserve, inability to satisfy myself, to be self-sufficient and to cut myself loose, that is what a first look at my condition revels to me" (Blondel 1984, p. 3).

way in which we function. That said, however, he also stresses a more critical view of this as well. Thus, he distinguishes between two characteristics of *Dasein*'s relationship to other beings, or objects, in the world. These are the famous *zuhanden*, or ready-to-hand, and *vorhanden*, or present-at-hand. The first of these to be discussed here is the ready-to-hand, which is the way a being presents itself as having the being of *Zuhandenheit*, or *handiness*.

Through this phenomenological approach, Heidegger noticed something fundamental about *Dasein*. That is, *Dasein* in relation to other beings seems to be focused on the immediate significance of all other beings to *itself*. That is to say, through this relation *Dasein* sees other beings as significant or relevant insofar as the other beings can fulfill a sort of need; that is, insofar as they provide some use. In fact, Heidegger even suggests that there is a tendency of *Dasein* to fail to recognize the presence of a being if it is not of immediate use. For example, a candle which is not burning and has no scent (a scent can be useful insofar as it is pleasurable) is relatively unnoticed until it is lighted, thus fulfilling its purpose. That said, it is also important to recognize that since this is the way in which *Dasein* is, this relationship is crucial to *Dasein* since "the more we take hold of it and use it, the more original our relation to it becomes" (Heidegger 2010, p. 69). Thus, the more we partake in the utilization of other beings, the more we understand our own being.

Although *Dasein* has as its being a relation to other beings that is based primarily in usefulness, there is another way in which beings relate to the world of *Dasein*; this is what Heidegger calls *present-at-hand*. *Presence-at-hand* is the mere presence of a being which is observable.[228] Thus, this is the relation to the world in which beings are observed simply as present, without regard to any specific use that could come out of the being. However, Heidegger's analysis suggests that this is a subsequent relation to the world, whereas the *ready-to-hand* is that which forms our primary relation to the world. The reasoning for this relation being subsequent to Heidegger's conception of *Dasein* is because "The presence of what is unusable still does not lack all handiness whatsoever; the useful thing *thus* present is still not a thing which just occurs somewhere" (ibid, p. 72). Consequently, the being that is *present-at-hand* does not simply appear to us as useless, but rather it is a being which is no longer *ready-to-hand*, that is able to be used, and so instead it is noticed as a being *present-at-hand*, a being that is simply there, almost like a nothingness.[229]

---

[228] For a discussion of *zuhanden* and *vorhanden* in Heidegger, especially in regard to its articulation of relationality, see David Weberman (2010) "Heidegger's Relationalism".
[229] Gregor Moder (2013), examines the relation between a being *present-at-hand* and nothingness in his article "Held Out Into the Nothingness of Being".

In other words, this relation becomes evident only after a being has been estimated as being meaningless; that is to say, after a being has become no longer useful.[230] As an example, we may consider a vase. So long as the vase fulfills its duty, it is noticed and we relate to its being through its use, its being *ready-to-hand*. If however the vase shatters, it is now noticed, but since it is judged as not able to perform its task, we relate to its being through its merely being in front of us, through its *presence-at-hand*.

It might initially seem as though *Dasein* has neediness as part of its being, for utilization or use-value always arises out of a need. For instance, a need to communicate is the source of a writing utensil's usefulness. Thus, the continuous tendency to see other beings as objects ready-to-hand must have *Dasein*'s neediness as a source, must it not? Despite this generally sounding reasonable, neediness is not the source of utilization. Rather, the source of the treatment of other beings as objects ready-to-hand is *Dasein* itself. It is the way in which *Dasein* is fundamentally; that is, *in the world*, and the world is relationality.

Having considered the relationality of the world of *Dasein* in Heidegger, we may now return to the two relations interpretation of Kant's distinction articulated at the end of Part One. An analysis of the concept of world was given, and we must now consider how this proposed interpretation adjusts how we must view *Dasein*. As was mentioned, and as seen in Heidegger as well, we experience and interact with the world of objects in a relational way. *Dasein* is actively engaged in its world, that is, it is concerned with its *being in the world*, through the mode of its being, *care*.

Due to *care* and active involvement in its being, *Dasein* must also have, as a mode of being, a sense of being futural. In other words, *Dasein*, as a being whose being is as a *being in the world*, is also a *being-toward-death*. When *Dasein* does not fall victim to the "they" and its being as a *being-toward-death* is recognized, *Dasein* also recognizes that, in its *being-toward-death*, it is and always has been *in the world* in this mode of being thrown. The world into which *Dasein* is thrown becomes recognized as meaningful insofar as it is filled with possibilities through this relationality of the world of *Dasein*.[231]

Additionally, however, we have indirect experience (that is, experience which we cannot cognize) of the noumenal world, the world of things-in-themselves, or of the world insofar as it exists apart from relations between things. It may not be immediately clear how this follows from the two relations interpre-

---

230 Tom Sparrow (2014), discusses usefulness and the role it plays in Heidegger's tool-analysis in *The End of Phenomenology: Metaphysics and the New Realism*.
231 For more on the possibilities of *Dasein*, see John Haugeland (2013) *Dasein Disclosed*.

tation; however, it is easy to demonstrate. To do so, it is helpful to discuss objects, which will also further differentiate between Langton's relational theory and my own.

Langton, I have argued, misapplies the relational and intrinsic aspect division. Before proceeding to articulate a new interpretation, it is necessary to further explicate why this is, so as to clarify where my own interpretation differs from hers. To do so, let us reflect briefly on objects and their properties, since it is objects to which Langton applies her division.

We must first determine what can be meant here by object. Various thinkers have stated that objects are possibly anything that is,[232] that they are distinguished from qualities or properties[233] or contrasted with the observer or subject,[234] and finally that objects are substances.[235] Perhaps the best way to consider an object is to identify its characteristics. This will indicate what we can expect to find in any object.

In that regard, I will here suggest those qualities of an object, and then briefly expound upon each.[236] An object must have these characteristics:
1. Relationality
2. Perceptibility
3. Affectability
4. Ontological Individuality

In the first instance, an object must be relational. That is to say, an object exists as an object insofar as it stands in relation to and amongst other objects as *particular*. If not distinguished from other objects *vis-à-vis* relationality, then there is no way for an object to be an object rather than that which is: a simple division between being and nonbeing. Once we enter the discussion of that which is, the breakdown of being into beings or objects, we are necessarily speaking of relations.

---

[232] Bertrand Russell (1937) offers such a view in *Principles of Mathematics*.
[233] D.M. Armstrong (1989) attempts to make this distinction in *Universals: An Opinionated Introduction*.
[234] That is, the body as *object versus* the body as *subject*. S.D. Edwards' (1998) article "The body as object versus the body as subject: The case of disability" gives a great discussion on this and furthermore ties the discussion into disability studies.
[235] E. J. Lowe (1994) for example argues so in his article "Primitive Substances".
[236] Each deserves a complete analysis; however, this is beyond the scope and intent of this work. Thus, only a brief discussion articulating the main points regarding each will be given here. This means it will necessarily be inadequate.

Insofar as we are concerned with relationality when discussing objects, we can conclude that objects must hold the primary properties of relationality, perceptibility and affectability. That which is relational is so in these two ways. First, it is necessarily able to be perceived. I here use the term "perceived" to indicate perception, not only as a mode of an object being represented to the mind, but also as meaning it can affect other objects: that is to suggest that being perceptible means to rouse affection in another object.[237] Second, an object, if it is to be an object, must itself be able to be affected. A cup unable to be affected in any way (one that cannot be touched, filled, etc.), is not an object. This is an absurd thought.[238] Third and finally, an object must be ontological. In other words, it must hold a claim beyond its pure ontic relationality. An object cannot be, absent an ontological grounding, for then it would have no being at all. Beyond this, without an ontological structure upon which a being may be relational, i.e, an object, then there can be no ontic properties of said object. This ontological structure represents pure *nonrelationality,* a major position held by object-oriented ontologists.

Such ontologists assert the non-*Dasein*-centered view that objects hold an equal ontological status with *Dasein*; that is, objects are not objects only insofar as they stand in relation to *Dasein*. In *Tool-Being,* Harman writes: "the tool-being of the object lives as if beneath the manifest presence of that object…At any point in reality, the world of the as-structure is only a belated echo of a deeper realm of brute efficacy" (2002, p. 220). Thus, underlying the ontic relationality of an object must be its ontological, that is, nonrelational framework.

We now return to the problem found in Langton's interpretation of Kant. While her claim to distinguish relational from intrinsic aspects of an object points in the right direction, she holds that intrinsic aspects are themselves relational. This is because those intrinsic aspects (as with the relational ones) are mere properties of the object. This reading would make Kant's distinction mean simply this: some properties of an object, namely intrinsic properties, do not make themselves known to us. Yet, this does not fit well with Kant's thought, which leans towards an unknown *thing*. Let us therefore consider my alternative.

I have proposed a two relations interpretation of Kantian worlds, of his distinction between noumena and phenomena. Under this interpretation, Kant's di-

---

237 As water flowing against a rock at a certain current affects the rock through erosion.
238 I can imagine resistance to this in the form of ideas as objects. I will not articulate a position one way or another on mental objects here, except what follows. Mental objects can be said to be affected immediately by other mental objects as well as intermediately through physical objects which give rise to mental objects.

vision indicates only the manner of our experience, be it relational or nonrelational. However, this interpretation provides not only for reading Kant in a way which is agreeable to his own interest – understanding the way we experience the world and the knowledge we can have of it – but also lends itself to understanding *Dasein*. We have discussed the world of *Dasein* in great length earlier, but as stated, it is necessarily one that is relational. If we also relate to the world in a nonrelational manner, what does this mean and how does it manifest? That which is nonrelational, the noumenal self or *transcendental* of *Dasein*, contrary to how Heidegger defined it,[239] is humanness, or that which makes *Dasein* what it is. It is the source of the fundamental ontology that has been the central theme in this first part. Thus, in order to understand the nonrelationality of *Dasein* and the world, we must inquire into the concept of humanness.

---

239 Heidegger defined the source explicitly in *Kant and the Problem of Metaphysics* as follows: "The ground for the source [*Quellgrund*] for laying the ground for metaphysics is human pure reason, so that it is precisely the humanness of reason, i.e., its finitude, which will be essential for the core of this problematic of ground-laying" (1997, p. 15).

Chapter Eight
The Systematic Expression of Humanness

Whenever, in whichever manner, and by whatever means we propose an investigation into the fundamental character of the being whose primary mode of Being[240] is *in-der-Welt-sein*,[241] we admit that the subject of our inquiry is the essential quality that makes this being the being that it is: i.e., the Being of its being. Humanness is the quality of that being which is characterized as *Dasein*. That is, humanness is that on which such an examination must be focused. The question of humanness has yet to be asked in any formal manner and has only previously been grazed past in order to articulate a proposition regarding this or that aspect of the being to which humanness belongs.[242]

---

240 Unless otherwise indicated in brackets, being with a lowercase "b" denotes the German *Seinde* whereas Being with a capital "B" denotes *Sein*.
241 That is *Dasein*
242 Due to the centrality of the question of humanness, it would be perhaps easier to denote those who have made no claim on the subject. Nonetheless, a non-exhaustive list of some of the most influential authors who address the question of humanness directly (though many more may be said to have done so indirectly), all of whom ought to be discussed in detail in this work if only space allowed, include the following: Plato (2016) in *The Republic of Plato* discusses everything from our sense experience in gaining knowledge to issues of character. Aristotle (1973) examines notions of character and reason at length in *Nicomachean Ethics* and even calls the human being ζῷον πολιτικόν in *Politica* (1957). René Descartes (1664) articulates the limits of sensation and the process of reasoning in *Principia Philosophiæ*. St. Augustine (2012) touches on issues of suffering, morality, and other aspects of the human condition in *Augustine Confessions*, much as St. Thomas Aquinas (1984) does in *Questions on the Soul*. John Locke (2012) focuses on the political aspect of human life and the ways that we bring politics to the world in *Two Treatises of Government*. Jean-Antoine-Nicolas De Caritat Condorcet (1979) in his *Sketch for a Historical Picture of the Progress of the Human Mind* considers the relationship between knowledge, morality, and autonomy. Niccolò Machiavelli's (1995) *The Prince* explores the human themes of will and power, among other things. Thomas Hobbes (1994) in *Leviathan* examines the nature of politics and what that means for human nature. David Hume's (1896) *A Treatise of Human Nature* discusses themes of knowledge, experience, consciousness, and even morality. Charles Darwin (2004) *The Descent of Man* considers the human being in its biological and evolutionary, as well as social conditions. Sigmund Freud (2016) *Civilization and its Discontents* centers on the social and psychological underpinnings of human development, and cultural and social development as well. François La Rochefoucauld (1959) in *Maxims* offers many insights into the nature of the human being. Julien Offray de La Mettrie (1996) gives one of the most detailed materialist perspectives on the human being in many of his works. Mary Wollstonecraft (1995) explores education and sensibility, among other topics, in one of the earliest proto-feminist works, *The Vindication of the Rights of Women*. Many others have discussed human nature or various aspects of it in different contexts.

Approaches to this topic have failed to address the question of humanness as they have concerned themselves only with the being itself, not with that which makes the being, Being.[243] If we are to propose, then, a delimitation of the concept of humanness, we must begin by explicating further what it is that we are asking about. We must make some preliminary remarks about the concept of humanness before proceeding.

Insofar as this quality of humanness is essential, we may call it the being [*Wesen*] or the *essence* [*Wesen*] of the being *Dasein*. Essence, as τὸ τί ἦν εἶναι,[244] is a prerequisite for a being to be the kind of being that it is. As a mode of Being we call it *necessary* if it is self-sufficient [*selbständige*] and *contingent* if it presupposes a being which causes it to exist [*existiert*].[245] As the *essence* of *Dasein*, it must be a mode of Being, *a priori* to the mode of being [*existieren*] that is most characteristic of *Dasein*, namely, *in-der-Welt-sein*. It is in this sense that we can call "humanness" *necessary*. Insofar as it is *necessary* as a *precondition* of Being the being of *Dasein*, we may call it *transcendental*. [246]

However, this does not provide for much in the way of a delimitation of humanness. The question of humanness has yet to be posed appropriately. When confronted with the possibility of the formulation of the question of humanness it becomes immediately clear that it is the most primary of questions, yet also that it does not readily allow for answers. For to pose the simple question, "what is humanness?" is to admit of nothing. The very act of questioning is performed with a premeditated end. Simply put, it asks about something; "Questioning is a knowing search for beings in their thatness and whatness" (Heidegger 2010, p. 4). As with any good research question, a quality that many philosophical questions may appear to lack, the question of humanness takes as its aim the pursuit of discovery [*Entdeckung*], and as such, *questioning qua questioning* necessitates the possibility of discovery: that is to say, the act of *questioning*

---

243 Even Heidegger's analytic remains only ontical, as was argued in Part One.
244 For more on Aristotle's examination of metaphysics generally, see Aristotle (2002) *Aristotle's Metaphysics*.
245 This necessity and contingency distinction goes back to the origins of philosophy. Most notably articulated by the determinism of the Atomists such as Leucippus and Democritus, and further elaborated on by Aristotle in his famous example of a battle at sea. Aristotle writes "it is necessary for there to be or not to be a sea-battle tomorrow; but it is not necessary for there to be a sea-battle tomorrow, nor for one to take place – though it is necessary for one to take place or not to take place" (1975, p. 53).
246 As defined by Kant in his *Critique of Pure Reason* when he writes, "I entitle *transcendental* all knowledge which is occupied not so much with objects as with the mode of our knowledge of objects in so far as this mode of knowledge is to be possible *a priori*" (2007, p. 59).

itself admits of the very ability of the question asked to admit discovery.[247] If the prospects of a *finding* [*Ergebnis*] disappear or are absent entirely, the question cannot be posed.

Thus, the question of humanness as "what is humanness?" is itself not a question, as it admits of no discovery; that is to say, the concept has yet to be made determinable through a critical examination.[248] Instead, humanness itself must be given meaning, that is, it must be delimited and made determinable. Thus, we must first ask, in what way can we undergo a delimitation of the concept of humanness? Where does this process commence?

Exposition on the Origin and Implementation of the Question of Humanness

The path to knowing humanness is through the awareness, pursued to the fullest extent, of those concepts with which humanness is in fundamental relation, until they become fully understood. First, we must settle what "humanness" means in the sense in which we use it. But how do we analyze a term which can be and has been interpreted in many different ways?[249] To do so, we must first trace out the concepts which are in necessary relation to humanness. But what are these concepts to which we continuously refer?

Let us begin by stating what it is that we do know, and work out what it is we do not.[250] First, it is certainly clear that this concept of humanness is attributed in some way to the notion of "human," as this is the foundation or root for the concept of humanness. Other than a linguistic relation, this alone does not provide enough of an explanation for what humanness is. Thus, it becomes indubitable that we must analyze the notion of "human" so that we may then gain a better understanding of what humanness might possibly be. But then, does this not express exactly that which we wish to know how to ask? If what we are seeking is an understanding of humanness, and we can easily conclude

---

247 For more on this see, Brian Paltridge and Aek Phakiti (2015) *Research Methods in Applied Linguistics: A Practical Resource*.
248 Leading to the issue brought up by Plato in the paradox of Meno.
249 "The human being has been called the animal who is always in heat, or the laughing animal, the naked ape, and many more things" (Desmond 1995, p. 106).
250 David C. Logan divides into "known knowns", "known unknowns", and "unknown unknowns". It is often through the former two that the latter is revealed. See David C. Logan (2009): "Known knowns, known unknowns, unknown unknowns and the propagation of scientific enquiry".

that humanness is the nature of "human," then this does in fact present us with the question of humanness.

But how do we know that humanness is the nature of "human"? Is humanness the same or separate from the conception of the human? It would make our task simple if it were to be the same as some critics might claim,[251] thus making the question of humanness the same as the question of *human nature*. But if humanness is the nature of the human, then must it not be distinct in itself? The nature or essence of something is never that which is exposed of the thing, i.e., its *representation*. It is always related; never the same. Jacobi emphasizes such a point, as Franco Cirulli correctly notes when he says that "we *could not* recognize anything at all if we stood at the mercy of an infinitely removed ground to connect an essence to an object" (2013, p. 15). So we may do away with this question, leaving us with the task we set out to accomplish.

But still, we are left with a new additional query: namely, what is human? We think of "human" in many ways. Human is the set of characteristics set forth by human beings. In other words, that which belongs only to the beings that are human in nature: that is, who have the character of *Dasein*. Should this not then make the concept of human separate and distinct from that of a human being? Clearly it must be so. Thus, we are left with a distinction between being human and being a human being. The latter specifies what it means to be the particular being that we are: namely, one that has the character of *Dasein*. The former designates the being that lies behind the being that we are.

Previous accounts of the nature of humanness have sought out the nature of being a human being, thus equating humanness with the concept of "human."[252] If we are instead to see these are two distinct concepts, where does this put humanness? If Being human as the nature of Being a human being articulates the Being of the being of *Dasein*, then humanness (insofar as it is the nature of being human), must be that which as *transcendental* serves as the necessary preconditions of those qualities that stem from the Being of the human being. What, then,

---

[251] Some examples of those who treat the two as the same, in addition to the terms' standard application in the sciences and social sciences, are Jonathan Marks (2009) in his chapter "The Nature of Humanness," in *The Oxford Handbook of Archaeology*, and, Jeroen Vaes, Paul G. Bain and Jacques-Philippe (2014) "Understanding humanness and dehumanization: Emerging themes and directions," in *Humanness and Dehumanization*. In this latter text, the authors indicate two senses of humanness, one which means human uniqueness, and the other human nature, neither of which are the way that I encourage the use of the term.

[252] For just a few examples see Norman Fairclough (2008) *Analysing Discourse: Textual Analysis for Social Research*, Larry J. Young (2009) "Being human: Love: Neuroscience reveals all", and Michael S. Gazzaniga (2009) *Human: The Science Behind What Makes Us Unique*.

is this necessary precondition of being human? That is the question of humanness which falls upon us here.

It is the question of humanness which will lead us to uncovering the meaning of the nature of being human. For not only does it make us certain of what humanness is, the nature of "human," but also points us to the very start of our analysis of humanness. If we are to understand it, then we must also know what being human means. Since we have determined that this is distinct from being a human being, we are left only to assume that it is somehow related, as the two are commonly believed to be the same. So first, we must come to a better understanding of being human through an understanding of the human being. Yet even this appears to be beyond our capabilities as of now, since there is still something left unaccounted for: the concept of being [*Sein*] itself which is continuously used here.

The Historical Articulation of the Question of Humanness

As has been mentioned, the question of humanness has never previously been asked in the fashion presented here; its formulation, grounding, and even timing has never been so perfectly coordinated. But why is this so? In what way is the timing, formulation, and grounding different? The preconceptions of humanness have only recently been called into question; that is to say, the question of humanness is in its infancy.[253] To show this, we must recall those preconceptions which have plagued and hidden the question of humanness under the veil of the human being, or of human nature.

Originally, the concern with the question of humanness was one of strict definition. "Featherless biped" was the first notable attempt at the postulation of an answer and was quickly rejected.[254] Upon such an utterance it was determined that the way to make for a definition is through characterization – descriptions of *how* and *the way in which* humanness manifests. "ζῷον πολιτικόν,"[255] "*Cogito*,"[256] and "Noble Savage,"[257] among others, have been put forth as the characteristics which establish humanness as unique.

---

[253] The "father" of philosophical anthropology was Max Scheler. See Manfred S. Frings (2001) *The Mind of Max Scheler: The First Comprehensive Guide Based on the Complete Works*.
[254] This definition was offered up by Plato only to be met with a plucked chicken by Diogenes of Sinope, according to the story. For more on this see Diogenes Laertius (2015), *The Lives and Opinions of Eminent Philosophers*.
[255] Aristotle in his work on politics writes in full "ἐκ τούτων οὖν φανερὸν ὅτι τῶν φύσει ἡ πόλις ἐστί, καὶ ὅτι ὁ ἄνθρωπος φύσει πολιτικὸν ζῷον" (1957, p. 3).

Other attempts aimed at definitions sought not characteristics, but rather valuations such as "selfish,"²⁵⁸ "good,"²⁵⁹ and "bad".²⁶⁰ These were *value-essences*, defining *natures* of humanness, centered on value judgements. Yet they admit of no answers to the question of humanness, but simply pose the question itself. For if humanness manifests as essentially "good," then what is humanness such that it can be so? The question remains unanswered, and is merely re-stated.

The first grace presented to the question of humanness came when it was hinted by Derrida that "None of the traits by which the most authorized philosophy or culture has thought it possible to recognize this 'proper of man' – none of them is, in all rigor, the exclusive reserve of what we humans call human" (2004, p. 66). Though this indicates that perhaps we may in fact not have anything "proper", a claim which I will argue strongly against, Derrida's statement also allows for the ability to raise again the question of humanness in its truest form, without the preconceptions with which it had been intertwined for over two millennia.²⁶¹ Thus emerges the existential analysis of humanness as it man-

---

256 In *Principles of Philosophy* René Descartes (1983) writes "*repugnat enim, ut putemus id quod cogitat, eo ipso tempore quo cogitat, non existere. Ac proinde haec cognitio, ego cogito, ergo sum, est omnium prima & certissima, quae cuilibet ordine philosophanti occurrat*" (1664, p. 2).

257 Applied to many interpretations of humanness, particularly that of Rousseau's happy, ignorant "man", the notion of a noble savage was first articulated by John Dreyden (1672) in *The Conquest of Grenada* when he wrote "I am as free as nature first made man/Ere the base laws of servitude began/When wild in woods the noble savage ran" (1672, p. 7). For more on Rousseau's "noble savage" see, Jean-Jacques Rousseau (1797) *Du contrat social*, and Asher Horowitz (1990) "'Laws and Customs Thrust Us Back into Infancy': Rousseau's Historical Anthropology".

258 See for example Hobbes' (1994) *Leviathan*, in which he claims "if any two men desire the same thing, which nevertheless both cannot enjoy, they become enemies; and in their way to the end, which is principally their own conservation...endeavour to destroy or subdue one another" (1994, p. 75).

259 Such a position is held by Mencius, among others, and articulated in the *Mencius* as "Human-heartedness is man's mind. Righteousness is man's path" (Soho 2002, p. 133).

260 This opposite position is held by many (likely because education and virtue seem to be meaningful only insofar as they cause us to "behave" in a way deemed better than we would having not been educated or left uncivilized), including Hsün Tzu [Xunzi] who in the *Hsun Tzu* wrote "it is clear that people's nature is bad, and their goodness is a matter of deliberate effort" (Xunzi 2014, p. 253). Due to the overwhelming majority of Eastern philosophical thought not taking a prominent role in this text, though it is nonetheless highly influential here, I will recommend two sources for the history of Eastern thought (specifically, in China). First, Benjamin Schwartz (1985), *The World of Thought in Ancient China*. Second, Youlan Feng and Derk Bodde (1952) *A History of Chinese Philosophy*.

261 Not unlike the question of Being in Heidegger. See Martin Heidegger (1961) *An Introduction to Metaphysics*.

ifests in itself, leaving aside essences, characteristics, and definitions. We will now address *Dasein*.

Heidegger's existential analytic focuses on the way in which humanness manifests itself in a particular way that gives rise to the many characteristics used previously to articulate definitions of humanness itself. Although Heidegger's concept of *Dasein* and his work in general is, as previously mentioned, ontic rather than ontological, and is thus not focused on humanness itself, and thus does not provide for an articulation of humanness in and of itself, it nevertheless leaves us in a position to accomplish precisely this.[262] Through understanding the mode of being which results from the manifestation of humanness, we may uncover humanness as humanness. To do so requires a different sort of analytic.

The Analytic of Humanness as Differentiated from The Existential Analytic of *Dasein*

It is in posing this question of humanness that the "I" itself comes under investigation. "The being of this being is always *mine*," as Heidegger writes (2010, p. 41). Humanness belongs solely to the individual being, to the "I" posing the question. However, insofar as humanness is a transcendental aspect of Being itself, not of the being of the being, it nevertheless applies, and as such belongs [*gehört*] to all who share in the Being of this being *Dasein*. Thus we require an investigation of not only the individual, but of the *metaphysica generalis* of the human being. Many accounts proposing to address the question of humanness have emerged from various traditions using different methodologies through which they hope to frame philosophical anthropology, whether it be cultural, (as with Cassier),[263] theological (the work of Coreth[264] or Maréchal),[265] existential (in the style of Buber),[266] or phenomenological (Plessner

---

[262] It is important to note that Heidegger himself sees the work done in *Sein und Zeit* as a setting-the-stage. In his later works, Heidegger places more emphasis on the ontological. However, if we keep in mind the distinction that ontic refers specifically to the relationality of a *thing, object,* or *being*, whereas ontological refers to the very relationship to Being-as-such. As will be seen later, this represents a nonrelational relation.
[263] Ernst Cassirer (1944) *An Essay on Man: An Introduction to Human Culture.*
[264] See, Emerich Coreth (1976) "Was ist der Mensch?" and Coreth (1991) *Antropologia filosofica.*
[265] See Joseph Maréchal (1970) *A Marechal Reader.*
[266] See Martin Buber (2002) *Between Man and Man.*

and others).²⁶⁷ However, philosophical anthropology has hitherto held as its focal point the question of the human being: namely, what does it mean to be the being that we are? As mentioned earlier, this question is best left strictly to anthropologists, biologists, or those philosophers who take as their starting point a concern with the nature of being a human being, not the nature of being human.²⁶⁸

This is not, however, the concern of the philosophical anthropologist, who takes as their central concern the delimitation of the concept of humanness. The philosophical anthropologist is not concerned with this or that human nor with humans generally speaking [*Menschen*]; indeed, they do not even singularly take the concept of human nature or "humanity" [*Menschheit*] as their aim. These are left for the other methodologies – the first for psychology, the second for anthropology, biology, and sociology, and the last for the philosophy of human nature. Instead, that which makes the human being [*Menschlichkeit*] what it is, or the quality of the human being such that it is this kind of being, humanness [*Seinsmenschlichkeit*] as such, is what comes under investigation by the philosophical anthropologist.²⁶⁹

Inasmuch as philosophical anthropology poses itself the question of humanness, so too must it carry with it its own methodology – one capable of setting itself such a task.²⁷⁰ Past accounts have focused largely on the insights awarded by taking an existential, or phenomenological approach.²⁷¹ It is by taking as their starting point the subjective experience of being *Dasein* that these accounts have maintained the ability to make human nature determinable. While this may in-

---

267 See Helmuth Plessner (1975) *Die Stufen Des Organischen Und Der Mensch: Einleitung in Die Philosophische Anthropologie*.
268 We will nevertheless engage with this question, though it will be, at best, underserved.
269 Along with this task comes the problem of origins and of history as such. A good commentary on the beginnings of and meaning of history can be found in Al-Ahsan's (1999) article "The Origin of Human History and the First Man".
270 As Jose Ortega y Gasset noted in *What is Philosophy?* "the philosopher must, for his own purposes, carry methodological strictness to an extreme when he is investigating and pursuing his truths" (1960, pp. 19-20).
271 As mentioned above, there are many beyond Plessner in this approach including but not limited to the following works: Jean-Paul Sartre (1991) *The Transcendence of the Ego*; Paul Ricœur (2016) *Hermeneutics and the Human Sciences: Essays on Language, Action, and Interpretation*; René Girard (1988) *"To Double Business Bound": Essays on Literature, Mimesis, and Anthropology*; Leonardo Polo (for more on Leonardo Polo see Salvador Piá Tarazona [2001] *El hombre como ser dual*), Paul Häberlin (1969) *Der Mensch: eine philosophische Anthropologie*; Maurice Merleau-Ponty (1976) *Les Sciences de l'homme et la phénoménologie*; Arnold Gehlen (2016) *Der Mensch Seine Natur und seine Stellung in der Welt*.

deed be an accurate claim, it is so only insofar as *Dasein* experiences its own nature, i.e., its subjective *everydayness* interpreted as human nature.

That is to say, such a methodological approach enables the investigation of human nature only in a particular *Dasein* in its subjective understanding of itself, not humanity as a whole. However, humanness cannot be considered to be experienced subjectively, as can human nature, as the latter is what is brought into being by the former, and as such is experienced in a different manner; it is experienced, in and of itself, as a noumenon. Before we proceed to the task that arises here, some preliminary remarks must be made regarding the primordial question of being.

Elucidation of Being

The first of the tasks before us lies in determining where the question of Being begins. This *purely ontological* concern focuses on that which *is* while itself remaining ever indecipherable, as nothing can be said about it. Historically, being is the first of the great questions, the question, that is, of what is called first philosophy. It was the pre-Socratics who took hold of the question first, each seeking to uncover the hidden principle or form which would be considered to underlie all that exists, a substance.

Beginning the Question of Being

An old story tells us that Thales of Miletus, the first philosopher, fell down a well full of water because he was looking up to the sky.[272] He then had an epiphany – that of which everything must consist is water. Since this postulation, a reductionism of being has occurred in an attempt to locate the singular substance which can compose everything that *is*. We know from Aristotle[273] that this search was characteristic of pre-Socratic philosophy and that the essential substance was proposed, by different philosophers at different times, to be *fire*,[274] *air*,[275]

---

[272] Plato (2014) shares this story with us in *Theaetetus*.
[273] Aristotle (2002) writes about this in his *Metaphysics*. Also see Mehdi Qavam Safari (2015) "Aristotelian Presocratics: A Look at Aristotle's Interpretation of Presocratic Philosophers" for a discussion on Aristotle's reaction to the Presocratic philosophers.
[274] A position attributed to Heraclitus. Two pieces of literature here are essential. First, David Wiggins' (1982) chapter "Heraclitus' Conceptions of Flux, Fire and Material Persistence" in *Language and Logos: Studies in Ancient Greek Philosophy Presented to G. E. L. Owen*. Second, the

harmonious order through *number*,[276] or the combination of what is commonly known as the classical elements:[277] namely, a mixture of fire, air, earth, and water.[278]

It is right, then, that Heidegger should claim that the question of being is the most primary, as it is in fact the question which began the Western tradition. However, he is also correct when he writes: "the decisive question is no longer merely 'What basic character do beings manifest?' or 'How may the being of beings be characterized?', but 'What is this "'being'" itself?' The decisive question is that of 'the meaning of being,' not merely that of the being of beings" (Heidegger 1991, p. 18). The pre-Socratic philosophers focused on the characterization of being; they focused on identifying being with something that was already immediately known to them. But how could being, the substance responsible for the existence of all that *is*, be identified with something that itself already *is*? Indeed, being must be something beyond that which is.

However, we cannot move past the pre-Socratics without noting their contributions to this question. Four proposed sources are worth mentioning, insofar as they align with what being *must* be, and two of them specifically have a direct influence on Heidegger. First, we can begin with the undefined *apeiron*, which is a step towards the assertion that Being is that which cannot be spoken of as doing so is to immediately limit what Being means.[279] The indefiniteness of Anaximander's *apeiron* is a crucial aspect of Being in Heideggerian philosophy, since for Heidegger too, Being is limited through its conceptualization and articulation.

Perhaps most influential in Heidegger's philosophy are the conflicting notions of being associated with Heraclitus and Parmenides: namely, *flux* and

---

surviving fragments of his work that can be found in Héraclite d'Éphèse, and Geoffrey Stephen Kirk (1954) *The Cosmic Fragments*.

275 Anaximenes held this view. A recent work of note that explores the lingering effect of Anaximenes in the theories of Levinas is Silvia Benso's (2018) essay "The breathing of the air" in *Atmospheres of Breathing*.

276 Pythagoras' position. For more on Pythagoras as well as the role of number in shaping reality see Richard Conn Henry (2005) "The mental universe".

277 Famously asserted by Empedocles. For more on this, see Denis O'Brien (2016) "Empedocles on the Identity of the Elements".

278 Additional claims include Xenophanes' view of Earth as the primary substance and Anaxagoras' *Nous*. Additional commentary on the pre-Socratics can be found in Mariano Iturb's (2015) essay "The Search for the Arche in the Pre-Socratic Philosophers (The Milesian School). A Path to Dialogue," In *The Cosmic Elements in Religion, Philosophy, Art and Literature*.

279 For more on the influence of the Pre-Socratic philosophers on the thought of Heidegger, see Włodzimierz Julian Korab-Karpowicz (2016) *The Presocratics in the Thought of Martin Heidegger*.

the *one*. Heraclitus' famous assertion of being, namely that it is *flux*, was articulated through Plato in his *Cratylus* as "πάντα χωρεῖ καὶ οὐδὲν μένει" καὶ "δὶς ἐς τὸν αὐτὸν ποταμὸν οὐκ ἂν ἐμβαίης" (1926, p. 66). Being, for Heraclitus, was an ever-changing or flowing which accounted for change in the world. Contrarily, Parmenides' *one* is an unchanging and eternal "*is*"ness. Parmenides' Being can be perfectly summarized as follows: "the existent neither has come into being, nor is perishable, and is entirely of one sort, without change and limit, neither past nor future, entirely included in the present" (Smith 1844, p. 124).

The last of the pre-Socratic notions of being or the essential substance worth mentioning is the atomistic theory of Leucippus and Democritus. Although this was proposed as an attempt to bring together Heraclitus and Parmenides, it is important for our purposes insofar as its influence stretches into modern scientific inquiry, especially regarding the essential qualities of beings. For this reason, it must be taken into consideration.[280]

Nonetheless, the pre-Socratics' concern is not a concern of Being, but one of substance. Here it may be added that Heidegger's project of a reawakening of the question of Being that he notes ended with pre-Socratic philosophy is at least partially misguided or misdirected, since the pre-Socratics were not exactly concerned with Being as such. A substance, insofar as it underlies that which it composes, is necessarily itself Being (*Sein*), and as such cannot be being itself, but rather only another being (*Seiendes*). In many ways Heidegger's claim that "For the Greeks, 'Being' fundamentally means presence" (1961, p. 64) captures the need for a greater distinction between substance and being, as the latter is something different that grounds the former.

Considering Heidegger's claim that the West had forgotten the question of being since pre-Socratic thought, and since we have just shown that pre-Socratic philosophy does not truly initiate the question of Being in the manner which Heidegger asserts, we may assume that it is Heidegger himself who first poses this question in this particular way. It is thus to Heidegger that we must turn in order to understand Being as such, and not only insofar as it manifests *in the world*. Instead, I will show that Being in Heidegger *is* world.

In order to argue that for Heidegger being and world are one and the same, a further reflection on his discussion of both being and world is necessary. This can be exceedingly difficult considering that for Heidegger, *Dasein* is itself the object through which we may access and evaluate Being.[281] In his project,

---

[280] For an excellent work on the development of inquiry into matter, see Jim Baggott (2017) *Mass: The Quest to Understand Matter From Greek Atoms to Quantum Fields*.
[281] Anna M. Rowan (2016) also notes as much in her article "*Dasein*, Authenticity, and Choice in Heidegger's Being and Time".

Heidegger himself immediately limits the question of Being to the question of the Being of a particular being, *Dasein*. This is because we have immediate access to our ownmost potentiality of being, and can thereby analyze Being. In other words, it is the only path for Heidegger. There is another path, as will be shown below: namely, through inquiring into the heart of Being as such by means of a reflection upon the different ways through which Being manifests. It is therefore important to our task that we avoid this form of the reductive analytic of being and that the concept of *Dasein* remain sidelined for the moment, to be considered only in the discussion of *Dasein* as a particular manifestation of Being, and not as our point of departure for a question of Being *qua* Being. That is to say, we must determine all we can about Being *qua* Being prior to the analytic of *Dasein*. The major aspects of being can be addressed within a discussion of the following themes:
1. Being as Nothingness
2. Being as Nature
3. Being as World.

Being as Nothingness

The question of being, as framed by Heidegger in his *Introduction to Metaphysics* is: "Why are there beings at all instead of nothing?" (1961, p. 1). Being is that which is responsible for the totality of what *is*, i.e., for existence as such. But as he points out, by asking such a question, "All that is not Nothing comes into the question, and in the end, even nothing itself – not, as it were, because it is something, a being, for after all we are talking about it, but because it 'is' Nothing" (ibid, p. 2). Nothing itself, then, cannot escape *being*, since it *is* just as everything else, including the not-being of everything also *is*, as in being with or possessing *being*.

How is it that nothing is still within *Being:* that it nevertheless "is"? This issue recalls the difficulty Heidegger has with understanding *Being* within the boundaries of language.[282] Our general understanding of "nothing" is that it represents, as Heidegger puts it, a "complete negation of the totality of what-is" (Kaufmann 2004, p. 246). Nothing has come to mean, for us, an absolute

---

[282] Robert Brandom (1994) argued that it is the semantic and linguistic framework of social practices that can reveal who we are as human beings in his work *Making it Explicit: Reasoning, Representing, and Discursive Commitment*.

emptiness that goes beyond being empty. But true nothingness is revealed to us through a sense of boredom and dread.[283]

Instead, it becomes understandable when Heidegger asserts that *Dasein* is always projected towards nothing, and thus "Nothing is that which makes the revelation of what-is as such possible for human existence" (ibid, p. 251). Nothing is an original part of essence, and is in fact *Being* as such. As James Robinson notes, "*Dasein*, held out into nothing, is beyond all beings, and has in this sense attained ultimate transcendence, the goal of metaphysics" (2008, p. 8). Insofar as *Dasein* can be said to be grounded in a nothingness, that is the nothing outside of itself or this ultimate transcendence of the nothingness of *Dasein*, nothing can be said to be the "answer to the metaphysical question" which nonetheless "is at the same time the end of metaphysics" (ibid).

But, we may wonder, how can nothing be the end of metaphysics? This, however, is nothing unique to Heidegger as the empirical predecessors of Kant, and in particular Hume had held very firmly on the potentiality of nothingness.[284] In *On Being and Nothing*, when discussing the empirical position, Jose A. Benardete writes that "If all matter of fact is contingent, then it is possible that nothing might exist" (1954, p. 364). But it is not only in Hume that nothing can be found to be made possible in relation to being: elsewhere it can be found to be considered equal with being.

In Book One of Hegel's *Science of Logic*, nothing is declared to be one and the same as being. This is not surprising if we consider the Hegelian dialectic. Hegel writes: "Being, the indeterminate immediate, is in fact *nothing*, and neither more nor less than nothing" and that "Nothing is therefore the same determination or rather absence of determination, and thus altogether the same as what *pure* being is" (2010, p. 59). Therefore for Hegel (and in *this* Heidegger is influenced by and amenable to his views) even though nothing is not a being, it is a part of *Being* as such. In addition, once anyone chooses to speak about nothing, they turn it into a being, and speak of it as if it was a something, thus making it part of *Being* as such.[285] It is obvious that nothing must then be included in *Being*. Nevertheless, we can also assert, with strong reason, that Being and nothing for Heidegger are equal. Erazim Kohák (1981) correctly notes the Hegelian in-

---

[283] For more on the concept of dread, anxiety, and the nothingness that gets revealed through them, see Stephan Strasser (1957) "The concept of Dread in the Philosophy of Heidegger".

[284] See David Hume (1896) *A Treatise of Human Nature* for more on his position on the subject of nothingness.

[285] In *An Introduction to Metaphysics*, Martin Heidegger writes: "Whoever talks about nothing knows not what he is doing. In speaking about Nothing, he makes it into a something" (1961, p. 25).

fluence on Heidegger regarding nothing when he suggests that the two, nothing and Being, are convertible in Heidegger's philosophy.

Considering the influence of Parmenides on Heidegger, it is unsurprising that nothing and Being in Heidegger can be understood as the same. Parmenides wrote: "For you could not know that which is not (that is impossible) nor utter it," a thing which Heidegger notes extensively about Being (Kirk, Raven and Schofield 1983, p. 269). However, to locate nothing within Being and not investigate its further relationships between being and other concepts in Heidegger would prove to be a fatal flaw in understanding Heidegger's Being. The reason for this will become clearer upon the further examination of being.

Being as Nature

It would not be too far off to recognize a connection between being and nature in Heidegger. Heidegger writes that "*Phusis* is Being itself, by virtue of which beings first come into being" (1961, p. 15). On this basis, it would seem like nature and Being are the same thing. However, the wording here is mischievous for the desperate scholar,[286] since it can be read as stating either that nature is being (as in that they are one and the same), or that nature *is* Being (that is, is *in* Being). Nevertheless, any accurate reading of Heidegger undoubtedly requires the latter of these. Insofar as nature is, if there are indeed laws of nature or a *kosmos* in the ancient Greek conception of the term, then it must be the case that these are *within being*. Being, then, is more primary than nature. This can be shown briefly through examining the characteristics of Being that may seem to suggest that being is the same as nature.

Being has a unique quality in that it is ultimately historical; this means that it changes gradually over time. But whether *Being* itself changes, or whether simply its presentation changes, may not be immediately clear. But for something to be "historical" means for it to be "natural": that is, naturally occurring or within nature. Therefore, there are some complexities in understanding the primacy of being which can easily lead to the false conclusion that being and nature are indeed the same. However, as articulated above, being must be the most primary of things, in no small part due to its not being strictly finite. Rather, Heidegger suggests the historicity of being more in the sense that the way being appears

---

[286] We are reminded of Shakespeare's "desperate men" in *Romeo and Juliet,* where he writes "O mischief, thou art swift/To enter in the thoughts of desperate men!" (1913, p. 260).

at different times is different, not that being *qua* being changes, as this would be impossible.

Thus it cannot be that Being, which is eternal, itself changes what it is, but instead deals with the way in which it appears differently over time. Simply put, it is *Dasein's* relation to being which changes over time, rather than being itself. This tends to be a popular reading of Heidegger's conception of *Being*, since it is what accounts for different understandings of various workings between past and current civilizations. Heidegger's work itself seems to indicate that this is the case with his reinterpretations of language – especially Greek – emphasizing that it is acceptable due to this historical component of being.

Nature, then, is a part of being, and being remains the most primary. It might be the case that nature and being appear to *act*[287] in a similar manner, "nevertheless Being is not properly grasped by the categories of Nature. For Nature, which Heidegger likes to call *das Vorhandene*, is also only a part of Being, something within the whole or in Being" (Gray 1952, p. 416). It is not enough, however, simply to assert this distinction without further noting what precisely the difference is; doing so leaves the ambiguity ill-defined and undiscussed. As such, we must here articulate that which makes being distinct from nature, that which makes it more primary.

Nature is a cause, since it is something that acts in such a way that it produces an effect which itself occurs necessarily.[288] Otherwise put, nature operates *vis-à-vis* a cause and effect relationship. This is why it used to be claimed that knowledge was to know the causes of given effects.[289] Being, on the other

---

[287] I use *act* here rather than *manifest* because being has the tendency to be itself a constant activity.

[288] Philip James Bailey in *The Festus Birthday* was very clear in pronouncing a similar statement, namely that "Nature means Necessity" (1857, p. 5).

[289] Many, including Aristotle, held such a position until challenged intimately by Hume. For example, Avicenna articulates an Aristotelian position in *On Medicine* writing "Now it is established in the sciences that no knowledge is acquired save through the study of its causes and beginnings, if it has had causes and beginnings; nor completed except by knowledge of its accidents and accompanying essentials. Of these causes there are four kinds: material, efficient, formal, and final" (1917, p. 90). It is also this notion which modern science, the investigation of nature and the natural, was founded upon in Francis Bacon's (2013) work *The Advancement of Learning* and again, it is precisely this kind of knowledge which Hume critiques and which leads to his skepticism, or what is known as "Hume's Fork" (see David Hume [1995] *An Enquiry concerning Human Understanding*). This type of knowledge was challenged previously, however, by the Phyrrianists – the first of the skeptics. Aenesidemus, for example, argues against any claim to absolute knowledge or certainty, no matter how small, and instead proposes *epoche* or suspension of belief, through what are called the *Ten Tropes of Aenesidemus*. For a good work on Aenesidemus which connects his philosophical skepticism with Kant's philosophy,

hand, is a source. This means that out of Being comes everything else, not because of any *action* of being, but rather because being encompasses all things and therefore they can only come to be if being itself is. If being is not, then not even nothing is.[290] In other words, being is the source of the cause of everything, yet it remains itself *not* the cause of everything, but only that which enables the cause, and likewise the effect, to occur. Nature is secondary, existing only out of *being, it* becomes the cause of everything, and being remains the sole source of all, since nature too arises only out of being as a source.

Being as World

Up to this point, it has been argued that being and nothing are convertible, and that nature is distinct from and secondary to being in Heidegger's thought. It must now be determined if there is more to being than nothing. Clearly, insofar as there is something, nothing cannot be the entirety of being. Hence, if they are the same, it is only insofar as nothing (much like nature) is a part of being, in combination with being as itself being a nothing, but not in such a way that being itself is comprised of nothingness. For being cannot be nothing, since as stated earlier, nothing is being. Thus being, if it is to be nothing, can only mean that being is *a* nothing, rather than that being is the same as nothing.

But if we are to suggest that there is more to being due to its being a source of that which *is*, and that which *is* includes the world, then it is useful to begin by articulating the four ways in which "world" can be meant according to Heidegger. Each of these meanings will be listed and examined in its relation to being.
1. "World is used as an ontic concept and signifies the totality of beings which can be objectively present within the world" (Heidegger 2010, p. 64).

In this first instance, world articulates that which exists; all that *is* becomes part of the expression of world. This conception of world is ontic, insofar as the totality of things within it are what constitute it itself as a concept, "world". This is what many who speak of the world refer to in their conceptualization. It is the

---

see Émile Edmond Saisset (1865) *Le scepticisme. Aenésidème, Pascal, Kant. Études pour servir à l'histoire critique du scepticisme ancien et modern.*
290 Sartre wrote something similar in *Being and Nothingness:* "Nothing has no meaning without Being" (1992, p. xxvi)

world of sensation, that is the sensible world, in the ancients, empiricists, and in Kant.[291]

2. "World functions as an ontological term and signifies the being of those beings we have just named in 1. Indeed, 'world' can name the region which embraces a multiplicity of beings. For example, when we speak of the 'world' of the mathematician, we mean the region of all possible mathematical objects" (ibid).

Following the previous meaning of the term world, insofar as there is a *place* in which the totality of things exist *within*, that place can be called "world". Since this conception of world "signifies the Being" of the beings that make up the totality of things, it is ontological rather than ontical, Heidegger says. In this sense, then, world can be said, as Heidegger notes, in the sense of "Extension in terms of length, breadth, and depth constitutes the real being of the corporeal substance that we call 'world'" (ibid, p. 88).

3. "world can be understood in an ontic sense, but not as beings essentially unlike Dasein that can be encountered withing the world; but, rather, as that '*in* which' a factical Dasein lives' as Dasein. Here world has a pre-ontological, existentiell meaning. There are various possibilities here: world can mean the 'public world of the we or one's 'own' and nearest (domestic) surrounding world" (ibid, p. 65)

We have now arrived at the third meaning of the concept "world", at that meaning which is most prevalent and which is to be designated by Heidegger's use of the term. This ontical "world" is the "*da*" of *Dasein*, the "thereness" of *Dasein's* being-in. It is "world" insofar as we are immediately confronted by it and as such turn it into that which is readily "mine", as in "my world", or the world with which I am in constant engagement.

4. "World designates the ontological and existential concept of worldliness. Worldliness itself can be modified into the respective structural totality of particular 'worlds,' but contains in itself the *a priori* of worldliness in general" (ibid).

This is the most general sense of world, and perhaps the most perplexing. Worldhood[292] is, Heidegger explains, "an ontological concept and designates the structure of a constitutive factor of being-in-the-world" (ibid, p. 64). In other words,

---

[291] As opposed to the intelligible world.
[292] I prefer to use the translation *worldhood* rather than *worldliness*.

worldhood is the essence of the world as defined in the third articulation. It is not a particular world but rather world generally and, as Heidegger notes, *a priori* to world in the sense of what he terms the *Umwelt,* the world surrounding *Dasein.*

Having outlined the four main senses of world, in what way is the concept of Being related to world in Heidegger? It is immediately clear that the first of the articulations of world relate only insofar as world designates the totality of things (that is, of beings), but is not itself expressive of Being *qua* Being, but only of beings. Being is certainly not world in the sense of its first articulation given here.

In the second articulation, world is ontological, and therefore worthy of consideration for its relationship to being as such. Insofar as being can be considered a source of that which *is,* this articulation of world seems to express a similarity to being. World, as the "realm of existing" of objects *in the world* (as in the first articulation or third articulation), can also be seen as that which "gives rise" to those objects, since without a "world" in this sense, there is no place of being and thereby no being of these objects. There is, then, an apparent connection between this conception of world and Being. However, this world is one that is more closely related to the conception of nature as it is something *within* and which encounters Being rather than being synonymous with Being.

In the third articulation, world is that to which *Dasein* becomes a subject; it constitutes the place of existence of *Dasein.* While the concept of *Dasein* as *in-der-Welt-sein* was discussed in full in an earlier chapter, it is important to note that this world, insofar as it is an ontic articulation of world, is related to Being only through *Dasein's* immediate relation to this world. Heidegger contends that through an understanding of *Dasein* as it *is* in this world, we may arrive at a conception of world in the final sense. Nevertheless, this articulation of world denotes nothing about Being as such in and of itself, but can at best hint at the Being of *Dasein* through *Dasein's* being-in.

The final articulation of world, which Heidegger notes as the goal at which the analytic of *Dasein* and the world of *Dasein* aims, is particularly interesting in the case of a Heideggerian project. Worldhood, in Heidegger's description, is that which accounts for the world as articulated in the third case. It is the being of the world of *Dasein* and as such the being of *Dasein* as *in-der-Welt-sein, Dasein's* most primary mode of being. It can therefore be said that worldhood is the Being of *Dasein.*

In each variation of world offered by Heidegger, "The constitution of the Being of existence was not interpreted from its openness to the prevailing world, but rather, conversely, the world was interpreted from the structure of existential (*daseinsmäßige*) world-formation" (Fink 2016, p. 69). What is challenging here is that Heidegger asserts that worldhood is non-differentiated between objects *in the world* (as in the first articulation) and yet, due to worldhood as defined in the fourth articulation resulting in its Being the Being of *Dasein*, and insofar as Heidegger claims that only *Dasein* has world, worldhood is thus reduced in the analytic of *Dasein* to the state of having a world, i.e, worldhood as *Dasein's* having a world. It is never discussed further, despite its being the ultimate goal of the project. It is therefore necessary, if we seek to provide an account of humanness, to reconsider worldhood in a different way, a way in which it can truly manifest as it is defined: namely, as the Being of world, and therefore as Being itself.

Being as Worldhood

Worldhood for Heidegger is that which makes possible the world of *Dasein*. Worldhood, or "worldliness" as it is sometimes translated, is the source of world in the other articulations. Insofar as worldhood is a source, it can also be said to be the being of world, and thus being itself. It is important to distinguish here between *cause* and *source*. *Worldhood* and *Being* both account for "what-is" insofar as they are sources of "what-is". However, they do not and cannot make up the cause of "what-is". The latter refers to an entity, whereas neither Being as such nor worldhood are entities. One cannot point in the direction of either. Nonetheless, without Being or without worldhood, nothing could actually *be:* that is, there could be no beings. In this regard, we may call them sources though not causes.

If worldhood is Being as such, then it is necessary to consider what precisely worldhood *is*. Heidegger claimed that it was only through the analytic of *Dasein*, our phenomenological access to world, that we could come to understand being and so too worldhood. However, many others have suggested various sources of the world;[293] what must be determined is where the source of world in each of the articulations can be found, as only that source can rightly be acquainted with Heidegger's worldhood.

---

[293] It should be noted that an adequate intellectual history of the concept of world as it is articulated in various accounts has hitherto not been compiled. As such, the assertions herein are drawn from claims and other statements that can be found in the sources and texts referenced, though they may not in themselves define a concept of world outright. According to Heidegger, the task of disclosing the meaning of "world" in philosophy is a fairly recent interest. "The concept of world, or the phenomenon thus designated, is what has hitherto not yet been recognized in philosophy" (1982, p. 165).

Unveiling the Categorization of Beings in the World

Our search for worldhood has led us to the question of humanness as originally articulated, and pushed us down the path of Heidegger. However, rather than skip to the analytic of *Dasein*, it is first necessary to consider the various components which account for the manifestation of being in the *world* of *Dasein*. This allows for an examination into the way in which beings *are*, as well as providing for further inquiry into worldhood, as we have determined that worldhood and being are both responsible for the coming to be of world, and since world in the first articulation represents the totality of things (that is, of beings,) commentary on beings can only aid in the unveiling of worldhood as such.

What is to be determined here is what is it to be a being in the world, and what are the characteristics of being a being? Insofar as being manifests itself and can do so in an infinite and unlimited way, there are also numerous ways in which things can exist. What kinds of things or beings are there? Heidegger's ontological difference between being and beings seems to denote only one general category, namely beings, which anything that is falls under.[294] We must then examine this claim to determine whether or not this can be said to be the case, or whether more than one category of existence is needed.

Heidegger describes beings as the category opposed to being as such. Heidegger is not the first nor last to hold such a view. Others have also suggested that only one categorization of beings is needed, though the category differs according to the respective philosophical view.[295] However, it is not the only mode of categorization of beings that has been expressed.

The traditional division into objects and subjects, which truly becomes a major focus in the philosophy of Descartes, can be helpful in categorizing existence. Indeed, it seems like a natural distinction insofar as a subject, as a conscious being *vis-à-vis* experience, engages with an object: that is, a being which is observed and experienced. Both subjects and objects consist of various properties which distinguish them from each other, yet nevertheless share in others. Each of these views will be addressed in order to determine an appropriate mode of categorization for beings.

---

294 A good follow-up discussion of this can be found in James Brown (1967) *Kierkegaard, Heidegger, Buber and Barth: Subject and Object in Modern Theology.*
295 Other examples of this view can be found in Gottlob Frege's (1995) "Function and Concept" in *Translations from the Philosophical Writings of Gottlob Frege* and in Peter Strawson's (1954) "Particular and General".

Subject-Object Orientation (Tools)

Beginning with Descartes, the categorization of beings into two classes, namely objects and subjects, took hold in the ontological question of what is. On the one hand, Descartes claimed extension was the underlying substance of material entities, whereas thought formed the basis of the subject.[296] Thus, the *cogito* as subject was ontologically distinct from the objects which were encountered, including the material part of the being, namely the body. This is why this view is commonly termed Cartesian dualism, emphasizing the distinction between body and mind.

The roots of this categorization can be clearly noted in the Platonic distinction between appearance and forms.[297] However, Descartes' emphasis on the "I" or *cogito* brought the subject to the forefront. Additionally, as noted earlier, Plato's forms were not entities with a separate and distinct existence from the appearance: that is, they were not considered to be entirely removed. The *cogito*, though, is both separated and distinct from the material body and the material world.[298] This is because the grounding property of the material world, namely extension, does not apply to thought, and therefore not to the *cogito*. The *cogito*, then, is entirely nonmaterial and removed from the material existence as an object.

Continuing in the trend of the distinction between the subject and the object, Kant's formulated categories are rooted in this mode of classification.[299] His categories of being, rather than being ontological, are purely mental, as can be seen from the very fact that they are categories of the understanding.[300] In other words, it is how we come to perceive the world: that is, how we *categorize* objects into an experience.

---

296 For more on Descartes' position on extension and subjectivity, refer to René Descartes (1983) *Principles of Philosophy*.
297 Aristotle also commented on the mind-body problem in *De Anima*, writing that "It is not necessary to seek out whether soul and body are one, any more than with wax and the shape molded in it, or generally with the material of each thing and that of which it is the material are one" (2001, p. 82).
298 Claudia Brodsky Lacour (1996) discusses Descartes' conception of the *cogito* at length in *Lines of Thought: Discourse, Architectonics and the Origin of Modern Philosophy*.
299 For a work which articulates the science behind Kant's categories see Phillip R. Sloan (2002) "Performing the Categories: Eighteenth-Century Generation Theory and the Biological Roots of Kant's A Priori".
300 Further commentary on the categories of Kant can be found in Lauchlan Chipman (1972) "Kant's Categories and their Schematism".

I do not wish here to provide a philosophical history on the subject, and will thus instead focus on the manner in which we classify objects as objects. In Part One I suggested that an object can be classified as such if it consists of four properties: affection, perception, ontic relationality, and nonrelationality (ontology). The task at hand, then, is to investigate whether this allows for a distinction between the object and the subject. To answer this, all that is needed is the proof that the subject can be made distinct.

Insofar as we are inclined to hold the position that there are objects which are perceived and subjects which perceive them, we must first pose the question: what does it mean to perceive? For it is certain, and few would suggest otherwise, that nonliving objects do not intuit, perceive, or cognize affections in another manner.[301] Nevertheless, it is without doubt that those objects can be affected in the very least sense of the term: physically.

To discover why this might be the case, we may recall Leibniz's thoughts on the topic when he proposed a compound machine which could have perceptions and which we could enter to see its inner workings. However, as Leibniz argues, we would not find any answer to the question of how perception works. He concludes, "*Ainsi c'est dans la substance simple, et non dans le composé, ou dans la machine qu'il la faut chercher*" (Leibniz 1886, p. 51). The so-called "simple substances" are what every being or object is composed of, and so it seems that all beings, insofar as they are composed of simple substances of some sort, must be granted some affectability and perception.

It is clear that perception and affection require, as a prerequisite, an ontic relationality. Objects are therefore necessarily relational, and insofar as objects co-exist *in the world* in a relational manner, every object *responds* to other objects. How can we categorize this act of *responding* which can be ascribed to objects? To be responsive means to *interact* in such a way that one movement initiates a *call* which requests from another an *answer*.[302] In this way we are speaking of relationality as such when we designate *responding* as interaction. This *relational interaction* takes a purely ontic form.

The physical manifestation of *responding* can be simple cause and effect relationality. A cause *calls*, an effect *responds*. But this *responding* need not be sparked by an immediate relation, i.e., a rock with its weight against a desk. An object may be *called* by another object from across the room, the city, and

---

301 For example, Tim Ingold holds such a view when he writes "the most fundamental property of all animals: unlike vases, they both perceive and act in their environments" (2002, p. 52).
302 This may bear similarities to the Actor-Network Theory (ANT) developed by Bruno Latour and others. For a great introduction to ANT see Bruno Latour (2005) *Reassembling the Social: An Introduction to Actor-Network-Theory*.

indeed the entire universe; this *call* creates an *echo* and *entangles* itself with the *responding* object.[303] This can occur because ontic relationality is applied to all beings insofar as they are in being; any being may *call* upon another and that other is *obligated*[304] to *respond* – this is the *law of Being*.

However, do objects perceive? Let us consider perception in its vaguest and broadest sense, so as to be inclusive of any opportunity to grant an affirmative answer. Insofar as *responding* is a form of relationality that all beings share, in such a way that one object affects another, there can be no doubt that this is a mode of perception – though most certainly not cognition – and affection as well; for, affection and perception necessitate each other such that an affection must occur if perception is to follow.

It may readily be granted that perception in this minimal use can be applied to objects; however, it will no doubt be contested that such a perception – if it is to be called that – remains merely on the physical plane and substantiates nothing intellectual as in perception in its typical use as applied to *Dasein*. In this case, it can be said, a distinction between objects and subjects is required: first because *Dasein* takes on the role of the *observer* such that, even if nonliving objects *act upon each other,* the real perception of this (the intellectual perception) necessitates a cognizant observer; second because if nonliving objects affect and perceive in the stated manner, then the former acts as the object and the latter becomes the subject.

Whichever of these positions one holds, they are flawed in their assumptions. These claims can be rejected in the first instance because the mode of perception identified with *responding* is indeed intellectual. Insofar as a physical, sensible relationality exists, that is, a sense perception, it must be accompanied by an intelligible perception – otherwise the sensible perception is itself never *perceived*, but is a mere moment.[305] Perception itself requires some mode of intelligibility such that even the sensible can be perceived in a way that can be deemed perception. We must therefore differentiate between the intelligibility of perception as *cognition* and *pure relationality*.

---

303 That is, through a process not unlike quantum entanglement, which has recently been shown to be possible at a macro level. For more on recent advances in quantum entanglement research, see R. Riedinger et al (2018) "Remote quantum entanglement between two micromechanical oscillators".
304 This operates as an ontological obligation. The very structure of an object's existence necessitates its response in such a way that to not respond would be to not exist in the same ontological structure.
305 As Herman Hesse wrote in *Steppenwolf,* "Eternity is a mere moment, just long enough for a joke" (1963, p. 97).

In the former, perception cannot be applied to all objects, but in the latter it is a necessary part of them. *Pure relationality* is that relation which exists in independence from its observability and empiricality. To say that the hammer *cognizes* the nail when it makes contact with it is undeniably false; yet to suggest that the hammer is in no way affected by the nail, by means of a perception, is just as much of a fiction as the former. *Experience* makes the difference complete.

We are constantly at the mercy of experientiality, even when that experience is non-*cognizable*.[306] This is true of all objects – insofar as an object is in being, and is therefore relational, it has an experience, whether or not its Being admits of such an experience in the form of *cognition*. That is to say, the hammer *experiences* the contact it makes with the nail, though its experience may be entirely *incognizable*; the hammer is nevertheless affected by the nail, and as mentioned previously, this occurs among all objects at all times. Such is the ontic-relationality of Being a being.

On the second account, the previous claims can be rejected because the supposed subject which arises from being an *observer* is nonetheless an object, first and foremost, in its ownmost potentiality of being.

> The subject itself is an object insofar as existence is implied by the idealist doctrine of constitution – there must be a subject so that it can constitute anything at all – insofar as this has been borrowed in turn, from the sphere of facticity. The concept of what 'is there' means nothing but what exists, and the subject as existent comes promptly under the heading of "object." As pure apperception however, the subject claims to be the downright Other of all existents (Groff 2014, p. 160).

All beings are Being and as such have Being as their most primordial mode of Being. Thus, all beings, insofar as they are being, are objects and can therefore be designated simply as beings, although on a secondary level of distinction we may formulate a selection of subjects among the objects. Such a claim returns our investigation to Heidegger, who voided the subject-object distinction in favor of a category of beings more generally.

---

[306] As Alan M. Olson writes in reference to the work of Karl Jaspers, "Thus the mere fact that a unified and therefore a universally valid *Weltanschauung* is not cognizable to an objectifying scientific inquiry, does not mean that it is non-existent" (1979, p. 14).

Object Orientation

The ontological difference between Being and beings, attributed to Heidegger, interprets only one class of objects: those that are Being, namely beings. In this case, even *Dasein* itself becomes a being among other beings. For this reason, it is often claimed that Heidegger moves beyond, or relativizes the subject-object distinction.[307] Instead, he simply reinvents it.

Rather than eliminating the subject-object distinction, Heidegger places *Dasein* in a position of *privilege*.[308] Insofar as *Dasein* has *cognition* of perception, it has "world" as in articulation three of Heidegger's discussion. World in this articulation is defined in terms of the possibilities which it presents to the being called *Dasein*. Only *Dasein* possesses such possibilities, since it is only *Dasein* that can *do something* about these possibilities: that is to say, *engage* with its world.[309] As I have suggested above, this *engagement* is not limited to *Dasein*. It is good to note that part of this engagement might be strictly limited to *Dasein*, namely the fact that one can question the Being of its own being. However, this again is centered on *cognition*, which is only one part of relationality as described above, and limits engagement to a point where engagement is centered on a mental process, rather than on the totality of various modes of engagement. The other modes of engagement, I argue, can be shared among all beings. In case such a position is still unclear, a different articulation will be made here.

The supposed limitation of *engagement* to *Dasein* can be said to stem from *intentionality*,[310] which in turn rests upon *mood* and *attunements*, which we may lump under the heading of *cognition* since the latter is a precondition of the former two. Insofar as *Dasein* can cognize objects, it can engage with them *inten-*

---

307 In *On Thinking and the World: John McDowell's Mind and World*, Sandra M. Dingli writes: "*Heidegger's* philosophy dissolves the *subject-object* distinction and therefore 're-instates' human beings in the world in which they live" (2005, p. 177). Also see Thomas Sheehan (ed.) (1981), *Heidegger: The Man and the Thinker*.
308 This privilege has been interpreted differently. For example, in *Reduction and Givenness: Investigations of Husserl, Heidegger, and Phenomenology* Jean-Luc Marion holds that "The privilege of *Dasein* is strictly phenomenological, not anthropological" (1998, p. 70), whereas in *The Inhuman Condition: Looking for Difference After Levinas and Heidegger* Rudi Visker notes that "The privilege of *Dasein* resides in that it exists ontologically" (2008, p. 52).
309 For additional commentary on the topic of the possibilities of *Dasein* through its engagement, see Glen L. Sherman (2009) "Martin Heidegger's Concept of Authenticity: A Philosophical Contribution to Student Affairs Theory". Also see Edith Wyschogrod (2000), *Emmanuel Levinas: The Problem of Ethical Metaphysics*.
310 For a good discussion of intentionality in Heidegger see Frederick A. Olafson (1975), "Consciousness and Intentionality in Heidegger's Thought".

tionally, and for *Dasein* that means with beings that are *zuhanden und vorhanden*. Nevertheless, through denying this engagement to other beings, Heidegger reveals a flaw in holding such a position consistently. If all beings are *in the world*,[311] and as such are fundamentally relational, then the engagement of *Dasein* cannot be due to its being in the world, but rather in the type of relationality it holds to that world – a type of relationality which other beings lack, namely a *cognitive* one. This however cannot be the case, since *cognition* alone is only one kind of intelligibility leading to perception, and as was shown previously *pure relationality* forms the other kind. To grant *Dasein* this privilege is to associate *zuhanden* and *vorhanden* with *cognition* rather than with *pure relationality:* an erroneous position, and one a solution for which can be found in object-oriented ontology.

To suggest that objects are present-at-hand only for *Dasein* and not for other objects as well is unwise, since even the slightest hint of relationality is that of *presence-at-hand*. This is the relationality that objects may have outside of usefulness, and as such can be easily attributed to objects outside of the *cognition* of *Dasein*. This is clear, for example, as a rock *on the table* is "present" *for* the table, and likewise the table has a presence *for* the rock. While at first it may seem counterintuitive to suggest a presence-at-hand among inanimate objects without the relationality of presence-at-hand, there is no *positionality*, no way for the rock to be actually *on* the table. However, it also becomes recognizable that the table is not merely present-at-hand, but very much ready-to-hand in such a scenario.

The table, insofar as it "holds" up the rock, provides a "service" to the rock – the service of holding it up – and as such provides some use to the rock, again, regardless of whether the rock holds any intention to this use or not. That is to say, *intentionality* does not ground the readiness-to-hand of a being. Readiness-to-hand, much like its counter presence-at-hand, are modes of relationality, which indicate the way in which one being relates to the other. In the case of the former, readiness-to-hand, this relation is one of direct correlation or *interaction*.

If we take readiness-to-hand, the signaling of a readiness to become useful as the indication of a potency of *significance* "for" or "to", then usefulness takes on a different meaning entirely. Usefulness is not determined by an ability to be "used" in the traditional sense,[312] but rather through the attribute of *significance*; that is to say, the table is useful to the rock since in its absence the rock would

---

[311] World here is to be understood as in articulation one from above.
[312] Like we use the hammer to pound the nail.

rest upon the ground rather than the table, and therefore the table holds *significance for* the rock.

The obviously immediate, though nonetheless parochial objection which arises claims that this is not true *significance* since it would require a conscious, that is *cognitive*, awareness – which the rock undoubtedly lacks. If the rock does not *care* about its being *on the table* rather than elsewhere, then its matter of place holds for it no *significance*. Such an objection, first, misunderstands the term *significance* as described above, and second, remains ignorant of the fundamental structure of *world*. The problem can be summed up as a confusion regarding the ontic-ontological distinction.

In the first case, the claim assumes that *significance* means *reflective meaning*, that is, a thoughtful consideration of an object's effect; this however is a fictitious form of meaning, and is much closer to *acknowledgement*. Indeed, an object such as a rock is incapable of such *acknowledgement* of *significance*, yet this does not diminish *significance* itself. We must here delimit what is precisely meant by *significance,* its origination and actualization.

Significance is rooted in both ontic and ontological relationality: that is, non-relational structure. It is the former which is most crucial here, for it is this which is attacked by the above claim. To reveal the *significance* which an object such as a rock is capable of interacting with, an example is necessary. Consider a rock placed too close to a moving river. It may be swept up by the current and carried to a different place, erosion can take an effect against it, along with other possible events.

Although it is certain that the rock does not *care* about its place, it nevertheless holds a specific relation to the water. This relationality is important because it determines the world of an object, even if that object cannot interact with its world in a way similar to *engagement*. Insofar as an object is in being among other beings, and is thus in relation to those beings, that object interacts *vis-à-vis* its relationality with other objects.[313] *Position* or *place* is one aspect of relationality and insofar as *place* alters, or along with any other aspect of relationality, the relationality of the object to another alters as well. Any alteration to relationality, regardless of its magnitude, is significant insofar as *significance* is in no small part determined by ontic relationality. *Significance* does not require a cognizant observer, but rather is significant due to its effect on the possibilities of world.

We turn now to comment on the second problem in the proposed objection, namely that it misunderstands the fundamental structure of *world*. While it is the

---

313 Though only in a minimal manner.

case that *world* here, as in articulation three, is the ontic-relational world (whether of *things* for *Dasein* or of the totality of beings more generally), to consider only this as world is notably wrong. The remaining two articulations of world must be accounted for: namely, world as a "realm of existence" and as the underlying structure of that realm, or worldhood.

The former of these, articulation two, namely world as the "place" within which all beings are, is *conceptual;* there is no *actual realm* that exists as a container housing the multitude of beings. This is simply a mode of categorization used as a means of understanding which, however, holds no actual being itself. In this respect, this articulation of world adds nothing of importance to the topic at hand. The latter, worldhood, is *ontological.* In other words, it consists of the necessary framework within which all beings are *in the world.*

It is this latter articulation of world that forms the ontological structure upon which ontic relationality becomes actualized. It is a *transcendental* necessity, and as such, *significance* is imbedded into the very structure of *world* as *ontological* and indeed *nonrelational.*[314] The rejection of *significance* for non-cognitive *objects* is a denial of *world* for those very same objects – something to which Heidegger clings to as well.[315] However, in doing so, the removing of *world* for objects only reinvents the subject in a new manner, and reinforces the division between subjects who *have* world, and objects that are merely *in* the world.[316] Instead, objects (if we are to eliminate the subject-object distinction) must be given equal ontological grounding *in the world.* Objects, even nonliving objects,[317] must *have world.*

If, then, we consider as proposed above that objects in the world exist independently of and with equal ontological status to *Dasein,* how does this affect our consideration of the meaning of being a being in the world? First of all, and crucially so, it immediately counters the conception that the world of *Dasein* is somehow more important ontologically, that is, that only *Dasein* has world. It is therefore mistaken to take this, as Heidegger does, to mean that *Dasein* has an ontological priority. A new proposition which can account for the *significance* of

---

314 There is a want to articulate *significance* in the same manner as meaning, namely as being "for" something. *Significance* as nonrelational cannot be "for" something, it is not significant because it *means* something to some being, but rather is *significant* insofar as it is the way in which it is.
315 Mark Tanzer (2016) discusses this at length in "Heidegger on Animality and Anthropocentrism".
316 To have world is differentiated from being in the world through *significance.* To have world means to have significance yielded. To be in the world simply means to be a being.
317 That is to say any being *in the world.*

objects themselves is required. We therefore turn to a recent development on this matter, namely object-oriented ontology.

Object-oriented ontology

Object-oriented ontology recognizes these problems in Heidegger's analysis of objects as "tools" and suggests instead – attempting to eliminate the ontological prioritization of *Dasein*, that is, the subject-object distinction – that the relationality of objects maintains their presence at hand. In many ways, it is an attempt to grant *significance* to objects, as Levi Bryant holds: "the world or the object related to through the agency of the human will becomes a mere prop or vehicle for human cognition, language, and intentions *without contributing anything of its own*" (2010, par. 3). Nonetheless, Heidegger holds that the facticity of beings or objects – the fact, for example, that fire is hot – will have an effect on the meaning that will be granted to it by means of *Dasein*, through *care*. Heidegger fails to recognize that this very facticity is part of what grants *significance*, not only through the *cognitive* vessel of *Dasein*, but in any and all of its relations; that is, fire *is* hot, not only "for" *Dasein* and through its interaction with *Dasein*, but in all cases, and that facticity is *significant* in and of itself.

In maintaining a Kantian noumenal quality, these objects (independent of relations either with *Dasein* or other objects) are never known in their entirety, in themselves, but only in their presence. On this, Harman insists that "If the human perception of a house or a tree is forever haunted by some hidden surplus in the things that never becomes present, the same is true of the sheer causal interaction between rocks or raindrops" (2002, p. 2).

Objects also *withdraw* from their relationality, according to object-oriented ontologists. Harman distinguishes between sensual and real objects, which can hold sensual or real qualities. The real object is the *withdrawn* object, and as such does not interact with other objects directly but rather through what he calls *vicarious causation*, requiring a third entity. "'Vicarious' means that objects confront one another only by proxy, through sensual profiles found only on the interior of some other entity" (Harman 2007, p. 201). Harman adds that there "is a constant meeting of asymmetrical partners on the interior of some unified object: a real one meeting the sensual vicar or deputy of another. Causation itself occurs when these obstacles are somehow broken or suspended" (ibid).

This distinction between real and sensual objects is not unlike the two objects (or two worlds) interpretation of Kant's phenomenon/noumenon distinction, and is in many ways a distinction between two worlds; one a perceptible, accessible world of relational sensual objects, and the other of nonrelational, metaphysical, real objects. Although at times Harman appears to be distinguishing between aspects of objects, it must in fact be the case that his position falls more in line with a differentiation of worlds. This is for two immediate reasons: first because real objects are nonrelational and second due to its metaphysics.

In the first, Harman's theory holds that real objects are nonrelational. Objects can be perceived only insofar as they are relational, and this is why real objects are unknown – real objects cannot present themselves to other objects in their entirety. This indicates that each object is removed from its relationality, and ultimately that objects are metaphysical. This is clear since the object in its relationality is different from the object itself as *withdrawn* – it is not merely a different presentation of itself, but is essentially different. That is to say, it is *real* rather than *perceived as real*.

It is also important to note that any entity is an object under this view, even if the entity is entirely fictitious; in this way such entities as "unicorns", "dragons" etc., all become objects, even if there is no physical manifestation of them. Harman thus proposes a theory which unifies entities, that is to say, grants all objects or beings equal ontological grounding, as objects first and foremost. This is crucial to our inquiry here, as under such a proposition, the world *as such* becomes an *object*. Part One above focused on world in Heidegger and Kant, but we are here tossed into a new consideration which must be thoughtfully examined: namely, what "is" *world* as an *object*?

World

In reconsidering the four qualities that an object must possess to be termed an "object", there can be no doubt that the world is an object in and of itself. The world is most clearly ontic-relational, and yet must necessarily then be ontological or nonrelational, as well. In other words, to say that the world is an object is to suggest that it is both relational and nonrelational. We must here consider what the world is as relational and nonrelational.

That the world is relational is abundantly clear from mere observation, in addition to what has been said up to this point. World consists of beings, or objects, all of which are in constant relation.[318] Relationality however, is not strictly internal to the object, but rather external – it is the connection that underlies all objects and binds them together with one another. This being the case, however,

---

[318] Even if we accept Harman's position, objects are in constant relation, only *real* objects are nonrelational.

it does not make sense to suggest that all beings, all objects, exist equally with regard to their ontological status *in the world* through asserting their nonrelationality, as Harman and other object-oriented ontologists do.

Nonetheless, the world is a being itself, since in my view, a being is simply that which cannot be anything other than relational. All that is being is necessarily in relation, if in no other manner it stands in relation to itself as being. Thus, the world consists only in relationality and so too all that is *in the world* is in relation. It was suggested, though, that world must be ontological, which necessitates a nonrelationality. The confusion comes from the different articulations of world discussed previously.

World in the first articulation (as the totality of what-is) is relational, as is articulation three, the world of *Dasein*. The second articulation of world is merely *conceptual,* as claimed earlier. However, the fourth articulation (that of worldhood) is ontological. It is the relational world that we mean here by "world": the world of objects. Insofar as anything *is* an object, or anything occurs, it is due to the relationality of the world.

For example, the fact that the rock may affect the table, or that *Dasein* may use the hammer to hit the nail, are both examples of the relationality of *world*. The world is thus experience, not of *Dasein*, but of *experientiality* as such. In other words, it is ontic relationality that makes world an object – worldhood only enables the being of world, its being an object in and of itself. Worldhood, however (the ontological sense of world) is nonrelational. How can we reconcile the necessity of the world to be ontic-relationality, and the necessary nonrelational, ontological, structure of world, i.e., worldhood?

The two relations interpretation of Kant, as presented in Part One, articulated that *Dasein* relates to the world as a relationality and a nonrelationality. This means that there is a relation to world and to worldhood, which in turn suggests some required division between the two. This two relations interpretation, applied to the world and to objects, indicates that objects also relate as both relationality and nonrelationality. It is Harman's *real objects*, then, which lack relationality, which are equal ontologically with *Dasein*.

Insofar as we may grant that objects hold equal ontological footing with *Dasein*, it must be in such a way so as to nullify relationality. Since our access to the world comes only through direct experience of it, and since that experience is rested upon relationality (which determines an ontological priority of our being), the equality of ontological bearing must arise from the nonrelationality of the object – which is the way it is even when we do not experience it. But since we too are objects of experience to another being, we must also find ourselves in nonrelationality with objects. In this way we can say that things can be categorized in two ways. First as a *relation*, and second as a nonrelation. Thus, we have one category of objects, namely beings, and these can be relational or nonrelational. Let us proceed to consider both.

Insofar as a being is relational, it is so through its entire being-so, that is, through its being in such-and-such a way. While an object is certainly relational with us, in such a way that we use it or experience it, objects are relational outside of our immediate experience with them as well. That is to say, position, temporality, quantity, quality, and the like, are all aspects of its relationality. For example, even number is relational since to say that there is an amount of an object, say two apples, is immediately to draw attention to its status as being *more than*. This *more than* need not compare the object with another actual object; it compares against itself. Thus, two apples are more than one apple and less than three.

It is easy to see then how all that is is relational. The composition of opposites, in its being-so, is rooted in a kind of negative relationality. A table is rectangular insofar as it is not round. While it can be argued that these relations are nevertheless grounded in our experience, that is to say an object is hot, and therefore is opposed to its being cold, is to experience it as hot and compare it to a previous experience of cold, this does not need to be the case. A cup of coffee, insofar as it *is*, regardless of my immediate perception or experience of it, will have a certain temperature, occupy a given space, etc., each – in virtue of being what it is – differentiating it from what it is not. Given this, it is in constant relationality; in its relationality to us specifically, we call this *referentiality*.

Objects are, however, not simply relational but also nonrelational. The necessity of this nonrelational aspect of an object's being was stated previously. But what does it mean for an object to be nonrelational? In one sense we may say that it is nonrelational with us; yet we may also say that it is nonrelational with other beings as well. In this regard, it is to consider the object as such, without consideration of its relationality: as it is in and of itself, independent of how it relates to the world.

This means that beings are relational insofar as they are *in the world*. If we are to suggest, then, that objects are both relational and nonrelational, what does this mean? Surely it would not make sense to suggest that a being as nonrelational exists independently of the same being as relational, since this would mean that it is entirely removed from its own being-as-such; therefore, it cannot be something completely distinct from the relationality of the being. Likewise, it is not coherent to claim that the relationality and nonrelationality of being are two aspects of the same being. For these are two aspects that repel one another: a being cannot be relational and nonrelational at one and the same time. That is to say, at any given time (t_1) a particular being (x) is necessarily relational in virtue of its very being.

Nevertheless, we still retain the same problem that the nonrelationality of any being cannot be claimed to be an aspect of the same being, since to be a being at all is to be relational. This must be so since a being is *in the world* and the *world* is itself relationality as such. There is no escape from relationality in the world. Thus, to be a being at all, is necessarily to be in relation. But what about these relations? Is a being ever exhausted by its relationality? Harman's response is to render beings ("objects" in his terminology) inexhaustible by relations so as to account for change. While it is easy to see the draw to suggest that change must be accounted for by unexhausted relations, further review will reveal that this tells only part of the story.

As I have noted, a being in the world is in constant relationality and must therefore be exhausted by its relations insofar as it is in the world. However, insofar as that very same being can be abstracted away from its relationality as it is in the *world itself* as a nonbeing, or as an aptitude, there is no such relationality to be exhausted from, but merely endless potentiality for relations. Thus, Harman is correct to assert that there is always something "withdrawn" or abstracted from relationality, though this does not implicate an inexhaustible relationality of the being in the world.

We may conceive of the relationality of each relation of any being as like a rubber band. Relations connect one being to another as if a rubber band were to stretch to encapsulate two beings and bind them together. Any single being cannot stand in relation to other beings any more than it does merely through its being-so. That is to say, as a being in the world it enters into all the relations it can, because it enters into relationality as such – it cannot be more relational than by being relational. But what about the issue of change?

As a rubber band stretches, its strength weakens as its tension increases. Relations function in a very similar fashion. Some relations are stronger while others are weaker. Some can be so weak as to barely form relations at all due to the vast distances between the beings in relation, but they nevertheless do. A glass on the table stands in a stronger relation to the table than it does to me. When I pick up the glass off the table the relations shift and stretch, so that the glass now stands in a stronger relation with myself than the table it once rested upon, allowing and accounting for the change.

Doubtless it will be objected that while this may explain relations among beings which are already *in the world* it does not account for relations which form as beings enter into the world: that is, as they are invented, produced, and the like. Upon manifestation as a being in the world as relational, a being is bound up in relationality such that it enters into relation with every other being in the world, and therefore it has exhausted relations. However, as another being manifests in the world, it too becomes bound up in relations to all other beings, including the aforementioned exhausted being. What, then, accounts for this seemingly inexhaustible exhaustion?

Beings, when abstracted from relationality (that is, when in the world itself) hold no relations as such, but contain every possible relation merely by virtue of the fact that it is what enables relationality as such; for without the world itself, there can be no world, meaning no relationality. Thus, even though the being is exhausted by relations upon being in the world, new relations form as new beings emerge in the world. As such, there is no "surplus" relation as is the case for Harman, but nonetheless, the exhaustion of the relationality of the being is itself only applicable to the being as it is *in the world*. As its world changes, as described above, or through the addition of new beings in the world, so too does its relationality. But to continue the analogy above, the exhausted being does not generate of itself a new relation upon a new emergence in the world, but rather such a relation streams outward from the emergent being. How then are we to make sense of the nonrelationality of being? If nonrelationality cannot be an aspect of or entirely distinct from the relationality of a being, how are we to determine its status?

Since a being by its nature is already determined to be relational, we must turn elsewhere and away from the being itself. This is due to relationality as a property of (the) world in which a being is. Thus relationality can also be ruled out as an aspect of a being since relationality is not grounded in the being itself, but is forced upon it by virtue of its being in the world. If, however, relationality is a property of the world as such, then is nonrelationality perhaps also a property of world?

Indeed, we know that it cannot be, since this would lead to the same problem. All that is being is *in the world*, and as such it is necessarily in constant relation. Nonrelationality must then be a property of that which has only an indirect influence on the being itself, since insofar as it *is*, and is *in the world*, it is relational. We must examine what could have nonrelationality as a property, such that a being can be nonrelational.

It is not possible that nonrelationality is a property of being itself, since being *is* and does not itself bear any properties as it is itself nothing, as described earlier. When looking at the *ontological order of existence,* that is, the ordering of coming into being necessary for the current given structure, it is clear that being manifests beings into the world, and as such the world of relationality exists insofar as there are beings. [319] Thus, the world that beings are *in* and what

---

[319] This is quite distinct from the classic medieval conception from the great chain of being,

we may call the world of relations (or simply world), arises insofar as there are beings at all, and like being it is itself nothing. It is, rather, relationality itself.[320]

This means, then, that world in this sense is not the same as world in Heidegger's second articulation of world, and thus the totality of beings do not have a "realm of existence" if we consider only world in the relational sense. This brings us back to the question of worldhood. Insofar as relationality is a property of world, and is world itself, nonrelationality must be a property of worldhood, insofar as it must serve as all four articulations; it must represent the totality of things, the realm of existence of the totality of things, as well as influence – at least indirectly – the world of *Dasein*.

Since we are missing a "world" in an actual sense, as the world of relationality is relationality itself and nothing actual, the worldhood of this world must itself be world, but an actualized world itself. We can call this, rightly, the world itself, as opposed to relationality.[321] We are now confronted with the necessity of the revealing of this world itself: of what does it consist, and how are we to know it?

World Itself

The answer to the latter is evident by virtue of its very necessity. It can be called necessary given that objects, as beings, are being, and anything that is being requires a place that is being within which it may reside. As mentioned, world is *pure relationality* insofar as it consists of beings, and as such is nothing actual; there is no *thing* that is world, but rather world is that relationality which pos-

---

though it bears a similar intent. Still the most excellent source to better understand the distinction is Arthur O. Lovejoy's (1978) *The Great Chain of Being*.

320 The terminology here is misleading – it is not that the world comes into existence with beings, but rather that there is no "place" or "thing" that is *a* or *the* world, but merely that "the" world is relationality itself. A wonderful work that strives to reveal the nonexistence of the world in this way is Markus Gabriel's (2017) *Why the World Does Not Exist*.

321 This is, in part, a similar approach taken by Tristan Garcia in *Form and Object,* insofar as it establishes the primacy of first considering objects themselves prior to our access to those objects. However, it designates a significant departure from the mode of classification of *kinds* of objects exemplified by Garcia, since for Garcia all things are things "n'importe quoi." Thus, it is in agreement with the first part of a major formulation: "Being enters the thing, being comes out of it. And a thing is nothing other than the *difference* between the being that enters and the being that comes out. Thus, the circuit of being is never halted" and far removed from the second half, "In the thing, there is never the thing-in-itself. And the thing is never in-itself, but outside of itself" (Garcia, Ohm, and Cogburn 2014, p. 19).

sesses all that is being. Thus, the fact that all objects have a "world" now means only that objects are relational.

Due to the rise of speculative realism, it will most certainly be claimed that the *world itself* as I have proposed it is nothing other than the ancestral realm of Meillassoux. In *After Finitude*, Meillassoux claims an ancestral realm which is antecedent to the relationality of human beings, as well as other living beings. He writes: "I will call ancestral any reality anterior to the emergence of the human species – or even anterior to every recognized form of life on earth" (Meillassoux 2017, p. 10). While this begins the attempt to remove the centricity of relationality, it is not difficult to recognize the difference between Meillassoux's ancestral realm and the *world itself*.

If the ancestral realm is antecedent to relationality of living beings to the world, it nevertheless cannot escape the relationality of itself, that is of the world, and therefore the *world itself* must be "antecedent" to the ancestral realm. However, the ancestral realm must be merely a primitive rendering of the *world itself* – a first attempt as it were – since it is in fact juxtaposed to the *world itself*. The *world itself* is contrasted with the world, the ancestral realm rests entirely within it.

Thus, Meillassoux does not break free from the true central restraint of correlationism which he so vehemently comes out against: the concept of "world". Meillasoux himself notes, though incorrectly, that:

> it makes no sense to say that the redness or heat can exist as qualities just as well without me as with me: without the *perception* of redness, there is no red thing; without the sensation of heat, there is no heat. Whether it be affective or perceptual, the sensible only exists as a *relation:* a relation between the world and the living creature I am. In actuality...the sensible...is the very relation between the thing and I (Meillassoux 2017, p. 2).

This mistakes the world as some *"thing"* outside of the very relationality which he casts strictly on the sensible.

World is the place in which and through which all things manifest; manifestation itself is a relation since that which actualizes out from its manifestation is by necessity *in the world,* that is, *relational*. By keeping the concept of world intact in such a manner, Meillassoux remains bound by correlationism, that is to say, the "ancestral" realm is a relationality in and of itself. This is clear by his use of the term "antecedent" to describe its positionality – both of which, position and time, are objects of *pure relationality*. As such, the world itself is far from the ancestral realm posited by Meillassoux.

Insofar then as beings cannot be without being *in*, and thus require a "place" that must form the ontological structure of the ontic relationality that is world, it is clear that the world itself is also being. However, unlike world as relationality and akin to being itself, the world itself is not a being: that is, not an object. It has no affection or perception and as such, no relationality in any form. It is purely ontological. Thus, that the world itself *is,* is evident in what has been said, and the latter question requires no further explanation.

However, the former becomes difficult. It is, however, clear that the world itself must be prior to relationality. We cannot say the same regarding beings, since beings require a place to be: namely the world, only insofar as they are relational, so the mere fact of beings does not necessitate the world itself. Likewise, the world itself requires beings, and so it cannot be *a priori* to all beings. Thus, we may claim that beings and the world itself are ontologically simultaneous. The *ontological order of existence* can then be reworked in the following way. Being expresses itself and gives rise to beings, which bring with them the world itself. The world itself then manifests beings as relational by means of a casting into the world. Let us explore more closely the process by which this occurs.

Being, as the primordial ontological expression, brings beings into being. Insofar as beings do not, by their own nature as such, stand in relation to other beings, they bring into being simultaneously with them the world itself, or nonrelationality. The world itself, then, manifests beings further into relationality: that is, into the world. But the question that requires greater exploration is this: how is it that beings get manifested twice?

It clearly cannot be the case that being manifests beings, which get manifested again by way of the transition of the world itself into the world: that is, nonrelationality into relationality. For once a being is manifested, it is fully expressed. Thus, we must locate the manifestation of the being at a single stage. On the one hand, once a being *is* it is relational, yet it cannot be relational in and of itself outside of the world, outside of relationality itself. Still, it is not immediately clear in what way a being can be in the world itself, that is nonrelational, if it must be relational by means of its very manifestation alone. Simply put, beings are necessarily relational. But how can a being that is necessarily relational exist in the world itself, which is fundamentally nonrelational?

There remains only one possibility: namely, that the being manifested by Being is not a being as such, but is a different kind of being, one which is in fact not a being at all. What does this mean? On the one hand it is clear that there must be some form of being if there is to be a world itself as has been here described. However, as stated, this being cannot be a being such as are in the world as the totality of things. Instead it must be a being which, not unlike

Being as such, gives rise to beings.[322] Thus, we may say that it is that which enables the being in the world to be in the way in which it is, it is in one sense, the essence of their Being.

However, in another sense it must be more than just an essence. It must, in fact, carry with its very being in what it is, the multitude of characteristics, or properties, of the being which is substantiated in the world. In some ways it may also be termed the *potency* which is actualized as beings in the world. Thus, for every being in the world, there exists by necessity a potency of the actualized being. We will term this potency the *thing-in-itself*.

Indeed, it must be a thing-in-itself if we follow the Kantian definition as "the way in which our senses are affected by this unknown something" as indicative of both being itself and the potency which enables its actualization (Kant 2004, p. 66). Indeed, the being itself insofar as it is necessarily relational in the world is that which we experience: that is, the appearance of the thing-in-itself as it exists in the world itself, nonrelationally. At this point we can therefore surmise that the world itself is comprised of potencies or things-in-themselves, which actualize and manifest in the world as relationality, and therefore are objects of our experience as they always appear to us through sense, which is determined via relations. In other words, beings carry into the world through their Being the very conditions of their Being in such a manner. For these conditions, potencies, or things-in-themselves, I propose to use the term "aptitudes".[323]

---

322 This is not entirely unlike (though nevertheless distinct from) Heidegger's conception of *Ereignis*.

323 It is crucial to note however, that this potency, that of aptitude, is *nonrestrictive* to the object. Those who criticize *potencies* do so often because they find it a limitation on the object, a determination of its being what it is now and for its future. Potencies are attached to objects, which leads to this problem; an object can only actualize qualities for which it contains potencies for. This, for example, is the case with Levi Bryant's position on *virtualities*. Aptitudes however, are not determinative for the object, they are not attached *to* the object, but *enable* the object to be in a certain way. The distinction here is subtle but crucial and avoids this problem of potencies. With potency, we think of an acorn actualizing as an oak tree. But an oak tree is not the aptitude of an acorn. Aptitudes are *unique* to the object itself, in this case the acorn, or the oak tree. Thus, my position differs from both Bryant's and Harman's own (as "hidden actualities"). I hope to make the distinction clearer in the following sections on aptitudes.

Chapter Nine
The Systematic Transcendental of Humanness

It has been proposed that beings other than *Dasein* must be given equal ontological footing, rather than a secondary status. As claimed above, this refers to the nonrelationality of beings in the world itself. Yet we are now left to address in what way this brings the question of humanness to the forefront, as stated at the onset of this work. To recapitulate, the question of humanness is that of the being of the particular being that is *Dasein*, or more simply the nature or essence of the being of *Dasein*. I have also shown in the first part that this question of humanness is the very same question which Heidegger puts forth as the question of the worldhood, or worldliness, of *Dasein*.

The question of the worldhood of the world has led to the postulation of the world itself. If the worldhood of the world must be the *a priori* structure of the world such that the world of relationality can be as it is at all, then, as we have devised it, the world itself (nonrelationality as such) fills this void. Thus, the world itself is that which makes possible a being's being relational; that is to say, without the world itself (nonrelationality) a being could not be in the world, could not be relational. In that sense, we may say that it is a precondition of the very possibility of being a being in the world. This may lead some to believe that it is a *transcendental*, but this line of thinking would be mistaken. For the world itself does not provide the possibility of experience for a particular being, but is itself what enables a transcendental. Insofar as a transcendental serves as a necessary precondition of experientiality, it *must be the source of the experience of, the inter-tanglement within, relationality as a particular being-in-the-world*. This is precisely what the world itself is not; the world itself is a precondition of relationality, nothing more nor less than this very specification.

If there is then a need of a transcendental, beyond merely the *pure intuitions* of space and time, which is capable of entangling our Being within the relationality of the world in the first place, such that we may experience this relationality through *pure intuitions*, which indeed as transcendental make experience possible, then the only place left for us to turn for this *transcendental* is to the concept of humanness. Humanness, if we are to claim it as transcendental, must be that which is responsible for the development of *Dasein* as the being that *Dasein* is *in its* relationality, without itself being relational.

To address this relationship between humanness and *Dasein* as a particular being, we must first add clarity to the meaning of humanness as an aptitude. In order that this may be accomplished, three tasks are at hand. They are as follows:

1. To show in what way humanness is an aptitude;
2. To reveal the hidden structure of the world itself;
3. To articulate the means by which humanness as an aptitude becomes something more than humanness itself.

To begin with the first of these, it must be clarified what precisely is meant by aptitude. It was stated that an aptitude is that which characterizes the particularities of the being of a being, yet what this itself means is not immediately clear. Indeed, a proper delimitation of "aptitude" is necessary here. In order to ensure that doing precisely this will provide a proper exegesis, the *world itself* will be further explained and expounded upon here.

If an aptitude may be said to characterize, for example, *Dasein* as *Dasein*, then we may also refer to aptitudes as essences, insofar as an aptitude is the essential aspect of a being. This, however, is too vague and unhelpful in its determination. To truly come to grips with the concept of aptitudes as used here, it is necessary to ask what the aptitudes of *Dasein* might be? It is humanness itself which confronts us here as the aptitude of the being *Dasein*. To fully articulate in what way humanness is the aptitude of *Dasein*, we must further reflect on the *world itself*, where aptitudes prosper.

We are confronted by two unique possibilities of the meaning of the *world itself*, the very same which are to this day debated in consideration of Kantian worlds. The two possibilities are:
1. There are two ontologically distinct worlds, the world and the world itself;
2. These "worlds" represent two aspects of a given being, its relationality (ontic) and nonrelationality (ontological).

In order to determine which is more suited to the world itself, we will set forth a pattern not unlike Kant's antinomies to view the positive and negative analyses regarding each of the propositions. Let us first consider the former.

A Case for the Distinctiveness Between Worlds

If we assume that the world and the world itself are ontologically distinct, then it is clear that all beings which can be said to exist in the *world itself* simultaneously exist ontologically in two different ways. This is because all beings necessarily exist in the world as relationality; to be a being at all means to be in relation to other beings as well as to being generally. It is impossible to be and not to be in relation to one's own being, for to do this would mean to not be rather than to be. Thus, any being which is a being at all must necessarily be in relationality. We therefore must presume that any being exists ontologically in the world.

The *world itself*, existing as a distinct world, must also contain beings. If it contains a being which also is ontologically in the world, then this being exists ontologically twice; it has two ontologies. It is unclear what having two ontologies truly means, as this is quite unfathomable and impossible. A thing either *is* or *is not*, but cannot be twice.

If, on the other hand, the *world itself* consists only of beings which are not *in the world* of relationality, then it follows from the above that it consists of the negation of the totality of what is: namely, nothingness. In this case, even if logically consistent, the postulation of the *world itself* holds no value or meaning as it contributes, quite literally, nothing. However, even nothing, as a being itself as Heidegger had shown, must then be relational. Thus, even the negation of the totality of being must itself be a relation.

If the *world itself*, as claimed, contains no relationality, then it must not consist of beings but rather only aspects of beings.

A Case for the Multiple Aspects of Beings

If we assume that the *world itself* consists only of attributes or aspects of beings, then there exist some accidents which are nonrelational. Attributes must exist in one of two ways, either: a) as a part of the being which they are attributes of without any existence of their own or b) as existences in and of themselves which merely attach to a specific being. If these accidents are a part of a being that is in the world as relationality, then they are relational in virtue of their being a part of a being in the world. Additionally, we may say that the attributes as being a part of a being are in necessary relationality to the being of which they are a part.

If on the other hand these accidents are to be nonrelational, an essential aspect of the world itself, then they must exist in and of themselves. This is possible only if they themselves transcend the world of relationality. The transcendence of the world of relationality requires the postulation of a world beyond the world of relationality in which such attributes may be said to *be*. This is because giving these attributes an existence of their own requires an ontological existence prior to the relationality of being a being.

If this is the case, then the *world itself* must exist as ontologically distinct from the world of relationality of being. Insofar as this is the case, the *world itself* cannot consist merely of aspects of beings, without the addition of a distinctive ontology. We must therefore conclude that the *world itself* is a separate ontological world.

A Case for Ontological Prioritization of Existence

It is clear from the above that the *world itself* cannot be understood in terms of Kantian worlds; that is to say, it is neither ontologically distinct from the world of relationality, nor does it merely consist of nonrelational aspects of a particular being. Nonetheless, it is also clear that aptitudes, insofar as they are nonrelational aspects of our being, in some way account for the world itself, and so too appear to account for an ontological distinctiveness. We must propose a solution to the contradiction presented here.

If the world itself is nonrelational, then it must be ontologically prior. However, as shown, it must not be ontologically distinct. Indeed, the *world itself* and the world must be one and the same world; only the former must precede the world in its prioritization. It can be said, then, that it serves as the foundation of relationality itself. Without the former, the latter cannot be.

This articulates the initial relationality, that of the *world itself* to the world; or, put differently, nonrelationality to relationality. It is not then that two aspects of the same being are represented by the *world itself* but rather two modes of a being's being-in, that is, two modes of relation. The first mode of relation, in the world, is as a being to another being: the common meaning of relationality. The second, as designated by the *world itself*, is as a nonrelationality. The latter relationality occurs only in the world – there is only one – but nevertheless precedes the relationality of the former.

Let us consider here this mode of relationality: that is, nonrelationality. What is nonrelational relationality? It is a transcendental relationality which, in its very own relationality, establishes all relations. We may think of it as follows. The world itself, as nonrelational, manifests as relationality in the world. Thus the preliminary relationality of nonrelationality, is the prospect of the emergence of relationality which springs out of nonrelationality necessarily. This is to say that nonrelationality carries with it, in virtue of its being so, relationality. We may rightly call this the *fundamental relation*.

However, the fundamental relation between nonrelationality and relationality cannot be known independently of something sharing in this fundamental relation: that is, something which must too be a part of the world itself. Here then, the precise nature of the world itself is revealed. It is not, as mentioned, either ontologically distinct or simple aspects of entities, but is itself a *type of* relation. Specifically, it is a mode of relationality between beings: a relationality that connects beings to the fundamental relation, a relation of nonrelationality. This is the same as claiming it is, in fact, both ontologically distinct and serves as an aspect of objects in the world of relationality.

Considering *Dasein*, then, we relate to the world in two ways: relationally and nonrelationally. The former is clear and requires no further explanation; however, the latter must be delineated. Insofar as all beings are in the world, they stand in relation to other beings. However, this does not take away from their ontological standing as beings in and of themselves, a part of the way it *is* in the world. This can be better articulated as a concern over *what* it is rather than *how* it is. As a being in the world, we too hold an existence unto ourselves outside of any mode of being in relation to something else, though we are indeed caught up in this relationality of our being-in.[324] Thus, this nonrelational self – indeed its relationality is to its own nonrelationality – stands in relation to other beings insofar as all beings have nonrelationality as a primary mode of their being: that is, are in the *world itself*. We may here conclude then, that the *world itself* is a mode of our very being.

Objects and their Nonbeing

Insofar as any being or object is necessarily relational, then the world itself, which consists in the abstraction of relationality, can only be conceivable in one of three ways each with regards to its objects, which we have called aptitudes. As stated previously, the world itself is not a separate ontological world, and thus its objects cannot be ontologically distinct either. Therefore, the three options are:
1. The world itself is a complete void;
2. Aptitudes are objects and are representative of the relational objects they correspond to; that is to say that objects exist nonrelationally;
3. There are *in fact* no objects in the world itself, and so thus aptitudes are not objects.

It is clear that the first of these is barely worth mentioning, and I would not have done so had it not been a position that is actually held.[325] The last of these seems to stand out as obvious, due to objects needing to be relational as mentioned earlier at the end of part two, however upon reconsideration it is not so simple.

---

324 For a commentary on the process by which *Dasein* falls (*Verfallen*) to the inauthenticity of *das Man*, see Tucker McKinney (2018) "'As One Does': Understanding Heidegger's Account of *das Man*".
325 This being the main tenet of traditional idealism.

Objects must be both relational *and* nonrelational. The latter option, as is clear, is necessary as the framework within which relationality occurs. We are thus left with the position articulated by the second proposition, a position in agreement with the claim of object-oriented ontology.

Just as object-oriented ontologists claim, objects are both relational and nonrelational. All beings are objects and, as such, must be both ontological and ontical. This rejection of pure *correlationism*, resulting in the granting of world to objects, also fits within the framework of the world itself. However, there is still something which is not suitable in the second claim above: namely, it does not seem that the world itself allows for such a claim. A quick reflection on all that has been said before is needed to make this clear.

Anything that *is*, is being. Being itself, however, is nothing and is not itself being, and so is not a being. All beings are also being and all beings, if we are to eliminate the subject-object distinction, are objects. Objects are both *in the world* as relational and *in the world itself* as nonrelational. Beings are therefore, insofar as they are being, relational.

What immediately becomes clear is the glaring problem that has plagued philosophy, including the position articulated here. The very first statement indicates precisely that anything that *is*, "*is*". Insofar as this is the case, it is impossible for anything that *is* not to be the case. Any being, that is, must necessarily be being, it cannot be nonbeing, for then it would not be being. This seemingly obvious proposition reveals a hidden truth: there is no nonbeing.

Nonetheless, it is certain that a being that is being becomes nonbeing. *Nonbeing is found in contradistinction to beings and not as a counterpart to being as such.* Indeed, as Heidegger rightly claimed, nothing is itself in being, and so too nonbeing must be in being. In this way, nonbeing becomes a way of *being in*. If relationality clings to all beings, then *nonbeing is the mode of being of nonrelationality, such that to be nonrelational means precisely to be in being with a mode of being as being a nonbeing.*

Returning to the above consideration regarding the claims of the world itself, we are left to consider if nonbeings are *objects*. In considering what Harman notes about fictionality and fantasy, it would appear that even these, which lack a reality, are nevertheless *objects*; however, even with their lack of a reality, these are objects specifically because they have been granted a status of being a being – a nonreal being conceived and transformed into an object.[326] This, however, cannot apply to a nonbeing, precisely because it is nonbeing.

---

[326] Must be granted in Being because otherwise even its fictionalization would not be.

Looking again at what Harman terms *real objects*, which are real insofar as they lack relationality and are the *thing-in-itself* grounding the *sensual object* of experience, it is clear that if they are nonrelational these must be *nonbeing*. While there are undoubtedly these *real objects*, it is my contention that to call them *objects* is misguided. A nonrelational object would be a nonbeing object, a proposition which is paradoxical.

But if objects are relational *and* nonrelational, and if to be nonrelational is to be a nonbeing, how does this fit into our understanding of objects, and in particular objects in the world itself? If nonrelationality and relationality must both apply to objects, then it can only be through the very being of the object itself. That is to say, since nonrelationality is the ontological structure of the world, of relationality itself, then objects (which are necessarily relational by virtue of their being a being *in the world*) must also have an underlying ontological nonrelationality that establishes and solidifies their very being, but which is itself not a being. It must rather be grounded in its very being a nonbeing, and therefore this nonrelationality that grounds the object in relationality of being a being, is not itself an object due to its being a nonbeing.

Thus, we are confronted here with a problem of the world itself; the nonrelational world itself (that is, the ontological structure of the world) does not consist of objects, since it in fact consists of no beings at all. We must therefore deny the second claim regarding objects in the world itself and admit the last. But if aptitudes cannot be considered objects, and further, if aptitudes are nonbeing, then what, if anything, can be said about aptitudes?

Harman adds something to the conversation which cannot be ignored here, namely, the idea of what he calls *forms* – though he takes the term in a very different sense from its historical use. Instead, Harman writes, forms

> are never identical either to that of which they are made or the ways in which they are described or known. The form of the object is that which hides midway between its material substrate and its concrete manifestation at any given moment in any given context. Forms are hidden in the floorboards of the world, and cannot be known by replacing them with something that seems to be known already: whether it be their constituent material or their effects (2015, p. 97).

This proposed new "formalism" faces head-on the challenge presented by materialism, particularly when philosophy is being pushed towards becoming more scientific. Yet, it stands firmly against the allure of immaterialism that haunts the non-materialist. Nonetheless, object-oriented ontology is often mistaken for a materialist philosophy. The problem of the world itself poses the question of aptitudes; we must here consider whether aptitudes are forms, in the manner of Harman, or whether they are something entirely distinct. In doing so, we will also consider if Harman's formalism can indeed account for what is perhaps the most difficult problem that affects immaterialist positions, that of *emergence*.

Aptitudes, Forms, and Emergence

It has been argued that the world itself consists of aptitudes, which have been designated as nonbeings. From this alone, it should be clear that aptitudes cannot be representative of a materialism; any reducibility to materiality, the physicality of atoms, quarks, or strings, is necessarily concerned with beings and not aptitudes, for a nonbeing is no being in and of itself. Materialism can explain only the relationality of beings in the world, but can do nothing of the sort as regards the nonrelationality of nonbeings in the *world itself*. As such, Harman is correct to dismiss it insofar as it has no ability to engage in discourse regarding nonrelationality. However, the above instantly raises the question of whether aptitudes must then be immaterial, and if so, whether the immaterialism of the formalism Harman proposes can ground aptitudes.

This new approach to formalism does not, however, result in an extreme push towards the darkest depths of immaterialism, as in the *idealism* espoused by Berkeley. Formalism as presented by Harman is immaterial only insofar as "forms" are not reducible to material properties: that is to say, it avoids the reductionism that plagues materialist philosophies. With forms, "there is no excess beneath the forms that are given, but because the excess is itself always formed" but rather "Reality consists of objects of all different scales, complicit in the production of other objects, which can never be identified either with the smaller objects that compose them or the larger objects that they compose" (Harman 2015, p. 100).

However, this "form" underlying objects is itself immaterial. It is here that the problem arises for such a theory. Immaterialism still emphasizes beings – "forms" are beings, aptitudes are nonbeings. This accounts for what I believe to be one of major differences between Harman's forms and aptitudes as described herein. In such a system, forms become a part of a metaphysical realism, which grants objects independence from a perceiver (ibid, p. 102).

Metaphysical realism is useful insofar as it presents a worthy challenge to anti-realist or idealist philosophical schemata. These latter two positions are hardly philosophical, being so steeped in metaphysics and mysticism that they no longer bears any semblance of an explanation for the reality of things. To reject a mind-independent totality of things has more in common with laziness than with philosophical rigor.

Such a proposition is true only insofar as one may assert (regardless of how narrowly) that conceptual schemata are purely cognitive. Rather, conceptual schemata should simply be taken to mean a "frame of reference": that is, of relationality, as discussed previously. In such an understanding, it becomes clear that this is not the case, and that even objects have a frame of reference that enables a conceptual scheme.

Nonetheless, this same position reveals that metaphysical realism is erroneous in its assertion that objects are independent of any conceptual schemata. *Contra* Harman, objects do in fact *act* as perceivers as previously articulated, and therefore can be said to possess a conceptual scheme, since objects are *by necessity* relational, as also discussed at length earlier. The nonrelationality of objects (that is, *aptitudes*) are *not objects themselves as they are nonbeings.* That which exists *independently of conceptual schemata,* that is, aptitudes, is *the ontological framework from which objects arise,* and in this way metaphysical realism gives way to a *metaphysical transcendentalism.*[327]

In *metaphysical transcendentalism*, what is real is not one or the other: neither objects in the mind-independent world, nor ideas in the mind, but both. Attitudes as *transcendental* are the ontological preconditions of objects *in the world*, of relationality itself. Thus, aptitudes are *in all senses* real as nonbeings, transcendental as preconditions, and so objects are real as relational beings in the world. Objects are not any less *real*, even if they are strictly relational and cannot be removed from relationality.

It will be noted, no doubt, that I have spent a great deal of effort above arguing that objects, including *Dasein*, relate to the world both relationally and as a nonrelation. While this still remains true, objects as nonrelational (that is, *aptitudes*) are no longer something we can term "objects," as they are nonbeing which immediately removes them from the realm of objects. Non-real objects can be deemed as such, as Harman does with fictionalism, since these entities are made into objects once they enter into being a being, since for Harman, "everything is an object". If it is a being, regardless of its reality or mere conceptuality, it is an object.

Yet aptitudes are not non-real, but are not beings at all. They are non-existent, not in the sense of a fictional character or an abstract entity (or even

---

[327] This position should not be confused with Iain Hamilton Grant's own *transcendental materialism*. For more on the latter, see Bryant, Srnicek, and Harman (2011) *The Speculative Turn: Continental Materialism and Realism*.

thought) that exists insofar as it has been conceived,[328] but rather nonexistent as such. That is to say, they exist in no form, no structure, and with no *essence*, they are essentially nothing *actual*. This is why I have also referred to them above as similar to potencies, which are also nothing actual until manifested.

But this difference between forms and aptitudes, namely that one is a being while the other is precisely nonbeing, is not the most crucial. The more crucial difference deals with the conception of *emergence*. Harman criticizes materialist philosophies for either the reductionism to physical entities such as particles or the *essentialism* or *oneness* of the likes of Heraclitus, through the claim that neither offers a strong account of *emergence* (2015, pp. 95–96). But does this new formalism or object-oriented ontology really provide this account any better?

In *The Universe of Things*, Steven Shaviro (2015) cautions against this belief, and claims that perhaps a return to *process philosophy*, in the style of Whitehead, may provide for a more accurate account of emergence. He suggests that in object-oriented ontology, despite some similarities with Whitehead's own work, objects are merely already and continuously present, and as such cannot really afford any account of emergence other than an object as already emerged.[329]

Although I believe Shaviro does not take into account many aspects of object-oriented ontology, and that there is indeed an element of *emergence* in it, this is nevertheless a concern I share. Object-oriented ontology cannot fully account for emergence when its view holds a constantly present object "already there". However, aptitudes circumvent this dilemma and enable a fuller expression of the emergence of objects as such.

Aptitudes enable us to give an account of the *emergence* of beings, that is objects, even though aptitudes themselves are not objects and are nonbeings. Insofar as all objects require an ontological structure which grants them ontic possibility, that is to say, the very possibility of relational existence – and indeed this is the only worldly existence – aptitudes, as the *pure ontological* expression of being, underlie all objects and are the manner through which objects may *emerge*. An object-oriented ontologist such as Harman, Bryant, and others, may well claim that this merely advances one of the two kinds of materialism which is rejected by such a tradition; a rejection which I myself have asserted above is well-founded.

---

[328] I am very much aware of the self-defeatism of this statement; unfortunately, however, I have had to give nonbeings the name "aptitudes" to convey the idea – which yes, makes them objects, though they are undoubtedly not so.
[329] For more on his position see Steven Shaviro (2014) *The Universe of Things: On Speculative Realism*.

Indeed, such a claim may be accurate; however, I would caution against it being made so immediately. While it is true that aptitudes *underlie* objects, this mode of "underlying" does not take the form of the traditional role of a substance or other underlying material, or even of a metaphysical *apeiron* in any way. Aptitudes *underlie* objects insofar as they represent the ontological nonrelationality of objects *in the world*; this does in fact allow for an account of emergence. Nevertheless, aptitudes do not *underlie* objects as a substance or as any other form of material reductionism.

It must be remembered that substances, be they physical entities (substances, physical particles, etc.) or metaphysical entities (the major one being form), are all beings and, as such, are *objects themselves*. Thus, it is correct to offer a critique of such materialist reductionism since, in fact, objects form the basic structure in this instance. That is to say, the reductionism of, for example, science into particles that *underlie* all objects, is in actuality a reductionism which offers no actual reduction – it reduces all objects into slightly smaller objects.

Of course, this indicates that materialist reductionism requires the reduction to objects, all of which must themselves be beings in the world. Aptitudes do not fit into such a category and could not do so, barring some perversion of the concept. Instead, aptitudes *underlie* only insofar as they are the *ontological structure of the world of objects*. This does not mean they are more "real" than objects, and in fact the opposite may be true. Rather, it only means that objects are ontic-relational, they are *in the world* as beings, while aptitudes are nonrelational and are not *in the world* but only *in the world itself*, as they are nonbeings.

There are therefore, as far as my proposition is concerned, no inaccuracies with the depiction of the *world of objects* as articulated by Harman and other object-oriented ontologists. It is perhaps the most accurate depiction of the *world* that has been posited in over two millennia of philosophic inquiry. Nonetheless, there is a point of disagreement and departure I wish to emphasize here (and it is certainly a major if not irreconcilable one), namely that the nonrelationality of an object is in fact itself an object.

But how is it that a theory such as object-oriented ontology can be so accurate in describing the world, and nevertheless fail to account for what I deem to be a fundamental aspect of the world and the objects within? I believe this can be accounted for by the treatment of objects only as they are *in the world*, not as *in the world itself*, as aptitudes. In other words, the problem arises in the lack of consideration for the entire spectrum of being, but only for a speck on that spectrum: that is, beings – a speck of which humanness is itself a part. Let us here consider what I call the *spectricity of humanness*.

Spectricity of Humanness

Let us continue to explore, then, in what precise way we may claim that aptitudes exist in the world itself and manifest in the world as relational.[330] Freedom, self-consciousness and the will, as discussed earlier, are characteristics of the aptitude of humanness: that is, the being of our being in the world. However, since the *world itself* is not ontologically distinct, it would be incorrect to posit humanness as existing in ontological distinction from *Dasein;* yet it is certain that it must be ontological. How may we rectify the contradiction in reference to the proposed two-relations perspective?

We must first consider the way in which humanness fits into the origination of beings in the being of the world. As mentioned earlier, this issue reflects the *ontological order of existence* which articulates the *ontological prioritization* and development of being in the world. If being in the world, relationality, is the resulting feature of the *ontological order of existence,* and if it is beyond debate that being must be the source (as it provides the source for all ontology) then we can easily place humanness somewhere in between, in the mediation of the process. For example:

Being→Humanness→World

This would also necessitate then that the world itself falls in between being and world; however, it is not immediately clear if it must be prior to or posterior to humanness. We may again consider both propositions.

If, on the one hand, the world itself is posterior to humanness, being originates beings initializing the process of origination. This would require, however, that relationality is brought into being immediately along with beings, as was shown earlier. On the other hand, if prior to humanness, this would mean that being has as its first motion the origination of a place rather than beings. This is problematic, however, as it treats the world itself as a place, as an ontologically distinct world.

If we know that *Dasein* as being-in-the world is necessarily relational, then *Dasein* is the being that emerges from the manifestation of humanness in the world. *Dasein* is necessarily ontical and is not primarily an ontological designation of the being which we are. For it represents a mode of Being in relation to other beings, that is it considers the "how" of what we are, but not precisely

---

[330] As previously mentioned, and as should be clear from the above discussion, this "manifestation" is less of an actualization of the aptitude itself, and more like an *emergence.*

"what" we are. In other words, it deals with the way humanness manifests itself in the world of relationality as the being *Dasein*. We can depict this as follows:

Being→Humanness→World→*Dasein*

This may at first resemble the Platonic world of forms; yet humanness, though in many ways it shares traits with the forms as treated by Plato in some of the dialogues, is not a form of the being *Dasein*, but instead can better conform to a reflection of *Dasein* as in the reflectability of Leibniz's *monads*.[331] We arrive at the world itself, not prior to being *Dasein*, but in reflection upon the ontological foundation of our ontical relationality to the world. Ultimately, then, the following is the best representation of the *ontological order of existence:*

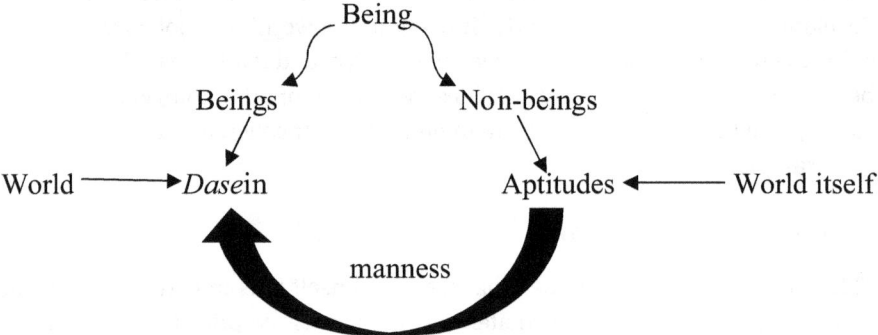

Fig. 1: Humanness as Filter

This illustrates the *ontological order of existence*, as must indeed be the case if we are to claim that humanness both precedes *Dasein* in *ontological prioritization* as well as not being ontologically distinct or prior to *Dasein* in its very existence, but comes about due to an abstraction. Thus, the world itself is the world abstracted away from relationality, rather than being an ontological world separate from relationality. Nonetheless, it is important to note that it is also the case that the world itself is ontologically prior to the world of relationality.[332] But

---

331 For more on Leibniz's view of substance and *monads*, see Gottfried Wilhelm Leibniz (1886).
332 A confusion regarding this concept is bound to arise as it is seemingly contradictory. In order to address those concerns sooner rather than later so as to avoid any unnecessary time on configuring the concept in a way in which it is immediately comprehensible, I would here like to provide some remarks.
  My first remark is that the world itself is ontologically prior because, indeed, the world of relationality *is not primarily* ontological. To show this, reconsider the distinction between the on-

tological and the ontic in, for example, Heidegger (2010), Bacon (1928), Hartman (1940), or any other numerous accounts. The ontic serves as a mere description of an ontologically existing entity. It does not claim anything essential, or we may say, about the very nature of that particular entity. The ontological does the latter. It accounts for the very structure, foundation, and general being of being, rather than the being of the particularities of a specific being. In this we may, or must, challenge the division established by Bhaskar in *Scientific Realism and Human Emancipation* when he writes: "I differentiate the "ontic" ("ontical" etc.) from the "ontological". I employ the former to refer to 1) whatever pertains to being generally, rather than some distinctively philosophical (or scientific) theory of it (ontology), so that in this sense, that of the $ontic_1$, we can speak of the ontic presuppositions of a work of art, a joke or a strike as much as a theory of knowledge; and, within this rubric, to 2) the intransitive objects of some specific, historically determinate, scientific investigation (or set of such investigations), the **$ontic_2$**.The $ontic_2$ is always specified, and only identified, by its relation, as the intransitive object(s) of some or other (denumerable set of) particular transitive process(es) of enquiry. It is cognitive process-, and level-specific; whereas the ontological (like the $ontic_1$) is not" (1986, p. 36-37).

Although a very thought out claim, the problem we can spot in this formulation is that ontic is split into $ontic_1$ and $ontic_2$ leaving ontological merely as the theory of the ontic. However, the correct division here is ontological as described in his first proposition and the ontic in the second. Note most crucially that Bhaskar articulates the ontic ($ontic_2$ in his division), is determined by virtue of its very relationality. Thus, relationality in its being the determination of the ontic, also determines the world of relationality as an *ontic world*.

My second remark follows thus: the confusion might also arise due to the intricacy of the concept of the world itself. However, I seek to make it very clear that this concept is in *no way* a mere escape, philosophical cop-out, or otherwise devised as a means by and through which an explanation can be afforded for that which otherwise remains inexplicable or contradictory or which threatens to void or moot a theoretical proposition. The world itself is a proper outcome, that is to say necessary and sufficient, of the division expounded upon in remark one (and through the first half of this work). Thus, the rejection of the world itself is a rejection of the ontological, a rejection of the claim that entities have a real existence quantified by their relationality (ontic), as well as an essential nature of that relationality which is itself nonrelational (ontological). While it is certainly possible, though very limiting, to reject the latter, the former cannot be rejected as its very rejection requires an ontological predication.

This leads directly into my third remark. This remark centers around the impossibility of the rejection of the world itself. It is not only incorrect to assume that the world itself can be rejected, but it is so because it is impossible to reject. I am certain that this claim has sparked some agitation among readers, so let me articulate a very detailed account of why this is the case. To do this I will state the reason, following up with the proof of this reason.

It is impossible to reject the world itself because the world itself is in fact, itself, nothing; to be more clear, it is nothing in and of itself. Proof: If a claim is to be rejected outright, it must rest on a false premise or a false conclusion. The premises of the world itself can be reduced to: 1) that the world of our everyday experience is pure relationality 2) entities in the world relate to that world both as relational and nonrelational. Of these, only the second seems to be deniable and so I shall focus on that one here. While one may reject that there is any possible nonrelational relation, I will here show otherwise (in case one missed this in the work itself).

This claim can be premised itself upon the following: 1) the distinction between ontic and ontological, as noted above 2) that anything which is ontic is necessarily ontological as well.

this leaves unaddressed this nonrelational relationality. What is it, and where does it come from? To address these questions, we must recall the previous discussion on objects and in particular, object-oriented ontological thought, which has in part led us here.

Aptitudes are the nonrelationality of objects *in the world* as they are *in the world itself*, meaning that they are abstracted from the entirety of their relations. This is to say that aptitudes are nonrelational and are therefore nonbeings. Objects, as relational, are beings. Thus, nonrelational relationality does not apply either to objects or aptitudes, but rather to something else entirely. It is not difficult to note that what begins to emerge from this position resembles a structure not altogether unfamiliar: namely, that of a spectrum.

The *fundamental relation*, as was previously discussed, is that between nonrelationality and relationality. It was also suggested that this relation itself, then, must be a nonrelational relationality. Being nonrelational, this nonrelationality must be a nonbeing, as with aptitudes, yet it contains relationality as well, which is noticeably absent in aptitudes. Therefore, this nonrelational relationality may *in fact* manifest itself. It is not difficult to posit this on the basis of the above. If nonrelationality yields aptitudes, and relationality yields objects, nonrelational relationality must yield hyper-objects.

Timothy Morton has suggested that there are hyperobjects: that is, objects which are not limited by spatiotemporality, at least not at the same scale as *Da-*

The latter is self-evident, the former can be and has been disagreed upon. However, the first is also clear from the use of the terms ontic and ontological. These claims entail the second premise of the major claim noted above. There is no reason for a rejection of the second premise then.

Considering the conclusion that there is a world itself, we return to my initial claim that it is impossible to reject. Insofar as one can agree that there is nonrelationality of entities, that is ontology, then they have themselves concluded that there is a world itself. Since the world itself is itself nothing other than the nonrelationality of entities insofar as they relate to each other in their being nonrelational, the world itself has been described. For it is a mere abstraction from the relationality of the world. Yet, as we have said that this nonrelationality is the ontological, it is also the essential, the realness (nature of/thing-in-itself) of the real (empirical appearance of the thing).

Thus, there is no possible way to reject the world itself as it is not something that is at all. I will end this lengthy footnote by stating very clearly, in case it remains unclear: there is nothing called the world itself that exists independently of the world which we are already within and consumed by, and in fact, there is nothing called the world itself that exists period; it is not capable of existence. It is nothing beyond a semantic tool used to differentiate between modes of being-in and to describe the absolute ontology of being *qua* being. If you hold an ontological position of any sort – there are very few who do not – then you make a claim to the world itself, whether you admit to it or not.

sein, in the same way that standard objects are and, in fact, although he includes objects such as styrofoam as an example, he also applies the term "hyperobject" to climate change.[333] If aptitudes are nonbeings, and objects are beings, then what is a hyperobject? Using this concept from Morton, and expanding on it based on the previous discussion, hyperobjects as nonrelational relationality must be that which (though in and of itself nonrelational) nevertheless manifests *in the world* of relationality, not necessarily as an object, but rather as a force.[334] Thus, I would argue against Morton that styrofoam and radioactive plutonium are simply objects, but that climate change is a prime example of a hyperobject.

If this is the case, then a manifested nonrelational relationality would be the being of such a being: that is to say, a hyperbeing. If aptitudes as nonrelational are nonbeings, which underlie objects (which themselves are relational as beings) then hyperbeing must be what underlies hyperobjects as a nonrelational relationality. This represents what I call spectral ontology, a spectrum of being and beings which brings with it a desperately needed connection between philosophy and other sciences by circumventing the traditional linear or circular modes of thinking about philosophy.

Returning to humanness, I have suggested that it *acts* as a filter of being: having briefly articulated the notion of a spectrum of being, it becomes vivid here that humanness is a filter. Although this has also been alluded to by Meillassoux, it serves a very different purpose in his work: namely, to battle correlationism. While Meillassoux is in the right to suggest "a line," "like a spectrum," which aims at bringing philosophical discourse back into scientific discourse – an end which I hold just as dear as Meillassoux – it is not to be contrasted with and seen as an escape from correlationism. In fact, correlationism should not be abandoned entirely at all, since to do so would be to disregard the spectrum. Correlationism is in fact a *part of* the spectrum.

---

333 For a discussion on hyperobjects and how they fit into an object-oriented philosophical position, see Timothy Morton's (2012) excellent and provocative work *The Ecological Thought*.
334 Although many will take this in a metaphysical, almost spiritual manner, it need not be. Gravity is a prime example. Gravity is not itself an *object* in and of itself (though an elementary particle has been suggested to possibly be at its root, namely the *graviton*), but rather is a concept we apply to a force. Gravity as a hyperobject, then, means that it is itself nonrelational and as such a nonbeing, which nevertheless, and indubitably, impacts as a relationality, that is, as a force. In regards to *Dasein*, it will be noted in the above articulation of the *ontological order of existence* that the distinguished concept of "human" was missing. Upon the addition of hyperbeings and hyperobjects, we could suggest the addition of "human" to the diagram above in the following way: as a branching off of *Dasein*'s self-reflection of its humanness, that is, a bridging of the world of relationality and the world itself.

Just as light penetrates a prism, only to be diversified into a spectrum of different colors, we have here the same picture for Being. Being, as the totality of what is, is the emergent spectrum of being itself. On that spectrum exist nonbeings, beings, and hyperbeing(s). Correlationism, then, is perfectly apt for the part of the spectrum to which *beings belong*. Humanness as a filter, as an aptitude, thus becomes the manner in which it is possible that a being emerges *in the world* as *Dasein*.

But more must be said about the *spectricity of* humanness. What does it mean to say that humanness, as an aptitude, is *spectral*? We mean this in two ways. The first, as noted above, refers to the placement of humanness, along with all aptitudes, on a position on a spectrum of being that looks something like this:

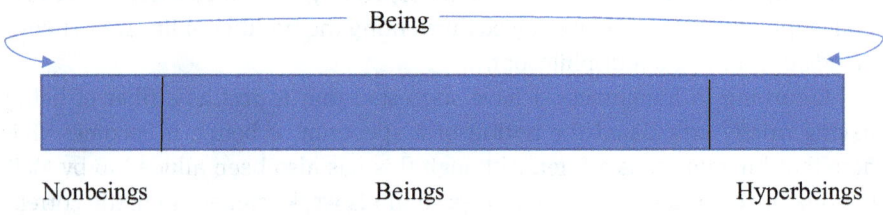

Fig. 2: Spectricity of Being

Therefore, under such an ontological structure, which can be called *Spectral Philosophy* or *Spectral Ontology,* Being is the constant emergence of beings along a spectrum which casts aptitudes as nonbeings, which enable the possibility of beings as such along with hyperbeings. Thinking about Being as a spectrum marks a divergence from the thought of Being as static, and forces us to reorient our ontological perspectives to include nontraditional Being, nonbeings and hyperbeings.

But spectricity, or the spectral, here means something different as well: namely, "ghostly", which is fitting of the name. For both humanness and aptitudes in general are nonbeings, yet they remain in being. Just like a spook or specter, aptitudes such as humanness are a non-there thereness which haunts the being itself which remains "thrown" *in the world*, a world lacking in aptitudes, since they are nonbeings. The *spectricity of humanness* thus also refers to the quieted specter or "ghost" of humanness which lurks behind every human being unsensed, unknown, and without relation to the *world*. It is this spectral nature of humanness through which we must confront fundamental ontology, and out of it that we may concern ourselves properly with *Dasein* as such.

A Brief Note on Spectricities

I would here like to articulate further the distinction between what I have termed aptitudes and the 'entity' of the spectral, the *spectricity*. We can denote the difference between the two, first and foremost, due to the particularity of the former. *Aptitudes* are always concerned with the particular Being of a particular being – such as the case with humanness, treeness, etc., much as the way in which Platonic forms are a generality of a particularity. As Jean Baudrillard famously wrote: "The real is not only what can be reproduced, but that which is already reproduced" (1980, p.146). Although all particular trees share in the generality, the form, or what I term, the *aptitude*, of treeness, this *aptitude* is itself a particular aptitude which does not apply as a generality to the Being of all beings.

Opposed to this particularity, the *spectricity* (as an 'entity', a 'noun') is complete and total generality, universality. It denotes nothing other than the very structure underlying the reality of the *world*, it is the structure of the *world itself*, as I have put forth earlier. The spectricity is itself the nonrelationality of the relationality that becomes the Being of a being and so, in this sense, it is the Being of the Being of any and all beings.

The Being of any particular being differs between each and every being, as can be seen in the example of treeness – it is always still a particular Being. However, the Being of that Being, the very structure of that Being, is forever universal. How can that be the case? There are two reasons that make this clear: 1) universality forms a necessary basis for particularity and 2) this Being of Being is itself the non-Being of Being.

In the first instance, we must note that even if we have a generality for any and every particular being, a Being of a being, we would still lack – and therefore require – a Being of beings. 'Treeness', as a Being of the being of a tree, as a Platonic form, and indeed as an *aptitude*, only determines how that Being manifests as relationality as a particular object of a tree. It does not, and cannot, exemplify anything regarding that Being in and of itself beyond its manifestation as a tree. That is to say, anything which could be said about treeness is necessarily something about a tree, or about trees, and is nothing about Being. Of course, I agree, along with Deleuze and Guattari, that "*Nous sommes fatigués de l'arbre*" (1980, p. 15).[335]

Each *aptitude* grants the being 'insight' (a relation) into the fundamental structure; each being has a different 'access point' to the Being of their being. As Paul Shepard notes: "Longer than memory we have known that each animal has its power and place, each a skill, virtue, wisdom, innocence – a special access to the structure and flow of the world" and, more importantly, continues "Together, sacred, they help hold the cosmos together" (1997, p. 173). This is true, of course, not just of treeness, or frogness, but of any object.

For certain, there must be a 'Beingness', a fundamental structure of the Being/Form/*Aptitude* of 'treeness.' If there is a universality between all beings which have the Being/Form/*Aptitude* of treeness, then there must also be a universality among all various forms of *aptitudes*, whether it be treeness or humanness. Although treeness and humanness vary greatly from one another, there must be a structure to each which is universal; a structure which, at the very least, enables such an *aptitude* to be manifested, a structure of Being that allows for its relationality as a being. If this was not universal in the very structure of the Being of Being, then we should have beings of trees, but not of humans, or of humans and not of trees. It should not be taken lightly then, as some spiritual or metaphysical jargon, when Giordano Bruno writes (emphasis added):

> Thus, everything in the universe, in relation to the universe, exists everywhere according to its capacity, whatever its relation might be with other particular bodies; for it is above, below, right, left, and so on, in keeping with all local differences, since, in the totality of the infinite, there are all these differences and none of them. **Whatever thing we take in the universe, it has in itself that which is entire everywhere, and hence comprehends, in its own way, the entire world soul** (although, as we have said, it does not comprehend it totally), **and that world soul is entire in every part of the universe** (1998, p. 91).

We should not treat that which Bruno speaks of here as spiritual (despite his use of 'soul'), but rather something very much real, concrete. Indeed, any 'form', any *aptitude* must contain within it this fundamental, universal structure of *spectricity*.

It is also important to note, however, that this fundamental structure, *spectricities*, are themselves non-entities. Here we must distinguish also between *aptitudes* as nonbeings in the *world itself* and *spectricities* as the Non-Being of the

---

[335] Deleuze and Guattari (1980, p. 15) continue on to note: "*Nous ne devons plus croire aux arbres, aux racines ni aux radicelles... Au contraire, rien n'est beau, rien n'est amoureux, rien n'est politique, sauf les tiges souterraines et les racines aériennes, l'adventice et le rhizome.*"

Being (which is itself a non-being) of beings. The former is the nonrelational 'entity' which manifests in the world of relations as a being, whereas the latter is the very structure of the non-being, the Being of the non-being. It is the *world itself* in and of itself.[336]

The Pathway to Philosophical Anthropology

Having discussed at length the concept of humanness, we have thus arrived at the point at which we have aimed – to pose the philosophical anthropological question of humanness. By way of a re-visitation of Kantian transcendental ontology through the lens of *Dasein*, a distinction between worlds has been claimed – a world of beings as manifested *in the world* as relational, and the *world itself* full of *spectral* nonbeings, or aptitudes as I have termed them, which form the very possibility of a being's relationality and thereby its manifestation, its worldliness. This *world itself* and the aptitudes contained within are abstracted away from relationality and are therefore nonrelational entities. Nevertheless, they are the fundamental building blocks of the world, of relationality itself, and therefore not only of beings themselves, but the very possibility of beings.

Thus, we have articulated the need for a reversal from the finitude of humanness, grounding *Dasein* in pure finitude, to the *transcendental* of humanness. *Dasein* is no longer rooted in finitude, but in transcendentality; that is to say, *Dasein* in its *worldliness* and relationality is constricted and exhausted by its finitude, but does not spring out of and is therefore not grounded in finitude. Rather, *Dasein* becomes *Dasein* only through its manifestation in the world, through its *relationality*. In the abstraction from this relationality of *the world*, and in the *world itself*, *Dasein* is no longer the *Dasein* of finitude, but transcendental humanness itself.

We are here to determine, that is, to reevaluate *Dasein* in these terms and with this greater recognition not only for the way in which *Dasein* is *in the world*, but also as *in the world itself*, albeit not as *Dasein* precisely, but rather as that very fundamental ontology of the being *Dasein*. This work has revealed that this fundamental ontology is best understood in terms of a spectrum of Being, originating first as a nonbeing aptitude, namely humanness, which emerges into a Being in the world as a human being. It is towards the latter that we must now turn and orient the future of philosophical anthropology. That is to say, we must consider

---

[336] *Spectricities* as such will be the subject of future work as will be necessary to provide any adequate account of them.

the *manifestation* of humanness as a *being in the world*, and in turn, arrive at a genuine philosophical anthropology articulated through a critique of humanness.

We ought here to delineate the pathway, or methodology, that such a critique should follow and the resulting form it would emulate. Philosophical anthropology is dialectical in that it is derived as a synthesis between the philosophical and the anthropological aspects, or approaches, to the study of the human being. Thus, phenomenology can only be part of a philosophical anthropological approach and should not be treated as a methodology which can pose for itself the whole of the question of humanness.

Heidegger writes that "Phenomenology is the way of access to, and the demonstrative manner of determination of, that which is to become the theme of ontology" (2010, p. 33). However, insofar as phenomenology is concerned with the individual experience of Being, it is set from the standpoint of a particular being, namely *Dasein*, and can never reach beyond this position. Thus, phenomenology as such is unfit for the study of the ontological, despite Heidegger's claims, but is rather an examination of the ontical.[337]

In determining the limits of anthropology, Heidegger writes: "over and above the attempt to determine the essence of 'human being' as a being, the question of its being has remained forgotten; rather, this Being is understood as something 'self-evident' in the sense of *being present* of created things" (ibid, p. 48). It is in this way and for this reason, that his existential analytic of *Dasein* can be said to be phenomenological, rather than comprising a philosophical anthropology. However, in his dismissal of the prospects of anthropology to address the fundamental ontology of the Being of *Dasein*, he has failed to discuss the most notable prospect of a philosophical anthropology as a methodology for doing so, which is, in fact, its posing of the question of humanness as better able to address this concern. It is the failure of anthropology, and all sciences for that matter, that they consider the beings of their investigation as merely present-at-hand.

This is why humanness means, in Heidegger, precisely the finite nature of the being called *Dasein*; humanness is the finitude of *Dasein*. Yet *Dasein*, as was shown in the first part, is not merely finite, but consists of nonfinite, infinite, and transcendental aspects as well. Furthermore, the transcendental – which is

---

337 Though the ontic of *Dasein* holds ontological foundations, which is what is being sought here. This is what enables eidetic reduction. Even though the ultimate goal of eidetic reduction is to uncover hidden essences through imaginative processes of perceptual elimination, this is a subjective experience which relies entirely on the individual and fails to account for what the individual brings into such a reduction. That is to say, the very act of eidetic reduction is grounded through perceptual means.

also the ontological rather than ontical since it is the pure framework or structure out of which relationality forms – was identified earlier in this work with the *transcendental ego*. It becomes clear that insofar as humanness forms the ontological foundation of *Dasein*, humanness must be the transcendental of *Dasein*, either jointly with the transcendental ego or prior to it, in which it gives rise to the latter. In such a case, the latter becomes *transcendent* insofar as it bridges the gap between ontic relationality and ontological singularity.[338]

The concern of the ontological, of Being *qua* Being as it relates to *Dasein* through the quality of humanness, is better addressed through philosophical anthropology, as it accounts for the individual experience of Being as well as being itself, since it takes the question of humanness as its primary mode of questioning. Humanness, as transcendental, must necessarily concern itself with the ontological, with Being as such. Thus, the method of philosophical anthropology begins with the ontological, proceeds to the anthropological, filters it through the philosophical, then synthesizes these into the philosophical anthropological question of humanness. This process of "filtering" refers to the rigorous evaluation of anthropological aspects of *Dasein* through what might be termed the metaphysics of *Dasein*. Thus, the resulting philosophical anthropology, centered on the question of humanness, is a dialectic formed from the disparity between the two. It is for this reason that there is no existing complete philosophical anthropology.[339]

The analytic of humanness will then ultimately follow this procedure. Whereas the existential analytic of *Dasein* takes the form of a phenomenology, it is an analytic of *in-der-Welt-sein* and the everyday experience of the being of *Dasein*, the fundamental aspects of *Dasein's* interaction with the world. The analytic of humanness requires a breakdown of the fundamental aspects of *Dasein* as a being. We must, then, sketch the structure of the analytic of humanness, which mimics the modes of *Dasein* in Part One.[340]

The Fundamental Structure of the Critique of Humanness

In following the dialectical methodology espoused by philosophical anthropology, through which the conflict between the anthropological approach – and in-

---

338 For more on the transcendence of the ego, particularly in Sartre's work from which I draw from here, see Phyllis Morris (1985) "Sartre on the Transcendence of the Ego".
339 As Hans Peter Rickman notes, "Philosophical anthropology is concerned with the whole range of philosophic problems" (1960, p. 12).
340 See footnotes for each question below for the representative form.

deed that of any positive science – to the study of *Dasein* and the metaphysics of *Dasein* finds resolution, it becomes possible to outline the structure of the analytic of humanness. From what has been articulated, it is clear that we must discuss in what way humanness is attributed to a particular being called *Dasein*. This cannot be accomplished, however, without noting what possibilities are brought along with the very immanence of being a particular being generally. We must then first address the issues which derive from this immediate, existential relation to Being.

Indeed, *Dasein* as a being is not strictly a being, but is a particular kind of being. If we are to pose the question of humanness appropriately, then we must also develop further the consideration of *Dasein* insofar as *Dasein* has the character of *in-der-Welt-sein*. This will require a deeper plunge into the empirical study of the being *Dasein* as opposed to a strictly phenomenological one. It must be outlined precisely what it means to be this particular kind of being as differentiated between other particular beings. Here we must articulate all aspects of human beings insofar as humanness is related to them. That is to say, we must consider the origin and characteristics of human beings as well as the consciousness that gives rise to these traits possessed by *Dasein*.

In doing so, it will be necessary to draw upon the cognitive and positive sciences in order to form a complete picture of *Dasein*.[341] In addition to these characteristics which will be discussed in light of cognitive and positive science, it will be necessary to discuss the many metaphysical aspects of *Dasein* such as reason, freedom, identity, and the like, which are the primary concern of the philosophy of human nature. Despite Heidegger's concern over the treatment of beings as present-at-hand in anthropology and other sciences, it is in fact Heidegger's analytic which limits the investigation, since the philosophical anthropological methodology of investigating humanness itself, as it manifests *in the world* does not fall victim to this oversimplification of the being under investigation.

It should be noted, however, that it is through the presence-at-hand of a being (in this case, *Dasein*) that we become acquainted with fundamental ontology, *contra* Heidegger. The readiness-to-hand aspect of *Dasein's* relation to the world and to Being as such, is antecedent to its presence-at-hand. *Dasein* engages with the readiness-to-hand of beings in the world; this is to say that it is not a property of *Dasein* itself, but rather a mode of relation – it is an ontic relationality. The dialogue established out of the interconnection between the cognitive

---

[341] This is a similar approach to understanding philosophical anthropology associated with E.M Adams (2007) "On Being a Human Being".

or positive sciences and philosophy brings to the forefront the synthesis of philosophical anthropology, as alluded to earlier, and that is precisely why in philosophical anthropology, it has been remarked, all aspects of the human must be considered.[342]

Nevertheless, *Dasein* is a particular kind of being. We must dive deeper and pose the question as to what is the fundamental, primary nature of this particular kind of being whose primary mode of being is *in-der-Welt-sein*. Heidegger's mistake here is in thinking that the question, namely the question of Being as such, is the answer. *In-der-Welt-sein,* as a mode of being of *Dasein,* is not also the primary *nature* of what it means to be *Dasein*. For *Dasein* is a particular kind of being, namely a human being. It is thus not enough to provide an analytic of *Dasein,* even if it is (we may say) more complete than Heidegger's own, as otherwise we still stop two steps short. The "Human" itself must be addressed and dealt with intricately.

The necessity of this cannot be overstated. There are then four questions which make up the whole of the fundamental inquiry of humanness. For the purpose of clarity, we can here state them and explicate their relation to the inquiry as follows:

1. What is Being?[343]

This ontological question is perhaps the most general and most fundamental. It is the question which has been addressed in this work and which serves as the grounding for a philosophical anthropology.

2. What does it mean to be a being?[344]

This is a very distinct question and addresses a unique concern. Armed with the *ontological difference*, as it has been termed,[345] this difference is quite easily recognized. However, this question is more unique than simply through its being distinguished from the question concerning Being. The uniqueness of this question is imparted through its particularity, its singularity. The addition of an article

---

342 For some different interpretations see, H.O. Pappe (1961) "On philosophical anthropology", Richard M. Zaner (1966) "An Approach to a Philosophical Anthropology" and Richard Schacht (1990) "Philosophical Anthropology: What, Why and How".
343 Being represents the infinite mode of *Dasein*. Insofar as *Dasein* is *a being* it will remain in Being infinitely so; that is to say that being is infinite.
344 Being a being represents the finite mode of *Dasein*. A being will ultimately become a non-being, due to its finitude.
345 While this concept has been articulated in Heidegger by many scholars, a great examination of it can be found in Graeme Nicholson (1996) "The Ontological Difference".

in the question immediately asks about something definite, particular, and singular. It does not pose itself towards objects, but towards this or that object or category of objects, thus placing it as the primary question of *finitude*. No question which can be posed in the aftermath of this question can remove itself from its particularity, its directedness. Even if one were to ask about everything that *is*, it is posing itself only in a finite way and is therefore limited to its finitude, its particularity.

3. What does it mean to be a human being?[346]

This question, which has taken hold of many past inquiries, is in fact less substantial than has been claimed. For such a question is simply one in which what is being asked about is a particular kind of a particular. In this case, we are interested in the particular being which can be classified as human. This question, shifting away from a purely ontological or philosophical question, is also a physical one, grounded in anthropology – as well as its taking an interest in other sciences such as biology and physiology, insofar as these relate to the particular being in question. For even if one argues that the fundamental characteristic of our being is the very relation between our being and Being (as is the case with Heidegger), when viewed through the lens of philosophical anthropology, when centered on the manifestation of humanness, these other sciences cannot be diverged from the question.

We should discuss here what about this particular being's composition ensures that it is what it is, rather than what it is not: namely, a different being. Thus, it is not limited to the physical or the philosophical, but includes both, as it must address metaphysics of this being such as the concept of freedom as expressed in the human being. Indeed, it is the focus on this question which accounts for the vast majority of philosophy centering on anthropology, or philosophical anthropology. Heidegger's own analytic of *Dasein* poses this question, though it can be noted that it also begins to extend itself into the following question.

4. What does it mean to be human?[347]

The removal of the particular in this question returns us towards the primordial question of Being. We are here not asking about *how* we are *in the world*, that is what makes us what we are insofar as we are a particular kind of being. Instead,

---

[346] Being a human being, insofar as it is simply an articulation of a *kind of* being, is also representative of the finitude of *Dasein*.

[347] Being "human" represents the *nonfinitude* of *Dasein*.

we are posing the question of what makes us this type of being. That is to say, with this question we are concerned with the Being of the being that is *Dasein*. This concerns itself with the sociality, and more closely and deeply, the metaphysics of *Dasein*. Thus, while the previous question concerns itself with the way in which we exist in the world (phenomenology) and the way in which we actively *engage* with the world (anthropology), this question forces us to consider the nature of that existence. It is here that one can locate, as the name suggests, the philosophy of human nature.

These are the four main questions as previously articulated, listed in a precise way in the manner of our investigation. Although the final question is closer to the fundamental inquiry which we here pose, it does not pose for itself the question of the *nature* of this nature of the being *Dasein:* that is, the question of humanness.[348] Nevertheless, due to the complexity of the question of humanness, we may not simply ask the question prior to proceeding through the structure above. In this way, then, we have provided for the complete structure necessary for a critique of humanness, the starting point of a philosophical anthropology.

The Continuing Procedure of the Critique of Humanness

More must be said with regards to philosophical anthropology as a procedure for uncovering or unveiling humanness; this requires the articulation not only of the thematic under investigation but also the mode through which it is to be discovered. Above I have outlined a philosophical anthropology; however, it has not yet been well established how philosophical anthropology, which poses to itself the question of humanness, can at the same time be the eventual outcome of the philosophical inquiry. That is to ask the paradoxical question: how is it that through philosophical anthropology we are to arrive at a philosophical anthropology? A reflection upon past attempts towards philosophical anthropology will indicate in what way this may be the case as well as reveal to what extent previous inquiries were led astray.

We shall start with Max Scheler, one of the founders of philosophical anthropology, who correctly noted that if it is to be complete it must take into account the totality of the human being, including that which traditionally lies outside of the boundaries of philosophy: such as biological, psychological, and physiological aspects. This totality, however, was never fully articulated, likely due to his

---

348 Humanness as stated is transcendental.

premature death. For many philosophical anthropologists, the totality of man is, essentially, what Heidegger terms *Dasein:* namely, the being-in-the-world, that is, the human being, though only the few following in his wake use it in the same sense.

Martin Buber, for example, who agrees with Max Scheler, writes "philosophical anthropology... where the subject is man in his wholeness" still brings into the discussion the Heideggerian phenomenology of *Dasein,* stating that "the investigator cannot content himself ... with considering man as another part of nature and with ignoring the fact that he, the investigator, is himself a man and experiences this humanity in his inner experience in a way that he simply cannot experience any part of nature" (Buber 2002, p. 147).[349] This phenomenological disposition[350] of the investigative subject approaches philosophical anthropology through the standpoint of a being-in-the-world, *Dasein.* Likewise, more contemporary philosophical anthropologists have focused on the inclusion of lifeworlds in the analysis of the human being.

This tends to be the focus of what Michael D. Jackson calls *existential anthropology.*[351] However, the very conception of a lifeworld, as Bjorn Kraus notes: "Lifeworld means a person's subjective construction of reality, which he or she forms under the condition of his or her life circumstances" (2015, p. 4). It is a construction that emerges out of *Dasein's being-in-the-world.* Leonardo Polo's *Transcendental Anthropology*[352] also clings to the importance of lifeworlds, though this is not explicit, as he emphasizes the relation of the human being with other human beings, something which grounds *Dasein* as fundamentally in the world and which Heidegger notes as a mode of *being-in,* as a victimization of the they-self (*das Man*) as a way of being-with.

Rudolf Steiner differs in his approach to philosophical anthropology and he articulates his position through what he terms anthroposophy. Anthroposophy suggests an extrasensory or spiritual consciousness which connects the human being to a spiritual world, which includes formless spiritual beings

---

349 It should be noted that this refers most significantly to the inherent relation that we have to subjectivity, than to a strict Heideggarian framework.
350 Although Buber does not call for a necessarily phenomenological approach.
351 For more on existential anthropology see Michael Jackson (2008) *Existential Anthropology: Events, Exigencies, and Effects.*
352 Leonardo Polo (1999) offers his view in its most complete form in *Antropología Trascendental I & II.*

that predate the material world, as Steiner wrote about in detail.[353] Although much of Steiner's anthroposophy need not be critiqued here, as this has been done exhaustively by others,[354] one interesting aspect he includes in his treatment of the human being is a consciousness which is extrasensory.

Where Scheler differs from other philosophical anthropologists, and which we must outline here, is in his conception of *Wertsein*, or value-being. While the ontology of this was never fully articulated either, I believe that it may bear similarities to, or at the very least form the outcome of, my suggestion regarding philosophical anthropology: namely that it is both the question and the answer. Additionally, Scheler notes that the human being, insofar as it cannot be defined (as he held) is therefore not a static being but rather, and in every sense, a becoming, making the task of philosophical anthropology an attempt to expose the becoming nature of the human being.[355] That is to suggest, the delimitation of the manifestation of humanness as *being-in-the-world*.

Furthermore, Scheler begins a trend for philosophical anthropology toward the focus on the concreteness of the human being (*Dasein*) and, what becomes introduced in Plessner as, the excentric positionality of this being.[356] For Plessner, this means that *Dasein* is the kind of being which exists most fundamentally, at a boundary between its physicality and the world. This creates an "openness" to the world. Joachim Fischer finds this concept to be the identifying and unifying concept of philosophical anthropology after Scheler. Fischer offers an exceptional overview of the concept as follows:

> Excentric positionality is the most artificial category of the theoretical program; at the same time, it lends particular clarity to the typical philosophical-anthropological thought process. It follows the same approach to categorization as that employed by Scheler. In order to formulate a conceptual understanding of the human sphere, Plessner explicitly begins within the subject-object relation, with the experience of the entity that is confronted with the subject. It is his intention to distinguish the "'living thing'" from the non-living thing at the level of the object. His hypothesis is that the living thing is distinguished from all other things, not only by virtue of its border, which marks the point where it begins

---

[353] Rudolf Steiner (1991) offers his thoughts on anthroposophy and philosophical anthropology in *Man as Symphony of the Creative Word: Twelve Lectures given in Dornach, Switzerland from October 19th to November 11th, 1923*.
[354] For a wonderful introduction to the general points of Steiner's "anthroposophy" and criticisms of it, see Colin Wilson (1986) *Rudolf Steiner: The Man and His Vision: an Introduction to the Life and Ideas of the Founder of Anthroposophy*.
[355] For Scheler's complete approach to philosophical anthropology see Max Scheler (1972) *Vom Umsturz der Werte*.
[356] To explore this in more detail see Helmuth Plessner's (1975) *Die Stufen Des Organischen Und Der Mensch: Einleitung in Die Philosophische Anthropologie*.

or ends, but by virtue of the "'boundary'" nature of its layer. The living thing is characterized by border traffic in relation to its environment, it is a boundary-setting thing (Fischer 2009, p. 160).

Thus, while his anthropology was never completed, Scheler's impact on the field is extraordinary. Additionally, as Buber noted,[357] enough can be gleaned from what works Scheler did publish[358] such that his position is made clear and continues to make an impact on the continuation of philosophical anthropology.[359]

In keeping with and expanding upon Scheler, rather than treating philosophical anthropology as a discipline of philosophy that studies the totality of human being, much as ontology studies being, a true philosophical anthropology is also a methodology of its own; in this sense it is similar to phenomenology, being both a branch of philosophy and a philosophical methodology. Thus, one cannot approach philosophical anthropology from the standpoint of phenomenology, existentialism, or any of the other numerous philosophical schools and movements. Phenomenology, for example, studies consciousness, or more explicitly experience. Philosophical anthropology focuses its efforts on that which makes a human being human at all, or the very nature of the concept of human, namely, the concept of humanness. Therefore, it is out of necessity that this Critique of Humanness is composed.

But in what way is it to be composed? What is the structure, not of the Critique, but of philosophical anthropology? Insofar as we may claim that philosophical anthropology is both a movement or school as well as a methodology, what is the methodology of philosophical anthropology? It is a dialectic between, on the one hand, anthropological accounts and philosophical accounts. A philosophical anthropology, if it is to be worthy of the name, must incorporate both of these. This is what many mean when they say that philosophical anthropology includes "all aspects of man" as mentioned previously. Thus, many philosophical anthropological works and projects focus purely on this methodology, attempting to utilize tools and information from both disciplines whilst not recognizing that this necessarily entails the question of humanness.

---

[357] Martin Buber (1945) suggests as much in his article on Scheler "The Philosophical Anthropology of Max Scheler".
[358] In works such as Scheler's (1975) *Die Stellung des Menschen im Kosmos*.
[359] It is my contention that, even if enough of his position were to have been made clear, then it could not have challenged Heidegger's dismissal of anthropology to the point of enabling the full formation and categorization of philosophical anthropology as it now stands. For a good overview of Scheler's critique against Heidegger's "fundamental ontology" of *Dasein* see Daniel O. Dahlstrom's (2002) essay "Scheler's Critique of Heidegger's Fundamental Ontology," in *Max Scheler's Acting Persons: New Perspectives*.

Therefore, the methodological procedure for the fundamental inquiry into the question of humanness will require a dedication to the inclusivity of both anthropological – and by extension psychological, biological, and physiological – accounts, and those that are philosophical. To do so, both of the thematics subjected to investigation, the human being and being human, as indicated by the above articulated questions, will be broken down and evaluated based on both the anthropological and philosophical components and considerations.

It is in following the above methodological approach that the question of humanness is required to be addressed. Following from the investigation of humanness considered in this work, the manifestation of the aptitude of humanness must now be the focus of any Critique of Humanness. What has been determined here is the fundamental ontology of *Dasein*. What remains to be determined is the precise meaning of being human which can now be thoroughly examined through a philosophical anthropology. It is clear, however, with humanness as the nature of being human and all that has been articulated in the preceding discussion, that when considering both the anthropological aspects and the metaphysics of *Dasein*, being human must in some way be that which allows for the bridging of the *world* of relations and the *world itself.*

Bibliography

Absher, Brandon (2016): "'Speaking of Being: Language, Speech, and Silence' in *Being and Time*". In: *The Journal of Speculative Philosophy* 30 (2): pp. 204-231.
Achourioti, Theodora and Michiel van Lambalgen (2011): "A Formalization of Kant's Transcendental Logic". In: *Review of Symbolic Logic* 4 (2): pp. 254-289.
Adams, David (1991): "Metaphors for Mankind: The Development of Hans Blumenberg's Anthropological Metaphorology". In: *Journal of the History of Ideas* 52 (1): pp. 152-166. doi:10.2307/2709587.
Adams, E. M (2007): "On Being a Human Being." In: *The Pluralist* 2 (1): pp. 1-15.
Adams, Robert Merrihew (1997): "Things in Themselves." In: *Philosophy and Phenomenological Research* 57 (4): pp. 801-285. doi:10.2307/2953804.
Adams, Douglas (1993): *Mostly Harmless* (Hitchhiker's Trilogy, No 5). New York: Ballantine Books.
Ainslie, Donald C (2015): *Hume's True Scepticism*. Oxford: Oxford University Press.
Al-Ahsan, Abullah (1999): "The Origin of Human History and the First Man." In: *Islamic Studies* 38 (1): pp. 63-86.
Alighieri, Dante (1921): *The Divine Comedy of Dante Alighieri. The Italian Text with a Translation in English Blank Verse and a Commentary by Courtney Langdon, Vol. 3 Paradiso*. Cambridge (MA): Harvard University Press.
Allais, Lucy (2004): "Kant's One World: Interpreting 'Transcendental Idealism'". In *British Journal for the History of Philosophy* 12 (4): pp. 655–684.
Allison, Henry E (1976): "The Non-spatiality of Things in Themselves for Kant." In: *Journal of the History of Philosophy* 14 (3): pp. 313-321.
Allison, Henry E (1978): "Things in Themselves, Noumena, and the Transcendental Object." In: *Dialectica* 32 (1): pp. 41-76.
Allison, Henry E (2004): *Kant's Transcendental Idealism: An Interpretation and Defense; Revised and Enlarged Edition*. New Haven; London: Yale University Press
Allison, Henry E (2009): "Kant's Transcendental Idealism." In: Bird, Graham (Ed.): *A Companion to Kant*. Oxford: Blackwell Publishing Ltd, pp. 111-124.
Allison, Henry E. (1973): "Kant's critique of Berkeley". In: *Journal of the History of Philosophy* 11 (1): pp. 43-63.
Almog, Joseph (2014): *Everything In Its Right Place: Spinoza and Life By The Light Of Nature*. New York: Oxford University Press.
Aportone, Anselmo (2009): *Gestalten der Transzendentalen Einheit: Bedingungen der Synthesis bei Kant*. Berlin; New York: De Gruyter.
Aquila, Richard E (1998): "Self-consciousness, Self-determination, and Imagination in Kant." In: *Topoi* 7 (1): pp. 65-79.
Aquila, Richard E (2009): "The Relationship between Pure and Empirical Intuition in Kant." In: *Kant-Studien* 68 (1-4): pp. 275-289.
Aquinas, Thomas (1984): *Questions on the Soul*. Milwaukee: Marquette University Press.
Aquinas, Thomas (2012): *Summa Theologiae: Complete Set*. New York: Aquinas Institute.
Arendt, Hannah (1958): *The Human Condition*. Chicago: University of Chicago Press.
Aristotle (1957): *Politica* [Translated by W.D. Ross]. Oxford: Clarendon Press.
Aristotle (1973): *Nicomachean Ethics* [Translated by Leonard Hugh Graham Greenwood]. New York: Arno Press.

Aristotle (1975): *Categories and De Interpretione* [Translated by J. L. Ackrill]. Oxford: Clarendon Press.
Aristotle (2001) *De Anima* [Translated by Joe Sachs]. Santa Fe, NM: Green Lion Press.
Aristotle (2002): *Aristotle's Metaphysics* [Translated by Joe Sachs]. Santa Fe, NM: Green Lion Press.
Aristotle (2017): *Physica* [Translated by Rosin Waterfield and David Bostak]. New York: Dover publications.
Armstrong, David Malet (1989): *Universals: An Opinionated Introduction*. Boulder: Westview.
Arnold, Sir Edwin (1898): *The Light of Asia: Or, The Great Renunciation (Mahâbhinishkramana)*. Boston: Roberts Brothers.
Auden, W. H. (1940): "As I Walked Out One Evening." In: *Another Time; Poems*. New York: Random House.
Avicenna (1917): "Avicenna On Medicine." In Charles Francis Horne (Ed.): *The Sacred Books & Early Literature of the East*. New York: Parke, Austin, and Lipscomb inc.
Azeri, Siyaves (2010): "Transcendental Subject vs Empirical Self: On Kant's Account of Subjectivity." In: *Filozofia* 65 (3): pp. 269–283.
Bacon, Francis (2013): *The Advancement of Learning: Book I*. Cambridge (UK): Cambridge University Press.
Bacon, Roger (1928): *Opus Majus* [Translation by Robert Burke]. Philadelphia: University of Pennsylvania Press.
Badiou, Alain (2005): *Le siècle*. Paris: Éditions du Seuil.
Baggott, Jim. (2017): *Mass: The Quest to Understand Matter from Greek Atoms to Quantum Fields*. Oxford: Oxford University Press.
Baier, Kurt (2008): "The Meaning of Life." In Klemke, E.D. and Steven M. Cahn (Ed.): *The Meaning of Life* 3rd edition. New York: Oxford University Press, pp. 101–132.
Bailey, Philip James (1857): *The Festus Birthday*. Boston: Sanborn, Carter, Bazin & Co.
Ballard, Edward G., James K Feibleman, Paul G. Morrison, Andrew J. Reck, Robert C. Whittemore (1962): *Studies in Social Philosophy*. The Hague: Springer.
Banham, Gary (2005): *Kant's Transcendental Imagination*. London: Palgrave Macmillan
Bartlett, Anthony W. (2003): "A Flight of God: M. Heidegger and R. Girard." In: *Revista Portuguesa De Filosofia* 59 (4): 101-120.
Baudrillard, Jean (1980): *Simulations*. New York: Semiotext.
Beare, John I. (1906): *Greek Theories of Elementary Cognition: From Alcmaeon to Aristotle*. Eastford: Martino Press.
Beck, W. David (2002): "The Cosmological Argument: A Current Bibliographical Appraisal." In: *Philosophia Christi* 2 (2): pp. 283-304.
Beerling, R. F. (1955): "Power and Human Nature." In: *Philosophy and Phenomenological Research* 16 (2): pp. 214-22. doi:10.2307/2103774.
Beiser, Frederick C. (2002): *German Idealism: The Struggle against Subjectivism, 1781-1801*. Cambridge (MA): Harvard University Press.
Benardete, José A. (1954): "On Being and Nothing." In: *Review of Metaphysics* 7 (3): pp. 363-367.
Bencivenga, Ermanno (1987): *Kant's Copernican Revolution*. Oxford: Oxford University Press.
Bennett, Jonathan (1968): "Strawson on Kant." In: *The Philosophical Review* 77 (3): pp. 340-49. doi:10.2307/2183571.

Benso, Silvia (2018): "The Breathing of the Air: Presocratic Echoes in Levinas." In Škof, Lenart and Petri Berndtson (ed.): *Atmospheres of Breathing*, Albany: SUNY Press.
Bentham, Jeremy (1879): *An Introduction to the Principles of Morals and Legislation*. Oxford: Clarendon Press.
Bergson, Henri (1911): *Creative Evolution* [Translated by Arthur Mitchell]. New York: H. Holt.
Berkeley, George (1995). *A Treatise concerning the Principles of Human Knowledge* [Edited by Kenneth Winkler]. Indianapolis: Hackett Publishing.
Bird, Graham (2006): *The Revolutionary Kant: A Commentary on the Critique of Pure Reason*. Chicago: Open Court.
Blondel, Maurice (1984): *Action*. Indiana: Notre Dame Press.
Blumenberg, Hans (2010): *Paradigms for a Metaphorology*. Ithaca (NY): Cornell University Press.
Borsari, Andrea (2009): "Notes on 'Philosophical Anthropology' in Germany. An Introduction". In: *Iris* 1 (1): pp. 113-129.
Boswell, James (1831): *The Life of Samuel Johnson*. London: John Murray.
Boyle, Matthew (2009): "Two Kinds of Self-Knowledge." In: *Philosophy and Phenomenological Research* 78 (1): pp. 133-64.
Boym, Svetlana (2009): "From Love to Worldliness: Hannah Arendt and Martin Heidegger." In: *The Yearbook of Comparative Literature* 55: pp. 106–128.
Brandom, Robert B. (1994): *Making it Explicit: Reasoning, Representing, and Discursive Commitment*. Cambridge (MA): Harvard University Press.
Bremer, Manuel (2008): "Transcendental Logic Redefined." In: *Review of Contemporary Philosophy* 7.
Brittan, Gordon G. (2015): *Kant's Theory of Science*. Princeton: Princeton University Press.
Brown, Donald E. (1999): "Human Nature and History." In: *History and Theory* 38 (4): pp. 138-57.
Brown, James (1967): *Kierkegaard, Heidegger, Buber and Barth: Subject and object in modern theology*. New York: Collier.
Bruno, Giordano (1998): *Giordano Bruno: Cause, Principle and Unity: And Essays on Magic* [Edited by Richard J. Blackwell and Robert de Lucca]. Cambridge: Cambridge University Press.
Bryant, Levi R. (2010): "Onticology– A Manifesto for Object-oriented ontology Part I." [Larval Subjects] https://larvalsubjects.wordpress.com/2010/01/12/object-oriented-ontology-a-manifesto-part-i/, Accessed September 9, 2017.
Bryant, Levi R., Nick Srnicek, and Graham Harman (2011): *The Speculative Turn: Continental Materialism and Realism*. Melbourne: re.Press.
Buber, Martin (1945): "The Philosophical Anthropology of Max Scheler." In: *Philosophy and Phenomenological Research* 6 (2): pp. 307-321. doi:10.2307/2102887.
Buber, Martin (1997): *Ich und Du*. Gütersloh: Gütersloher Verlagshaus.
Buber, Martin (2002): *Between Man and Man*. London; New York: Routledge
Bultmann, Rudolf (1991): *Rudolf Bultmann: Interpreting Faith for the Modern Era* [Edited by Roger A. Johnson]. Minneapolis: Fortress Press.
Buroker, Jill Vance (1981): *Space and Incongruence: The Origin of Kant's Idealism*. Dordrecht: Reidel.
Butts, Robert E. (1959): "Hume's Scepticism." In: *Journal of the History of Ideas* 20 (3): pp. 413-419.

Byron, George Gordon (Lord). (1885): *Childe Harold* [Edited by H.F. Tozer]. Oxford: Clarendon Press.
Cajori, Florian (1899): *A History of Physics in Its Elementary Branches: Including the Evolution of Physical Laboratories*. New York: Macmillan.
Camus, Albert (1991): *The Myth of Sisyphus and Other Essays* [Translated by Justin O'Brien]. New York: Vintage.
Caputo, John D (1983): "The Thought of Being and the Conversation of Mankind: The Case of Heidegger and Rorty." In: *The Review of Metaphysics* 36 (3): pp. 661-85.
Carbone, Guelfo (2016): "Kant's Antinomies Concerning the World Problem Starting from Cassirer-Heidegger's Debate in Davos (1929)". In *The Cosmos and the Creative Imagination*. Analecta Husserliana (The Yearbook of Phenomenological Research) [Edited by AT. Tymieniecka, P. Trutty-Coohill] vol. 119. New York: Springer.
Carnap, Rudolph (1934): *The Unity of Science* [Translated by Max Black]. London: K. Paul, Trench, Trubner & Co.
Carr, David (1977): "Kant, Husserl, and the Nonempirical Ego." In: *The Journal of Philosophy* 74 (11): pp. 682-690. doi:10.2307/2025771.
Carr, David (1987): "The Problem of the Non-Empirical Ego: Husserl and Kant." In *Interpreting Husserl*. Phaenomenologica (Collection Fondée par H.L. van Breda et Publiée Sous le Patronage Des Centres D'Archives-Husserl), vol 106. Dordrecht: Springer, pp. 137–156.
Carr, David (1994): "The Question of the Subject: Heidegger and the Transcendental Tradition." In: *Human Studies* 17 (4): pp. 403-418.
Carus, Paul (1915): "Kant's Antinomies and their Solution." In: *The Monist* 25 (4): pp. 627–632.
Cassirer, E. (1944). An Essay on Man: An Introduction to Human Culture. New Haven: Yale University Press.
Chalmers, David (1996): *The Conscious Mind: In Search of a Fundamental Theory*. New York; Oxford: Oxford University Press.
Chipman, Lauchlan (1972): "Kant's Categories and their Schematism." In: *Kant-Studien* 63 (1-4): pp. 36-50.
Chomsky, Noam (1957): *Syntactic Structures*. The Hague: Mouton.
Chong, Woei Lien (1999): "Combining Marx with Kant: The Philosophical Anthropology of Li Zehou." In: *Philosophy East and West* 49 (2): pp. 120-149. doi:10.2307/1400199.
Cicero, Marcus Tullius (1834): *Oeuvres Completes De Ciceron* [Edited by M. Matter]. Paris: C.L.F. Panckoucke.
Cirulli, Franco (2013): *Hegel's Critique of Essence: A Reading of the Wesenlogic*. London: Routledge.
Clark, Stephan R. L. (1975) *Aristotle's Man: Speculations upon Aristotelian Anthropology*. Oxford: Clarendon Press.
Cole, Andrew (2013): "The Call of Things: A Critique of Object-Oriented Ontologies." In: *The Minnesota Review* 80: pp. 106–118.
Condorcet, Jean-Antoine-Nicolas De Caritat (1979): *Sketch for a Historical Picture of the Progress of the Human Mind* [Translated by June Barraclough]. Westport (CT): Hyperion Press.
Coreth, Emerich (1976): "Was ist der Mensch?" In *Zeitschrift für Philosophische Forschung* 30 (4): pp. 634–638.
Coreth, Emerich (1991): *Antropologia filosofica*. Brescia: Morcelliana.

Craig, William Lane (1979): *The Kalām Cosmological Argument*. London: MacMillan.
Dahlstrom, Daniel O. (2002): "Scheler's Critique of Heidegger's Fundamental Ontology." In Schneck, Stephen (ed.): *Max Scheler's Acting Persons: New Perspectives*. Amsterdam: Rodopi, pp. 67-92.
Dahlstrom, Daniel O. (2017): "Rethinking Difference." In Zaborowski H. (ed.): *Heidegger's Question of Being*. Washington, D.C.: Catholic University of America Press, pp. 8-25.
Dallmayr, Fred R. (1980): "Heidegger on Intersubjectivity." In: *Human Studies* 3 (3): pp. 221-46.
Dallmayr, Fred R. (1987): "Politics of the Kingdom: Pannenberg's Anthropology." In: *The Review of Politics* 49 (1): pp. 85-111.
Darwin, Charles (2004): *The Descent of Man, and Selection in Relation to Sex* [Edited by Adrian J. Desmond, and James R. Moore]. London: Penguin.
de La Bruyère, Jean (1836): *Les caractères de La Bruyère: Suivis des Caractères de Théophraste* [Edited by Jean-Joseph-François Dussault]. Paris: Chez Lefèvre.
Delille, Jacques (1833): *Oeuvres de J. Delille*. Paris: Lefevre.
Deleuze, Gilles, and Félix Guattari (1980): *Mille Plateau*. Paris: Éditions de minuit.
Dennett, Daniel (1988): "Quining Qualia". In: Marcel, A. J., and E. Bisiach (ed.): *Consciousness in Contemporary Science*. Oxford: Clarendon Press.
Derrida, Jacques (2004): *For What Tomorrow: A Dialogue*. Stanford: Stanford University Press.
Descartes, Rene (1664): *Principia Philosophiæ*. Amstelodami: apud Danielem Elzevirium.
Descartes, René (1908): *Discours de la méthode de Descartes: avec notes tirées de ses oeuvres, de celles de ses disciples et des méthodistes*. Paris: Librairie Cerf.
Descartes, René (2011): *Meditations on First Philosophy: With Selections from the Objections and Replies* [Translated by John Cottingham]. Cambridge: Cambridge University Press.
Desmond, William (1995): *Being and the Between*. Albany: SUNY Press.
Dewey, John (2008): *The Later Works of John Dewey, 1925–1953* [Edited by Jo Ann Boydston]. Carbondale (IL): Southern Illinois University.
Dicker, Georges (2004): *Kant's Theory of Knowledge: An Analytical Introduction*. New York: Oxford University Press.
Dicker, Georges (2011): *Berkeley's Idealism: A Critical Examination*. Oxford: Oxford University Press.
Diels, Hermann (1903): *Die Fragmente der Vorsokratiker Griechisch und Deutsch*. Berlin: Weidmann.
Dingli, Sandra M. (2005): *On Thinking and the World: John McDowell's Mind and World*. Aldershot: Ashgate.
Diogenes Laertius (2015): *The Lives and Opinions of Eminent Philosophers* [Translated by Charles Duke Yonge]. Rochester: Scholar's Choice.
Dreyfus, Hubert (2008): "Interpreting Heidegger on *Das Man*." In: *Inquiry* 38 (4): pp. 423-430.
Dryden, John (1672): *The Conquest of Granada by the Spaniards*. London: H. Herringman.
Du Sautoy, Marcus (2008): *Symmetry: A Journey Into the Patterns of Nature*. New York: Harper.
Easterling, H. J. (1976): "The Unmoved Mover in Early Aristotle." In: *Phronesis* 21 (3): pp. 252-65.
Edwards, Steven D (1998): "The body as object versus the body as subject: The case of disability." In: *Medicine, Health Care, Philosophy* 1: pp. 47–56.

Elpidorou, Andreas, and Laura Freeman (2015): "Affectivity in Heidegger I: Moods and Emotions in Being and Time." In: *Philosophy Compass* 10: pp. 661-671.
Emerson, Ralph W. (1903): *Essays*. Boston; New York: Houghton, Mifflin, and Company.
Emerson, Ralph W. (1904): *The Complete Works Of Ralph Waldo Emerson: Letters And Social Aims [Vol. 8]*. Edited by Edward Waldo Emerson. Boston; New York: Mifflin Houghton.
Empiricus, Sextus (2000): *Sextus Empiricus IV: Against the Professors* [Translated by R.G. Bury]. Cambridge (MA): Harvard University Press.
Evans, Joseph Claude (1984): *The Metaphysics of Transcendental Subjectivity: Descartes, Kant, and W. Sellars*. Amsterdam: B.R. Grüner.
Fairclough, Norman (2008). *Analysing Discourse: Textual Analysis for Social Research*. London: Routledge.
Feng, Youlan (1952): *A History of Chinese Philosophy* [Translated by Derek Bodde]. Princeton: Princeton University Press.
Fichte, Johann Gottlieb (1994): *Introductions to the Wissenschaftslehre and Other Writings* [Translated by Daniel Breazeale]. Indianapolis: Hackett Publishing Company.
Fink, Eugen (2016): *Play as Symbol of the World and Other Writings* [Translated by Ian Alexander Moore and Christopher Turner]. Bloomington, Indiana: Indiana University Press.
Fischer, Joachim (2009): "Exploring the Core Identity of Philosophical Anthropology Through the Works of Max Scheler, Helmuth Plessner, and Arnold Gehlen". In: *Iris* 1 (1): pp. 153-170.
Forster, Michael N. (2009): *Kant and Skepticism*. Princeton: Princeton University Press.
Frege, Gottlob (1995): *Translations from the Philosophical Writings of Gottlob Frege* [Edited by Peter Geach and Max Black]. Oxford: Blackwell, 1995.
Friedman, Lawrence (1954): "Kant's Theory of Time." In: *The Review of Metaphysics* 7 (3): pp. 379-388.
Frings, Manfred S. (2001): *The Mind of Max Scheler: The First Comprehensive Guide Based on the Complete Works*. Milwaukee: Marquette University Press.
Gabriel, Markus (2015): *Fields of Sense: A New Realist Ontology*. Edinburgh: Edinburgh University Press.
Gabriel, Markus (2017): *Why the World Does Not Exist* [Translated by Gregory S. Moss]. Cambridge: Polity Press.
Garcia, Tristan (2014): *Form and Object: A Treatise on Things* [Translated by Mark Allan Ohm, and Jon Cogburn]. Edinburgh: Edinburgh University Press.
Gass, Michael (1994): "Kant's Causal Conception of Autonomy." In: *History of Philosophy Quarterly 11* (1): pp. 53–70.
Gaston, Sean (2013): *The Concept of World from Kant to Derrida*. London; New York: Rowman & Littlefield International.
Gazzaniga, Michael S. (2009): *Human: The Science Behind What Makes Us Unique*. New York: Harper Perennial.
Gehlen, Arnold (2016): *Der Mensch Seine Natur und seine Stellung in der Welt* [Edited by Karl-Siegbert Rehberg]. Frankfurt am Main: Klostermann Vittorio.
Giovanelli, Marco (2011): *Reality and Negation – Kant's Principle of Anticipations of Perception*. New York: Springer.
Girard, René (1988): *"To Double Business Bound": Essays on Literature, Mimesis, and Anthropology*. London: Athlone.

Glass, Ronald (1971): "The Contradictions in Kant's Examples." In: *Philosophical Studies: An International Journal for Philosophy in the Analytic Tradition* 22 (5/6): pp. 65-70.
Golob, Sacha (2013): "Heidegger on Kant, Time and the 'Form' of Intentionality." In: *British Journal for the History of Philosophy* 21 (2): pp. 345-367.
Gotterbarn, Donald (2009): "Kant, Hume and Analyticity." In: *Kant-Studien* 65 (1-4): pp. 274-283.
Gould, Stephen J. (1992): *Ever Since Darwin: Reflections in Natural History.* New York; London: W. W. Norton.
Grabau, Richard F. (1963): "Kant's Concept of the Thing-in-itself: An Interpretation." In: *The Review of Metaphysics* 16 (4): pp. 770–779.
Gram, Moltke S. (1981): "Intellectual Intuition: The Continuity Thesis." In: *Journal of the History of Ideas* 42 (2): pp. 287-304.
Gray, J. Glenn (1952): "Heidegger's 'Being'". In: *The Journal of Philosophy* 49 (12): pp. 415-422.
Greenberg, Robert (2001): *Kant's Theory of a Priori Knowledge.* University Park: Pennsylvania State University Press.
Grenberg, Jeanine (2011): "Making Sense of the Relationship of Reason and Sensibility in Kant's Ethics". In: *Kantian Review* 16 (3): pp. 461–472.
Groff, Ruth (2014): *Subject and Object: Frankfurt School Writings on Epistemology, Ontology, and Method.* London: Bloomsbury.
Guidi, Lucilla (2017): "Moods as Groundlessness of the Human Experience. Heidegger and Wittgenstein on Stimmung." In: Philosophia 45 (4): pp. 1599-1611.
Gurwitsch, Aron (1966): *Studies in Phenomenology and Psychology.* Evanston: Northwestern University Press.
Guyer, Paul (2005): *Kant's System of Nature and Freedom: Selected Essays.* Oxford: Clarendon Press.
Häberlin, Paul (1969): *Der Mensch, eine philosophische Anthropologie.* Zürich: Schweizer Spiegel Verlag.
Harman, Graham (2002): *Tool-Being: Heidegger and the Metaphysics of Objects.* Chicago: Open Court.
Harman, Graham (2007): "On Vicarious Causation." In Mackay, Robin (ed): *Collapse II.* Windsor: Urbanomic, pp. 171–206.
Harman, Graham (2010): "Technology, Objects and Things in Heidegger." In: *Cambridge Journal of Economics* 34 (19): pp. 17-25.
Harman, Graham (2011): *The Quadruple Object.* Winchester: Zero Books.
Harman, Graham (2012): *Weird Realism: Lovecraft and Philosophy.* Winchester: Zero Books.
Harman, Graham (2015): "Materialism is Not the Solution: On Matter, Form, and Mimesis." In: *Nordic Journal of Aesthetics* 24 (47): pp. 94-110.
Harris, Sam (2014): *Waking Up: A Guide To Spirituality Without Religion.* New York: Simon & Schuster.
Harris, William T. (1894): "Kant's Third Antinomy and His Fallacy Regarding the First Cause." In: *The Philosophical Review* 3 (1): pp. 1-13. doi:10.2307/2175451.
Hartmann, Nicolai (1940): *Der Aufbau der realen Welt: Grundriß d. allg. Kategorienlehre.* Berlin: De Gruyter.

Hatfield, Gary (2006): "Kant on the perception of space (and time)." In Guyer, Paul (ed.): *The Cambridge Companion to Kant and Modern Philosophy.* Cambridge: Cambridge University Press, pp. 61-93.
Haugeland, John (2013): *Dasein Disclosed* [Edited by Joseph Rouse]. Cambridge (MA): Harvard University Press.
Hawking, Steven, and Leonard Mlodinow (2010): *The Grand Design: New Answers to the Ultimate Questions of Life.* London: Bantam Press.
Hegel, Georg Wilhelm Friedrich (1977): *Phenomenology of Spirit* [Translated by A.V. Miller]. Oxford: Oxford University Press.
Hegel, Georg Wilhelm Friedrich (2010): *The Science of Logic* [Translated and Edited by George Di Giovanni]. Cambridge: Cambridge University Press.
Heidegger, Martin (1961): *An Introduction to Metaphysics* [Translated by Ralph Manheim]. New York: Doubleday, Anchor Books.
Heidegger, Martin (1977): "Letter on Humanism." In David Farrell Krell (Ed.): *Basic writings: Second edition, revised and expanded.* New York: Harper & Row, pp. 189–242.
Heidegger, Martin (1982): *The Basic Problems of Phenomenology* [Translated by Albert Hofstadter]. Bloomington: Indiana University Press.
Heidegger, Martin (1991): *Nietzsche vol. 1* [Edited by David Krell]. San Francisco: Harper.
Heidegger, Martin (1997): *Kant and the Problem of Metaphysics.* Bloomington: Indiana University Press.
Heidegger, Martin (2010): *Being and Time* [Translated by Joan Stambaugh]. Albany: SUNY Press.
Heidegger, Martin (2011): *The Concept of Time* [Translated by Ingo Farin]. New York: Continuum.
Heidegger, Martin (2018): "Was ist Metaphysik? Urfassung" [Edited by Dieter Thoma]. In: *Philosophy Today* 63 (3): pp. 733-751.
Heidegger, Martin (2001): *Poetry, Language, Thought* [Translated by Alfred Hofstadter]. New York: HarperCollins.
Heisenberg, Werner (2000): *Physics and Philosophy: The Revolution in Modern Science.* London: Penguin Classics.
Henry, Michel (1993): "The Soul According to Descartes." In: Voss, Stephen (ed.): *Essays on the Philosophy and Science of Rene Descartes.* New York; Oxford: Oxford University Press.
Henry, Richard Conn (2005): "The Mental Universe." In: *Nature* 436 (7047): pp. 29.
Héraclite d'Éphèse (1954): *The Cosmic Fragments* [Translated by Geoffrey Stephen Kirk]. Cambridge: Cambridge University Press.
Hesse, Herman (1963): *Steppenwolf.* New York: Henry Holt & Company.
Hobbes, Thomas (1994): *Leviathan: With Selected Variants from the Latin Edition of 1668* [Translated by E. M. Curley]. Indianapolis: Hackett Publishing.
Hogan, Desmond (2009a): "Three Kinds of Rationalism and the Non-Spatiality of Things in Themselves." In: *Journal of the History of Philosophy* 47 (3): pp. 355-382.
Hogan, Desmond (2009b): "How to Know Unknowable Things in Themselves." In: *Noûs* 43: pp. 49-63.
Horowitz, Asher (1990): "'Laws and Customs Thrust Us Back into Infancy': Rousseau's Historical Anthropology." In: *The Review of Politics* 52 (2): pp. 215-241.

Howell, Robert (1992): *Kant's Transcendental Deduction: An Analysis of Main Themes in His Critical Philosophy*. Dordrecht: Kluwer Academic Publishing.
Hume, David (1896): *A Treatise of Human Nature* [Edited by Lewis Amherst Selby-Bigge]. Oxford: Clarendon Press.
Hume, David (1995): *An Enquiry concerning Human Understanding* [Edited by Eric Steinberg]. Indianapolis: Hackett.
Husserl, Edmund (1964): *The Idea of Phenomenology* [Translated by William P. Alston and George Nakhnikian]. The Hague: Martinus Nijhoff.
Ingold, Tim (2002): "Culture and the perception of the environment." In: Croll, Elisabeth and David Parkin (ed.): *Bush Base, Forest Farm*. London: Routledge, pp. 51-68
Jackson, Michael (2008): *Existential Anthropology: Events, Exigencies, and Effects*. New York: Berghahn Books.
Jacobi, Friedrich Heinrich (1976): *Friedrich Heinrich Jacobi Werke Vol. 2* [Edited by Friedrich Roth and J.G Hamann]. Darmstadt: Wissenschaftliche Buchgesellschaft.
Jeans, James (2009): *Physics and Philosophy*. Cambridge: Cambridge University Press.
Jenkins, Scott (2010): "Hegel on Space: A Critique of Kant's Transcendental Philosophy." In: *Inquiry* 53 (4): pp.326-355.
Jiménez, Juan Ramón (1957): *Selected Writings of Juan Ramon Jimenez* [Translated by H. R. Hays and Edited by Eugenio Florit]. New York: Farrar, Straus, and Giroux.
Johnston, Adrian (2008): *Žižek's Ontology: A Transcendental Materialist Theory of Subjectivity*. Evanston: Northwestern University Press.
Justin, Gale D (1977): "Re-Relating Kant and Berkeley." In: *Kant-Studien* 68 (1): pp. 77.
Juvenal and Persius (2004): *Juvenal and Persius* [Translated by Susanna Morton Braund]. Cambridge (MA): Harvard University Press.
Kant, Immanuel (1807): *Monadologia Physica: diss. hab. anno 1756*. Königsberg.
Kant, Immanuel (1976): *Allgemeine Naturgeschichte und Theorie des Himmels, oder, Versuch von der Verfassung und dem mechanischen Ursprunge des ganzen Weltgebäudes nach Newtonischen Grundsätzen abgehandelt*. New York: Readex Microprint Corporation.
Kant, Immanuel (1992): "On the form and principles of the sensible and the intelligible world [inaugural dissertation]." In: Walford, David and Ralf Meerbote (ed.): *The Cambridge Edition of the Works of Immanuel Kant. Theoretical Philosophy 1755-1770*. Cambridge: Cambridge University Press, pp. 377-416.
Kant, Immanuel (2003): "The Only Possible Argument In Support of A Demonstration of The Existence Of God (1763)." In: Walford, David and Ralf Meerbote (ed.): *The Cambridge Edition of the Works of Immanuel Kant. Theoretical Philosophy 1755-1770*. Cambridge: Cambridge University Press, pp. 107–202.
Kant, Immanuel (2004): *Prolegomena to Any Future Metaphysics: That Will Be Able to Come Forward as Science: With Selections from the Critique of Pure Reason* [Edited by Gary Hatfield]. Cambridge (UK): Cambridge University Press.
Kant, Immanuel (2007): *Critique of Pure Reason* [Translated by Norman Kemp Smith]. Basingstoke: Palgrave Macmillan.
Kant, Immanuel (2013): *Anthropology, History, and Education*. [Edited by Robert B. Louden]. Cambridge: Cambridge University Press.
Käufer, Stephan (2005): "The Nothing and the Ontological Difference in Heidegger's *What is Metaphysics?*" In: *Inquiry* 48 (6): pp. *482-506*.
Kaufmann, Walter (2004): *Existentialism: From Dostoevsky to Sartre*. New York: Penguin.

Kaye, Lawrence J. (2015): *Kant's Transcendental Deduction of the Categories: Unity, Representation, and Apperception*. Lanham: Lexington Books.
Keller, Pierre (1999): *Kant and the Demands of Self-Consciousness*. Cambridge: Cambridge University Press.
Kelly, Derek A. (1968): "Richard M. Zaner on Philosophical Anthropology." In: *Philosophy and Phenomenological Research* 29 (1): pp. 119-122. doi:10.2307/2105824.
Kierkegaard, Søren (2019): *Concluding Unscientific Postscript* [Translated by David F. Swenson, Walter Lowrie and Joseph Campbell]. Princeton: Princeton University Press.
Kirk, Geoffrey S., John E. Raven, and Malcolm Schofield (1983): *The Presocratic Philosophers: A Critical History with a Selection of Texts*. Cambridge: Cambridge University Press.
Kisiel, Theodore (1992): "Das Kriegsnotsemester 1919: Heideggers Durchbruch zur hermeneutischen Phànomenologie." In: *Philosophisches Jahrbuch* 99: pp. 105-122.
Kisiel, Theodore (2014): "Why the First Draft of *Being and Time* was Never Published." In: *Journal of the British Society for Phenomenology* 20 (1): pp. 3-22.
Kitcher, Patricia (1996): "Kant's Epistemological Problem and Its Coherent Solution." In: *Philosophical Perspectives* 13: pp. 415-441.
Kleingeld, Pauline (2017): "Contradiction and Kant's Formula of Universal Law." In: *Kant-Studien* 108 (1): pp. 89-115.
Kline, Morris (1974): *Mathematical Thought from Ancient to Modern times*. New York: Oxford University Press.
Kneller, Jane (2007): *Kant and the Power of Imagination*. Cambridge: Cambridge University Press.
Kohák, Erazim (1981): "Anti-Gorgias: Being and Nothing as Experience." In: *Human Studies* 4 (3): pp. 209-222.
Koons, Robert C. (1997): "A New Look at the Cosmological Argument." In: *American Philosophical Quarterly* 34 (2): pp. 193–212
Korab-Karpowicz, Włodzimierz Julian (2016): *The Presocratics in the Thought of Martin Heidegger*. Bern: Peter Lang.
Kraus, Björn 2015): "The Life We Live and the Life We Experience: Introducing the Epistemological Difference between 'Lifeworld' (Lebenswelt) and 'Life Conditions' (Lebenslage)." In: *Social Work and Society International Online Journal* 13 (2): 4.
Krausser, Peter (1973): "'Form of Intuition' and 'Formal Intuition' in Kant's Theory of Experience and Science." In: *Studies in History and Philosophy of Science Part A* 4 (3): pp. 279-287.
Krebs, Angelika and Ben-Ze'ev, Aaron (2017): "Preface to the Meaning of Moods." In: *Philosophia* 45: 1395–1397.
Kripke, Saul (1980): *Naming and Necessity*. Cambridge (MA): Harvard University Press.
La Mettrie, Julien Offray de (1996): *La Mettrie: Machine Man and Other Writings* [Edited by Ann Thomson]. Cambridge: Cambridge University Press.
La Rochefoucauld, François (1959): *Maxims*. New York: Random House.
Lachs, John (1990): "Human Natures." In: *Proceedings and Addresses of the American Philosophical Association* 63 (7): pp. 29-39. doi:10.2307/3130184.
Lacour, Claudia Brodsky (1996): *Lines of Thought: Discourse, Architectonics and the Origin of Modern Philosophy*. Durham: Duke University Press.
Land, Thomas (2006): "Kant's Spontaneity Thesis." In: *Philosophical Topics* 34 (1): pp. 189–220.

Langsam, Harold (1994): "Kant, Hume, and Our Ordinary Concept of Causation." In: *Philosophy and Phenomenological Research* 54 (3): pp. 625-647.
Langton, Rae (1998): *Kantian Humility: Our Ignorance of Things in Themselves*. Oxford: Oxford University Press.
Latour, Bruno (2005): *Reassembling the Social: An Introduction to Actor-Network-Theory*. Oxford: Oxford University Press.
Lau, Chong-Fuk (2010): "Kant's Epistemological Reorientation of Ontology." In: *Kant Yearbook* 2: pp. 123-146.
Lautréamont, Comte de (1874): *Les Chants de Maldoror*. Paris; Bruxelles: En vente chez tous les libraires.
Leary, David E. (1982): "Immanuel Kant and the Development of Modern Psychology." In: Woodward, William Ray and Mitchell G. Ash (ed.): *The Problematic Science: Psychology in Nineteenth-Century Thought*. New York: Praeger, pp. 17-42.
Leibniz, Gottfried W. (1907): *Discours de métaphysique*. France: Félix Alcan.
Leibniz, Gottfried W. (1886): *La Monadologie ed. Bertrand*. Paris: Eugene Belin.
Leibniz, Gottfried W. (1991): *Discourse on Metaphysics and Other Essays* [Translated by Daniel Garber, and Roger Ariew]. Indianapolis: Hackett.
Liang, Yibin (2017): "Kant on Consciousness, Obscure Representations and Cognitive Availability." In: *The Philosophical Forum* 48: pp. 345-368.
Locke, John (2012): *Two Treatises of Government* [Edited by Peter Laslett]. Cambridge: Cambridge University Press.
Locke, John. (1824): *The Works of John Locke, in nine volumes*. London: C. and J. Rivington.
Logan, David C. (2009): "Known knowns, known unknowns, unknown unknowns and the propagation of scientific enquiry." In: *Journal of Experimental Botany* 60 (3): pp. 712-714.
Loke, Andrew (2014): "A Modified Philosophical Argument for A Beginning of The Universe." In: *Think* 13: pp. 71–83
Longuenesse, Béatrice (1998): *Kant and the Capacity to Judge: Sensibility and Discursivity in the Transcendental Analytic of the 'Critique of Pure Reason'*. Princeton: Princeton University Press.
Lovecraft, H.P. (2007): *Collected Works, vol. 5* [Edited by S. T. Joshi]. New York: Hippocampus Press.
Lovejoy, Arthur O. (1978): *The Great Chain of Being: A Study of the History of an Idea*. Cambridge (MA): Harvard University Press.
Lowe, Edward Jonathan (1994): "Primitive Substances." In: *Philosophy and Phenomenological Research* 55 (3): pp. 531-52.
Lucretius (1948): *Lucretius On the Nature of Things* [Translated by Cyril Bailey]. Oxford: Clarendon Press.
Lucretius (2008): *De Rerum Natura: The Latin Text of Lucretius* [Edited by William Ellery Leonard and Stanley Barney Smith]. Madison: University of Wisconsin Press.
Lytton, Edward Robert Bulwer (1867): *Clytemnestra: And Poems Lyrical and Descriptive*. London: Chapman and Hall.
Machiavelli, Niccolò (1995): *The Prince* [Edited by Quentin Skinner and Russell Price]. Cambridge: Cambridge University Press.
Mainländer, Philipp (1894): *Die Philosophie der Erlösung*. Frankfurt a. M: Jaeger.
Mandt, A. J. (1997): "Fichte, Kant's Legacy, and the Meaning of Modern Philosophy." In: *The Review of Metaphysics* 50 (3): pp. 591-633.

Maréchal, Joseph (1970): *A Marechal Reader* [Edited by Joseph F. Donceel]. New York: Herder.
Marion, Jean-Luc (1998): *Reduction and Givenness: Investigations of Husserl, Heidegger, and Phenomenology*. Evanston: Northwestern University Press.
Marks, Jonathan (2009): "The Nature of Humanness." In: Gosden, Chris, Rosemary A. Joyce, and Barry Cunliffe (ed.): *The Oxford Handbook of Archaeology*. Oxford: Oxford University Press, pp. 237-254.
Marshall, Colin (2010): "Kant's Metaphysics of the Self." In: *Philosophers' Imprint* 10: pp. 1-21.
Marvin, Walter Taylor (1903): *An Introduction to Systematic Philosophy*. New York: Columbia University Press.
McCarty, Richard (2009): *Kant's Theory of Action*. Oxford: Oxford University Press.
McCullers, Carson (2000*): Reflections in a Golden Eye*. Boston; New York: Houghton Mifflin.
McKenna, Terrence (1992): *The Archaic Revival: Speculations on Psychedelic Mushrooms, The Amazon, Virtual Reality, UFOs, Evolution, Shamanism, The Rebirth of the Goddess, and the End of History*. New York: HarperCollins.
McKinney, Tucker (2018): "'As One Does': Understanding Heidegger's Account of *das Man*." In: *European Journal of Philosophy* 26: pp. 430–448. doi: 10.1111/ejop.12257.
Meillassoux, Quentin (2017): *After Finitude: An Essay on the Necessity of Contingency* [Translated by Ray Brassier]. London: Bloomsbury Academic.
Melnick, Arthur (1989): *Space, Time, and Thought in Kant*. Dordrecht: Kluwer Academic.
Mencken, Henry L. (1930): *Treatise on the Gods*. London; New York: A. A. Knopf.
Merleau-Ponty, Maurice (1976): *Les Sciences de l'homme et la phénoménologie*. Paris: Centre de documentation universitaire.
Messina, James (2011): "Answering Aenesidemus: Schulze's Attack on Reinholdian Representationalism and Its Importance for Fichte." In: *Journal of the History of Philosophy* 49 (3): pp. 339-369.
Moder, Gregor (2013): "Held Out into the Nothingness of Being". In: *Filozofski vestnik, letnik* 34 (2): pp. 97-114.
Moore, George (1923): *Hail and Farewell!: Salve*. New York: Bonnie & Liveright.
Morgan, Vance G. (1993): "Kant and dogmatic idealism: a defense of Kant's refutation of Berkeley." In: *The Southern journal of philosophy* 31 (2): pp. 217-237.
Morris, Phyllis (1985): "Sartre on the Transcendence of the Ego." In: *Philosophy and Phenomenological Research* 46 (2): pp. 179–198.
Morton, Timothy (2012): *The Ecological Thought*. Cambridge (MA): Harvard University Press.
Neiman, Susan (1997): *The Unity of Reason: Rereading Kant*. Oxford: Oxford University Press.
Newton, Issac (1704): *Opticks: Or, a Treatise of the Reflexions, Refractions, Inflexions and Colours of Light. Also Two Treatises of the Species and Magnitude of Curvilinear Figures*. London: Smith and Walford.
Nicholson, Graeme (1996): "The Ontological Difference." In: *American Philosophical Quarterly* 33 (4): pp. 357-374.
Nietzsche, Friedrich W, (1989): *Friedrich Nietzsche on Rhetoric and Language*. [Edited by Sander L. Gilman, Carole Blair, and David J. Parent]. New York: Oxford University Press.
Noailles, Anna de (1901): *Le Cœur Innombrable*. Paris: Calmann Lévy.
Norris, Christopher (2011): *"Hawking Co*ntra Philosophy". In: *Philosophy Now* 82: pp. 21–24.
Oberst, Michael (2015): "Two Worlds and Two Aspects: on Kant's Distinction between Things in Themselves and Appearances." In: *Kantian Review* 20 (1): pp. 53–75.

O'Brien, Denis (2016): "Empedocles on the Identity of the Elements." In: *Elenchos* 37 (1/2): pp. 5-32.
Oizerman, Teodor I. (1981): "Kant's Doctrine of the "Things in Themselves" and Noumena." In: *Philosophy and Phenomenological Research* 41 (3): pp. 333-350. doi:10.2307/2107456.
Olafson, Frederick A. (1972): "Consciousness and Intentionality in Heidegger's Thought." In: *American Philosophical Quarterly* 12 (2): pp. 91-103.
Olson, Alan M. (1979): *Transcendence and Hermeneutics: An Interpretation of the Philosophy of Karl Jaspers*. The Hague: Springer.
Olson, R. Michael (2013): "Aristotle on God: Divine Nous as Unmoved Mover." In Diller, Jeanine and Asa Kasher (Ed.): *Models of God and Alternative Ultimate Realities*. Dordrecht: Springer: pp. 101–111.
Onol, Tugba Ayas (2015): "Reflections on Kant's View of the Imagination." In: *Ideas y Valores* 64 (157): pp. 53–69.
Oppy, Graham (2001): "Time, Successive Addition, and Kalam Cosmological Arguments." In: *Philosophia Christi* 3 (1): pp. 181-192.
Ortega y Gasset, Jose (1960): *What Is Philosophy?* [Translated by Mildred Adams]. New York: W.W. Norton.
Pagels, Heinz R. (1982): *The Cosmic Code: Quantum Physics as the Language of Nature*. New York: Dover Publications.
Paltridge, Brian, and Aek Phakiti (2015): *Research Methods in Applied Linguistics: A Practical Resource*. New York: Bloomsbury.
Pappe, H.O. (1961): "On Philosophical Anthropology." In: *Australasian Journal of Philosophy* 39 (1): pp. 47–64, doi: 10.1080/00048406112341031
Pascal, Blaise (1858): *Pensées de Pascal: Précédées de Sa Vie*. Paris: Librairie de Firmin Didot Frères.
Pasternack, Lawrence (2014): "Kant on Opinion: Assent, Hypothesis, and the Norms of General Applied Logic." In: *Kant-Studien* 105 (1): pp. 41-82.
Paton, Herbert James (1935): "Kant's Analysis of Experience." In: *Proceedings of the Aristotelian Society* 36: pp. 187-206.
Paton, Herbert James (1936): *Kant's Metaphysic of Experience*. New York: Macmillan.
Paulsen, Friedrich (1963): *Immanuel Kant: his life and doctrine* [Translated by James Edwin Creighton and Albert Lefevre]. New York: Frederick Ungar Publishing Co.
Pereboom, Derk (1991): "Is Kant's Transcendental Philosophy Inconsistent?" In: *History of Philosophy Quarterly* 8 (4): pp. 357-372.
Pereboom, Derk (2005): "Defending Hard Incompatibilism." In: *Midwest Studies in Philosophy* 29 (1): pp. 228-247.
Persius (1987): *The Satires of Persius* [Translation by Guy Lee]. Liverpool: Cairns.
Piché, Claude (2004): "Kant and the Problem of Affection." In: *Symposium: Canadian Journal of Continental Philosophy/Revue canadienne de philosophie continentale* 8 (2): pp. 275-297.
Pike, Albert (1950): *Morals and Dogma of the Ancient and Accepted Scottish Rite of Freemasonry*. Charleston: Society.
Piyong, Liu (2013): "On Plato's Theory of Forms." In: *Canadian Social Science* 9 (4): pp. 206-208.

Plato (1926). *Plato: Cratylus, Parmenides, Greater Hippias, Lesser Hippias* [Translated by Harold North Fowler]. Cambridge (MA): Harvard University Press.
Plato (1956): *Plato's Phaedrus* [Translated by W. C. Helmbold, and Wilson Gerson Rabinowitz]. New York: Liberal Arts Press.
Plato (2002): *Five Dialogues* [Translated by G. M. A. Grube]. Indianapolis: Hackett.
Plato (2014): *Theaetetus* [Translated by John McDowell]. Oxford: Oxford University Press.
Plato (2016): *The Republic of Plato* [Translated by Allan Bloom]. New York: Basic Books.
Plessner, Helmuth (1975): *Die Stufen Des Organischen Und Der Mensch: Einleitung in Die Philosophische Anthropologie*. Berlin: De Gruyter.
Poincaré, Henri (2001): *The Value of Science: Essential Writings of Henri Poincaré* [Edited by Stephen Jay Gould]. New York: Modern Library.
Polo, Leonardo (1999): *Antropología Trascendental I & II*. Pamplona: Eunsa.
Putnam, Hilary (1983): *Realism and Reason: Philosophical Papers. vol. 3*. New York: Cambridge University Press.
Putnam, Hilary (1985): *Mathematics, Matter, and Method. Philosophical Papers, vol. 1*. Cambridge: Cambridge University Press.
Queloz, Matthieu (2016): "Wittgenstein on the Chain of Reasons." In: *Wittgenstein-Studien* 7 (1): pp. 105-130.
Quine, Willard V. (1953): *From a Logical Point of View*. New York: Harper and Row.
Rae, Gavin (2010): "Re-Thinking the Human: Heidegger, Fundamental Ontology, and Humanism." In: *Human Studies* 33 (1): pp. 23-39.
Rao, K. Ramakrishna (2002): *Consciousness Studies: Cross-Cultural Perspectives*. Jefferson: McFarland.
Reinhold, Karl Leonhard (2011): *Essay on A New Theory of the Human Capacity for Representation* [Translated by Timothy J. Mehigan and Barry Empson]. Berlin: De Gruyter.
Rickman, Hans Peter (1960): "Philosophical Anthropology and the Problem of Meaning." In: *The Philosophical Quarterly (1950-)* 10 (38): pp. 12-20. doi:10.2307/2217313
Ricœur, Paul (1998): *Hermeneutics and the Human Sciences: Essays on Language, Action, and Interpretation* [Edited and Translated by John B. Thompson]. Cambridge: Cambridge University Press.
Riedinger, Ralf, Andreas Wallucks, Igor Marinković, Clemens Löschnauer, Markus Aspelmeyer, Sungkun Hong, and Simon Gröblacher (2018): "Remote quantum entanglement between two micromechanical oscillators." In: *Nature* 556 (7702): 473.
Robinson, Hoke (1994): "Two perspectives on Kant's appearances and things in themselves." In: *Journal of the History of Philosophy* 32 (3): 411-441.
Robinson, James M. (2008): *Language, Hermeneutic, and History: Theology After Barth and Bultmann*. Oregon: Cascade Books.
Rogerson, Kenneth F. (1988): "Kant On the Ideality of Space." In: *Canadian Journal of Philosophy* 18: pp. 271-286.
Rosen, Stanley (2001): "Is Thinking Spontaneous?" In Predrag, Cicovacki (ed.): *Kant's Legacy: Essays in Honor of Lewis White Beck*. Suffolk (UK): Boydell and Brewer, pp. 3–24.
Rousseau Jean-Jacques (1797): *Du Contrat Social*. Paris: Chez Mourer et Pinparé.
Routley, Richard (2010): "Necessary Limits to Knowledge: Unknowable Truths." In: *Synthese* 173 (1): pp. 107–122.
Rowan, Anna M. (2016): "*Dasein*, Authenticity, and Choice in Heidegger's Being and Time." In: *Logos i Ethos* 22 (1): pp. 87-105.

Russell, Bertrand (1937): *Principles of Mathematics*. London: Routledge.
Russell, Bertrand (1997): *The Problems of Philosophy*. New York: Oxford University Press.
Safari, Mehdi Qavam (2015): "Aristotelian Presocratics: A Look at Aristotle's Interpretation of Presocratic Philosophers." In: *Metaphysik* 6 (18): pp. 17-32.
Saisset, Émile Edmond (1865): *Le scepticisme. Aenésidème, Pascal, Kant Études pour servir à l'histoire critique du scepticisme ancien et moderne*. Paris: Didier.
Sartre, Jean-Paul (1964): *Nausea* [Translated by Lloyd Alexander]. Norfolk: New Directions.
Sartre, Jean-Paul (1991): *The Transcendence of the Ego* [Translated by Forrest Williams and Robert Kirkpatrick]. New York: Hill and Wang.
Sartre, Jean-Paul (1992): *Being and Nothingness* [Translated by Hazel E. Barnes]. New York: Simon and Schuster.
Schacht, Richard (1990): "Philosophical Anthropology: What, Why and How." In: *Philosophy and Phenomenological Research* 50: pp. 155-176. doi:10.2307/2108037.
Schaub, Edward (1912): "Hegel's Criticisms of Fichte's Subjectivism. I." In: *The Philosophical Review* 21 (5): pp. 566-584. doi:10.2307/2177178
Schaub, Edward (1913): "Hegel's Criticisms of Fichte's Subjectivism. II." In: *The Philosophical Review* 22 (1): pp. 17-37. doi:10.2307/2178155.
Scheler, Max 1975): *Die Stellung des Menschen im Kosmos*. Bern: Francke.
Schlegel, Friedrich von (1971): *Friedrich Schlegel's Lucinde and the Fragments* [Translated by Peter Firchow]. Minneapolis: University of Minnesota and Lund Press.
Schneck, Stephen Frederick (2002): *Max Scheler's Acting Persons: New Perspectives*. Amsterdam: Rodopi.
Schopenhauer, Arthur (1969): *The World as Will and Representation*. New York: Dover Publications.
Schulze, Gottlob Ernst (1996): *Aenesidemus, oder, Über die Fundamente der von dem Herrn Professor Reinhold in Jena gelieferten Elementar-Philosophie: nebst einer Verteidigung des Skeptizismus gegen die Anmassungen der Vernunftkritik* [Edited by Manfred Frank]. Hamburg: F. Meiner.
Schumacher, Ralph (2001): "Kant und Berkeley über die Idealität des Raumes." In: Schumacher, Ralph, Rolf-Peter Horstmann and Volker Gerhardt (ed.): *Kant Und Die Berliner Aufklärung: Akten des Ix. Internationalen Kant-Kongresses*. Bd. I: Hauptvorträge. Bd. Ii: Sektionen I-V. Bd. Iii: Sektionen Vi-X: Bd. Iv: Sektionen Xi-Xiv. Bd. V: Sektionen Xv-Xviii. Berlin: De Gruyter, pp. 238-248.
Schuster, Graham (2014): "Is Reason Contradictory When Applied to Metaphysical Questions?" In: *Journal of Cognition and Neuroethics* 2 (1): pp. 1–11.
Serck-Hanssen, Camilla (2015): "Towards Fundamental Ontology: Heidegger's Phenomenological reading of Kant." In: *Continental Philosophy Review* 48 (2): pp. 217-235.
Shakespeare, William (1913): *Romeo and Juliet* [Edited by Horace Howard Furness]. London: JB Lippencolt.
Shakespeare, William (1899): *The Complete Works of Shakespeare* [Edited by William George Clark and William Aldis Wright]. Philadelphia: G. Barrie & Son.
Shaviro, Steven (2014): *The Universe of Things: On Speculative Realism*. Minneapolis: University of Minnesota Press.
Sheehan, Thomas (1981): *Heidegger: The Man and the Thinker*. New Jersey: Transaction Publishers.

Shelley, Percy Bysshe (1813): *Queen Mab; a Philosophical Poem*. London: Printed by P. B. Shelley.
Shepard, Paul (1997): *The Others: How Animals Made Us Human*. Washington, D.C.: Island Press.
Sherman, Glen L. (2009): "Martin Heidegger's Concept of Authenticity: A Philosophical Contribution to Student Affairs Theory." In: *Journal of College and Character* 10 (7): pp. 1-9
Shiu-Ching, Wu (2016): "On the Priority of Relational Ontology: The Complementarity of Heidegger's Being-With and Ethics of Care". In: *KEMANUSIAAN 23* (2): pp. 71–87.
Sion, Avi (2014): *Logical Philosophy: A Compendium*. North Charleston, SC: CreateSpace Independent.
Sloan, Phillip R. (2002): "Performing the Categories: Eighteenth-Century Generation Theory and the Biological Roots of Kant's A Priori." In: *Journal of the History of Philosophy* 40 (2): pp. 229-253.
Smit, Houston (2000): "Kant on Marks and the Immediacy of Intuition." In: *The Philosophical Review* 109 (2): pp. 235-266.
Smith, William (1844): *Dictionary of Greek and Roman Biography and Mythology*. London: Taylor and Walton.
Soho, Takuan (2002): *The Unfettered Mind* [Translated by Williams Scott Wilson]. Tokyo: Kodansha International.
Somers-Hall, Henry (2012): *Hegel, Deleuze, and the Critique of Representation: Dialectics of Negation and Difference*. Albany: SUNY Press.
Sparrow, Tom (2014): *The End of Phenomenology: Metaphysics and the New Realism*. Edinburgh: Edinburgh University Press.
Spinoza, Benedictus de (1905): *Ethica: Ordine geometrico demonstrata* [Edited by Johannes van Vloten and J. P. N. Land]. Hagae Comitis: M. Nijhoff.
Spiro, Melford E. (1999): "Anthropology and Human Nature." In: *Ethos* 27 (1): pp. 7-14.
St. Augustine (2003): *The City of God* [Translated by Henry Bettensen] [Edited by G.R. Evans]. London: Penguin Classics.
St. Augustine (2012): *Augustine Confessions* [Translated by James Joseph O'Donnell]. Oxford: Oxford University Press.
Stang, Nicholas F. (2012): "Kant on Complete Determination and Infinite Judgement." In: *British Journal for the History of Philosophy* 20 (6): pp. 1117-1139.
Stang, Nicholas F. (2014): "The Non-Identity of Appearances and Things in Themselves." In: *Noûs* 48 (1): pp. 106–136.
Steiner, Rudolf (2001): *Man as Symphony of the Creative Word: Twelve Lectures given in Dornach, Switzerland from October 19th to November 11th, 1923*. Sussex (UK): Rudolf Steiner Press.
Strauss, Daniel F. M. (2000): "Kant and modern physics—The synthetic a priori and the distinction between modal function and entity." In: *South African Journal of Philosophy*, vol. 19 (1): pp. 26-40.
Strawson, Peter F. (1954): "Particular and General." In: *Proceedings of the Aristotelian Society* 54: pp. 233–260.
Strawson, Peter F. (2007): *The Bounds of Sense: An Essay on Kant's Critique of Pure Reason*. London: Routledge.

Sturm, Thomas, and Falk Wunderlich (2010): "Kant and the Scientific Study of Consciousness." In: *History of the Human Sciences* 23 (3): pp. 48–71.

Tanzer, Mark (2016): "Heidegger on Animality and Anthropocentrism." In: *Journal of the British Society for Phenomenology* 47 (1): pp. *18-32*. doi: 10.1080/ 00071773.2015.1097406

Tarazona, Salvador Piá (2001): *El hombre como ser dual. Estudio de las dualidades radicales según la Antropología trascendental de Leonardo Polo*. Pamplona: Ediciones Universidad de Navarra.

Taylor, Henry Osborn (1919): *The Mediaeval Mind: A History of the Development of Thought and Emotion in the Middle Ages*. New York: Macmillan.

Tomaszewska, Anna (2007): "The Transcendental Object and the 'Problem of Affection.' Remarks on some Difficulties of Kant's Theory of Empirical Cognition". In: *Diametros* 11: pp. 61-82.

Turbayne, Colin M. (1955): "Kant's refutation of dogmatic idealism." In: *The Philosophical Quarterly (1950-)* 5 (20): pp. 225-244.

Vaes, Jeroen, Paul G. Bain, and Jacques-Philippe Leyens (2014): "Understanding humanness and dehumanization: Emerging themes and directions," In: Vaes Jeroen, Paul G. Bain, and Jacques-Philippe Leyens (ed.): *Humanness and Dehumanization*. New York: Psychology Press, pp. 323-335.

Vallega, Alejandro (2003): *Heidegger and the Issue of Space: Thinking on Exilic Grounds*. Pennsylvania: Pennsylvania State University Press.

Van Cleve, James (2003) *Problems from Kant*. Oxford: Oxford University Press.

Van Inwagen, Peter (1998): "Meta-ontology." In: *Erkenntnis* 48 (2–3): pp. 233–250.

Visker, Rudi (2008): *The Inhuman Condition: Looking for Difference After Levinas and Heidegger*. Pittsburgh: Duquesne University Press.

Voltaire (1817): *Oeuvres complètes de Voltaire, vol VII*. Paris: chez Th. Desoer.

Wagner, Steven (1984): "Descartes on the Parts of the Soul." In: *Philosophy and Phenomenological Research* 45 (1): pp. 51-70. doi:10.2307/2107326.

Walker, Ralph C. S. (1985): "Idealism, Kant and Berkeley." In: Foster, John and Howard Robinson (ed.): *Essays on Berkeley: A Tercentennial Celebration*. Oxford: Oxford University Press.

Walker, Ralph C. S. (2010): "Kant on the Number of Worlds." In: *British Journal for the History of Philosophy* 18 (5): pp. *821-843*.

Walter, Johnston Estep (1915): *Subject and Object*. West Newton: Johnston and Penny.

Warren, Daniel (1998): "Kant and the apriority of space." In: Philosophical Review 107 (2): pp. 179-224.

Watkins, Eric (2009): *Kant's Critique of Pure Reason: Background Source Materials*. Cambridge: Cambridge University Press.

Wawrytko, Sandra A. "The Buddhist Challenge to the Noumenal: Analyzing Epistemological Deconstruction". In: Mou, Bo and Richard Tieszen (ed.): *Constructive Engagement of Analytic and Continental Approaches in Philosophy*. Leiden: Brill.

Weberman, David (1996): "Heidegger and the Disclosive Character of the Emotions." In: *The Southern Journal of Philosophy* 34: pp. 379-410.

Weberman, David (2010): "Heidegger's Relationalism." In: *British Journal for the History of Philosophy* 9 (1): pp. 109-122.

Weinberger, David (1980): "Three Types of "Vorhandenheit". In: *Research in Phenomenology* 10: pp. 235-50.

Whitman, Walt (1882): *Leaves of Grass*. Philadelphia: Rees Walsh & Co.

Wiggins, David (1982): "Heraclitus' Conceptions of Flux, Fire and Material Persistence." In: Schofield, Malcolm and Martha Craven Nussbaum (ed.): *Language and Logos: Studies in Ancient Greek Philosophy Presented to G. E. L. Owen*. Cambridge: Cambridge University Press, pp. 1–32

Wike, Victoria S. (1982): *Kant's Antinomies of Reason: Their Origin and Their Resolution*. Washington, D.C.: University Press of America.

Williams, Robert R. (1985): "Hegel and Transcendental Philosophy." In: *The Journal of Philosophy 82* (11): pp. 595-606. doi:10.2307/2026413.

Williams, Robert R. (1992): *Recognition: Fichte and Hegel on the Other*. Albany: SUNY Press

Wilson, Catherine (1988): "Sensible and Intelligible Worlds in Leibniz and Kant." In: Woolhouse, Roger (ed.): *Metaphysics and Philosophy of Science in the Seventeenth and Eighteenth Centuries* [The University of Western Ontario Series in Philosophy of Science (A Series of Books in Philosophy of Science, Methodology, Epistemology, Logic, History of Science, and Related Fields)] vol 43. Dordrecht: Springer.

Wilson, Colin (1986): *Rudolf Steiner: The Man and His Vision: An Introduction to the Life and Ideas of the Founder of Anthroposophy*. Wellingborough: Aquarian Press.

Wilson, Kirk Dallas (1975): "Kant on Intuition." In: *The Philosophical Quarterly (1950-)* 25 (100): pp. 247-265.

Wilson, Margaret Dauler (1971): "Kant and 'The Dogmatic Idealism of Berkeley'. In: *Journal of the History of Philosophy 9* (4): pp. 459-475.

Winegar, Reed (2017): "Kant on Intuitive Understanding and Things in Themselves." In: *European Journal of Philosophy* 24 (2): pp. 305–329.

Wojtowicz, Randy (1997): "The Metaphysical Expositions of Space and Time." In: *Synthese* 113 (1): pp. 71-115.

Wolfendale, Peter (2014): *Object Oriented Philosophy: The Noumena's New Clothes*. Lulu Press, Inc.

Wuerth, Julian (2013): "Sense and Sensibility in Kant's Practical Agent: Against the Intellectualism of Korsgaard and Sidgwick." In: *European Journal of Philosophy* 21: pp. 1-36.

Wuerth, Julian (2014): *Kant on Mind, Action, and Ethics*, Oxford: Oxford University Press.

Wyschogrod, Edith (2000): *Emmanuel Levinas: The Problem of Ethical Metaphysics*. New York: Fordham University Press

Xunzi (2004): *Xunzi: The Complete Text* [Translated by Eric L. Hutton]. Princeton: Princeton University Press.

Young, J. Michael (2009): "Kant's Notion of Objectivity." In: *Kant-Studien*. 70 (1-4): pp. 131-148.

Young, Larry J. (2009): "Being Human: Love: Neuroscience reveals all." In: *Nature* 457 (7226): 148.

Zammito, John H. (1992): *The Genesis of Kant's Critique of Judgment*. Chicago: University of Chicago Press.

Zaner, Richard M. (1966): "An Approach to a Philosophical Anthropology." In: *Philosophy and Phenomenological Research* 27 (1): pp. 55-68. doi:10.2307/2106138.

Žižek, Slavoj (2012): *Less Than Nothing: Hegel and the Shadow of Dialectical Materialism*. London: Verso.
Žižek, Slavoj (2017): "The Persistence of Ontological Difference." In: Mitchell, Andrew and Peter Trawny (ed.): *Heidegger's Black Notebooks: Responses to Anti-Semitism*. New York: Columbia University Press, pp. 186-200.

Index

Aenesidemus 138n289
affectability, transcendental 109, 111n214; thing-in-itself and 109
affection, double 111
affectionability, transcendental 103
Allison, H.E. 104–6
Almog, J. 91
Anaxagoras 133n278
Anaximander 133
Anaximenes 133n275
anthropology, existential 188
anthropology, philosophical xv–xvi, 1–2, 7–8, 10–11, 130–1, 181–91; Dasein and 188; as methodology 190; ontology and 2, 183; see also Being
anthropology, transcendental 188
anthroposophy 188–9
antinomies see freedom and Kant, I. and reason
apeiron 133, 172
appearances 3, 34–5, 50n71, 53–4, 56, 57n99, 58–9, 62–4, 66–7, 70, 73, 75, 84, 87–8, 94–5, 97, 100–108, 110–11, 144, 161, 174n332; Kant and 58, 78, 81, 84, 100, 101n193, 102–3, 130n200, 104–5, 107, 111; mind-dependent and 102; ontology of 106; space and 63, 107; time and 107; see also thing-in-itself
apperception 58, 81, 86, 147; transcendental 81, 83–7; see also Kant, I.
aptitudes 10, 161, 161n323, 162–3, 165, 167–71, 171n328, 172–3, 173n330, 176–81; being and 165, 171, 179–81; essences and 163; forms and 168–71; materialism and 169; nonbeings and 10, 156, 168–70, 171n328, 172, 176–8, 180–1; universality and 180; see also Dasein and emergence and humanness and objects
Aristotle 27–8, 39, 41, 73, 132; Kant and 73; mind–body problem and 144n297

Baudrillard, J. 179
Being xiii–xiv, 11–12, 34, 40–1, 47–8, 52, 90–1, 116, 124–5, 132–42, 147, 160–1, 173, 178–83, 185–6; being and 125, 141, 147–8, 160, 167, 179–82, 184, 186; Being-as-such xiv, 43, 130n262, 134–6, 141–2, 160, 183–5; Being of being 127, 140, 186; Being of Being 90, 179–80; Being qua Being 135, 137, 141, 174n332, 183; cognition and 147; Heidegger and 133–41, 147, 182; historicity of 137; law of 146; metaphysics and xiv; nature and 135, 137–9, 187; nontraditional 178; nothing/nothingness and 135–9; philosophical anthropology and 181–3, 186, 188–9; Pre-Socratics and 132–4; question of 132–4, 185–6; relationality and 179–80; spectrum of 178, 181; substance and 134; thought-Being correlate 36–7; world and 135, 139–40, 178; see also Dasein and humanness
being 12, 14, 16, 18–19, 41, 43–6, 48, 54, 61, 68, 82–3, 87, 90–2, 113–14, 117–22, 124, 127, 130, 132–9, 141–7, 149, 154–72, 174n332, 178, 180–4; analytic of 1, 48, 135; being-as-such 46, 90, 90n162, 141, 143, 155, 160, 167; being of being 114, 130, 133, 163, 174n332; being qua being 137, 174n332; being-so 155–6; composition of 145; exhausted being 156–7, 181; in the world 149, 156–7, 162, 164, 166, 168, 173, 181, 187–9; nature and 137–8; necessity and 71–4; nonrelationality and 153–4, 155–7, 160, 162–3, 165–7, 174n332, 180; nothing and 139, 158; objects and 15–16, 147, 150, 154, 167, 170; question of 132–5, 182, 185; relationality and 90, 107, 154–60, 162–9, 173, 177, 180–1; spectrum of 172, 177–8; supreme 73; thought and 18, 21, 82; world and 154, 159, 162–4,

167–8, 172–3; see also Being and Dasein
being human 127–8, 131, 190–1; see also human being
Beingness 180
Benardete, J. 136
Bennett, J. 100
Bergson, H. 107, 110–11
Bhaskar, R. 174n332
Blondel, M. 118
Bruno, G. 180
Bryant, L. 152, 171
Buber, M. 118, 130, 188, 190

Camus, A. 96
Cartesianism 11–13, 31, 81–2, 86, 144; see also Descartes, R.
Cassier, E. 130
categories 14, 78n139, 83–4, 88, 138; Kant and 42n52, 80, 144
causality 67–73, 97, 152; freedom and 67–70; law of 69–71; nature and 67–8, 70, 138; self-causality 68n118; spontaneity and 68, 70, 96; transcendental 70
Chrysippus 26
Cirulli, F. 127
cognition 37, 52, 80, 146–9, 152
composites 64–7, 71
condition, human xv, 2, 2 n10, 124n242
consciousness 5, 30, 82–3, 124n242, 184, 189–90; consciousness qua consciousness 83; dialectical nature of 5; grounding and 5; recognition and 5; self-consciousness 5, 67, 79, 82, 86–7, 173; spiritual 188
contingency 71, 73, 125n245
Copernicus 44
Coreth, E. 130
correlation, transcendental 23
correlationism xvi, 8, 11–14, 18–19, 21, 23, 34–8, 46, 159, 167, 177–8; definition of 12, 18; see also emergence and Meillassoux, Q. and realism

Dasein: analytic of xiv, 2–3, 6–8, 40, 47–8, 55n89, 91, 93, 135, 141–2,
182–3, 185–6; appearances and 106–8; aptitudes and 163; attunement and 115–17, 148; Being and 47–8, 52, 127, 130, 134–5, 141, 182–5, 185nn343–4; being and 6, 47, 80, 91, 113–19, 125, 127, 130–1, 134, 137, 147–8, 159, 162, 173–4, 182–7; being-in 2, 40, 48–9, 54, 91–2, 113–14, 140–1, 165–7, 174n332, 188; being-in-the-world [in-der-Welt-sein] 2, 7, 40, 48, 52–3, 55, 74–5, 79, 91–2, 113–20, 124–5, 141, 148–9, 158, 173, 178, 181, 183–5, 187–8; being-together-with 114–15; being-toward-death [sein-zum-Tode] 54, 117–18, 120; being with 114; care [Sorge] and 10, 91, 117, 120, 152; cognition and 148–9, 152; defined 113; Ding an sich and 79; dread and 115n220; empirical 47; engagement and 148; essence [Wesen] and 125, 163; experience and 131; faculty of 108; finitude and 9–10, 41, 45–9, 54–5, 76, 181–2, 185n343, 186n346; freedom and 77; fundamentals of 42, 47; future and 117–18; handiness [Zuhandheit] 91, 119; Heidegger and xiv, 1–3, 7–9, 38, 41, 46–8, 91, 93, 94n172, 113–19, 130, 134–6, 141, 148, 151, 185–8; as human being 185–6, 189; infinitude of 9–10, 45–9, 55, 76, 185n344; intentionality and 148–9; intuition and 79–80; Kant and 9, 47, 79, 107, 181; knowledge and 45; magnitude and 53; metaphysics and xiv, 40–1, 44, 92–3, 106, 183–4, 187, 191; moods and 115–17, 148; nature of 131, 185, 187; neediness of 120; nonbeing and 117–18; nonfinitude of 9–10, 45–9, 55, 76, 186n347; nonrelationality and 123, 154; nothing and 136; noumena and 2, 77, 79–80, 92, 92n166; objects and 10, 12, 119–20, 122, 148–52, 154, 170; as observer 146; ontic and 7, 9, 47, 91, 173, 182, 182n337; ontic-existentiell 91; ontic-relationality and 184; ontology and xiv, 2, 7–9, 41, 45–6, 91, 93, 151–2, 173, 181, 183, 191; perception and 146, 148; phenomena and 9,

52–4, 79; phenomenology and xv, 9, 40, 183, 187–8; potentiality of 55; present-at-hand [vorhanden] and 7, 10, 91, 119, 119n228, 120, 138, 148–9, 184; privilege and 52, 148, 148n308, 149; projecting and 116–17; pure reason and 1, 92; ready-to-hand [zuhanden] and 10, 91, 119, 119n228, 120, 148–9; reason and 50, 52, 74–6, 92; recognition and 52, 80; relationality and 7, 47, 91, 119–20, 152, 154, 162, 173–4, 181; subjectivity and 131–2, 141; temporal nature of 49; "they" and 91, 118, 188; thing-in-itself and 8, 48, 79, 107; thrownness [Geworfenheit] 93, 116; transcendentalism of 9–10, 45–9, 80, 92, 123, 181, 183; world and 2, 7, 47, 53, 67, 74–5, 91, 93–4, 107, 112–20, 122–3, 140–3, 148, 150–1, 154, 158, 166, 170, 181, 183–4, 189; worldhood and 141, 162; wordliness [Weltlichkeit] 7, 67, 91, 162; see also ego, transcendental and humanness

Deleuze, G. 179
Democritus 134
Derrida, J. 129
Descartes, R. 11–13, 56, 58, 81, 124n242, 143–4; cogito and 56–7, 81, 86–7, 128, 144; dualism and 11–12, 31, 31n37, 32, 144; reason and 57; soul and 56, 56n97, 57–8; thought and 58
Dewey, J. 37
difference, ontological 90, 90n162, 143, 147, 185
Ding an sich see Kant, I. and noumena
dualism see Descartes, R.

ego, transcendental 5, 5n16, 6–7, 10, 48, 57n99, 80–1, 81n144, 82–7, 91–3, 108, 111–12, 183; apperception and 85, 85n156; Dasein and 10, 92–3; Fichte and 5–6; Heidegger and 6–7, 48; Kant and 5, 81–9, 92; necessity of 84, 89; as noumenon 108; as unifying factor 86, 89; see also objects
emergence 8, 12–14, 16–21, 24, 157, 169, 171–2, 173n330, 178; aptitudes and 171; correlationism and 13; relation and 13, 18, 157; see also objects and ontology, object-oriented
entities, nonrelational 181
existence, ontological order of 157, 160, 173–4, 177n334

Fichte, J.G. 2, 4–6, 13, 18, 39, 53n82; consciousness and 5; dialecticism and 5; Kant and 39–40; pure ego and 5–6, 81n144
first principles 1, 41
Fischer, J. 189
formalism 168–71; see also Harman, G.
forms, Platonic 16, 26–8, 31–2, 94n173, 144, 174, 179; objects and 26–7, 32
freedom 67–70, 76–7, 173, 184, 186; antinomy and 70, 97; causal 70–1; Kant and 77; transcendental 69, 97; see also Dasein and spontaneity

Garcia, T. 15, 158n321
Guattari, F. 179

Harman, G. xvi, 2, 12, 12n20, 13, 15, 17, 17n27, 19–20, 22–8, 30–1, 33–8, 41, 107, 152–4, 156–7, 161n323, 167, 169–71; Aristotle and 17n27, 27; correlationism and 23, 35–6, 38; emergence and 17, 19–20; fictionality and 167, 170; formalism/forms and 168–9; Heidegger and 37–8; Kant and 38; materialistic reductionism and 22–3, 171; nominalism and 22, 26; object-oriented ontology and 2, 13, 17, 19, 24, 26–31, 31n37, 32–8, 41, 153, 171–2; overmining and 19; Plato and 27–8; The Quadruple Object and 26; real objects and 19–20, 24, 26–9, 37, 152–3, 153n318, 154, 168, 170; tool-analysis and 38; Tool-Being and 12, 27, 122
Hawking, S. xiii
Hegel, G. 5; ego and 81n144; Geist and 85; Science and Logic and 136
Heidegger, M. xiii, xiiin1, xv–xvi, 1–3, 3n12, 6–11, 27, 31, 37–8, 40–1, 42n51, 43–7, 47n60, 48–9, 90–3, 104,

106–7, 112–15, 117–20, 123, 130, 133–43, 147–8, 151–3, 158, 162, 164, 167, 182, 184–8; anthropocentrism of 8, 31, 38; anthropology and 190n359; Being and Time [Sein und Zeit] 3, 3n12, 11, 31, 40, 55n89, 113, 114n217, 130n262; beings and 143, 147; Descartes and 11–12; finite transcendence and 48; Hegel and 136; Husserl and 6, 40; Introduction to Metaphysics and 135; Kant and 1–3, 5, 37, 43, 45, 47, 90–2, 104, 104n201, 112; Kant and the Problem of Metaphysics and 9; nature and 137; nothing/nothingness and 135–6, 136n285, 164, 167; objects and 27, 31, 152; Parmenides and 136–7; phenomenology and 182; reason and 46, 49n66, 55, 55n89; tool-analysis of 38, 152; transcendentalism and 7n18, 46, 48; world (der Welt) and 2, 7–8, 113–14, 118, 134, 139–42, 153, 158; worldhood 140–2; see also Being and Dasein and humanness

Heraclitus 27–8, 133–4, 171

human being xv, 11–12, 54, 90, 113, 124n242, 127–8, 130–1, 178, 181–2, 184–91; relationality and 159

humanness: analytic of 183–4; aptitudes and 162–3, 173, 178–9, 181, 191; Being and 124–5, 127, 130, 179, 183; being and 124–5, 127, 130–1, 181; being-in-the-world and 189; being human, concept of xvi, 10–11, 123, 124n242, 125–6, 131, 162, 181; critique of 2, 9, 91, 181, 183, 187, 190–1; Dasein and xv, 123–5, 127, 130, 162, 173–4, 177n334, 178, 181–4; definitions of 126–9; essence [Wesen] and 125; experience and 132; as filter of being 177–8; finitude and 181–2; forms and 174; Heidegger and 8, 130, 182; historical scholarship on 124, 124n242, 125, 127n252, 128, 128nn254–5, 129, 129nn256–60, 130; human beings and 126–8; manifestation of 181, 186; necessary 125; problem of xiii, xv; philosophical anthropology and 131, 181,

183–4, 187; philosophy and xiii, 11; problem of xiii, xv; quality of 124–5, 183; question of xv, 124n242, 125–30, 142, 162, 181–4, 187, 190; spectricity of 172–3, 178; spectrum and 178; transcendentalism and 125, 127, 130, 162, 181, 183, 187n348; world and 173–4; see also nature, human

Hume, D. 43–4, 84–5, 136

Husserl, E. 1, 6, 40

hyperbeings 177, 177n334, 178

idealism 6, 13, 18, 20, 59, 169; pure 102; speculative 14; transcendental 3, 7, 12, 104–5

Idealism, German 5, 13, 39, 85

interactions, relational 145

interpretation see objects

intuition 44, 50–1, 53, 57, 59, 61, 64–7, 78–80, 82–3, 86, 89, 95, 107, 109; empirical 81; intellectual 79–80, 80n143, 88; non-sensible 79, 88; pure 53, 66–7, 88, 94, 102, 108–11, 162; sensible 58, 67, 79–80; sensuous 111; supra-intellectual 107, 111

Jackson, M.D. 188

Kant, I: affection and 111; apperception and 58, 81, 86; antinomies and 56, 59–61, 64, 67–74, 74n131, 75, 95–8, 106, 163; Cartesian cogito and 81; Cartesian dualism and 31; categories and 42n52, 144; correlationism and 18, 34, 36–7, 46; Critique of Pure Reason 1–4, 9, 23, 39, 41–5, 55–9, 66n112, 81, 90, 94–5, 98, 103, 105, 125n246; Ding an sich 4–8, 15, 36, 40–1, 54n85, 57, 77–9, 87, 93, 98, 101, 107; epistemology and 1, 44; experience and 64, 100, 106, 108–10, 112n215, 144; Harman and 38; Heidegger and xvi, 2, 5–6, 8–9, 45, 47, 104, 136; humanness and xv–xvi; Hume and 84; idealism and 6, 102n197; infinity and 60–3; intelligible (noumenal) world and 6, 94, 94n173, 95, 98–9; knowledge and 42–4, 84–5, 100–101, 103,

125n246; kosmos and 1; magnitude and 52–3; metaphysics and 1, 3, 41, 43–4; noumena and 2, 5, 5n16, 6, 9, 31, 48, 77–80, 84–5, 88–9, 94n173, 95, 98–9, 152; objects and 18, 20, 44, 52–3, 84, 103, 107–8; On the Form of the Principles of the Sensible World 94; ontology and 9, 41–3, 48, 90–2, 94n173, 104, 106–7, 181; paralogisms and 56–8, 81; phenomena and 52, 85, 89, 98–9, 152; philosophical anthropology and 1, 1n9; Prolegomena to Any Future Metaphysics 43, 78; reason and 46, 49–50, 55, 55n89, 56–9, 73–5, 95–8, 100, 105; Reinhold and 3–4; self and 83; self-consciousness and 82, 86; sensible (phenomenal) world and 6, 98–9; soul and 56, 56n96, 57, 57n99, 57–8; space and 60, 63, 66–7, 94, 102, 105n204, 109–10; time and 61–3, 71, 94, 102, 105n204, 109–10; transcendentalism and xv–xvi, 5, 44, 58, 63, 81, 88, 92; world and 60–3, 93, 93n170, 94, 94n173, 95, 98–9, 103, 106, 112, 139, 153; see also Dasein and ego, transcendental and thing-in-itself
"Kantian problematic" 3
Kantian system xvi, 2–6, 9, 36–7, 39, 40n48, 41, 45, 47, 77–8, 92–3, 98–103, 105–6, 108–9; Fichte and 4, 6, 40; Harman and 37; Heidegger and 3, 6, 9, 47; idealism and 7, 102; transcendentalism and 103; two aspects interpretation 98, 103–4, 106, 108; two worlds interpretation and 27, 98–9, 101, 103, 108, 152, 154; see also Kantian worlds
Kantian worlds 2, 9, 55n91, 98, 98n184, 99, 105–6, 122–3, 163, 165; see also noumena and phenomena
Kohák, E. 136
kosmos 1, 137
Kraus, B. 188

Langton, R. 104–6, 111, 121–2
Leibniz, G.W. 66, 145; monads and 66, 66n112, 174

Leucippus 134
lifeworld, concept of 188
Locke, J. 13, 13n22, 14–15, 19, 29, qualities and 13–15, 19, 29

Maréchal, J. 130
materialism 168–9, 171; speculative 13, 19; transcendental 170n327
meaning, reflective 150
Meillassoux, Q. 12–13, 15–19, 23–4, 32, 36, 38, 159, 177; After Finitude 12–13, 159; correlationism and 13, 18, 23, 38, 159, 177; emergence and 16–17; objects and 15–16; speculative realism and 17, 23, 32, 38
metaontology 44n57
Mlodinow, L. xiii
monism 28, 32
Morton, T. 32–3, 176–7; The Ecological Thought and 32–3

Nakhnikian, G. 6
nature, human xiv–xv, 46, 124n242, 127–8, 131–2, 184; philosophy of 187
necessary being 71–74, 81
nominalism 21–4, 26, 30; speculative 21; undermining and 22
nonbeing 10, 42, 121, 167–72, 176–8, 180–1; see also Dasein and nonrelationality and objects and world
nonrelationality 122–3, 144, 150, 154, 163, 165, 167–8, 172, 174n332, 181; nonbeing and 10, 167–9, 176–7; ontological 168, 172; see also being and objects and relationality and world
noumena 2, 5, 5n16, 6–9, 31, 48, 59, 65, 77–9, 82, 88, 94n173, 95, 99, 103, 106, 106n205, 108, 120, 132, 152; affection and 102–3, 110; defined 77; Ding an sich and 77–8, 88; negative 79, 88; as non-sensible knowledge 77; phenomena and 2–3, 5, 31, 59, 77, 79, 82, 84–7, 89–91, 95, 98, 98n184, 99, 103–4, 108, 122–3, 152; positive 5n16, 6, 78n138, 79–80, 88–9; transcendental self and 84; unknowability of 95; see also affectionability, transcendental

and Dasein and Kant, I. and self and world

objects: affectability and 121–2; affection and 103, 144, 159; appearances and 64, 84, 103n200, 108, 110; aptitudes and 161n323, 166, 168–72, 176; categories of 14, 154, 186; classification of 20, 144, 158n321; defined 121; emergence and 171; experience and 20, 80, 105–8, 111, 144, 154, 161; hyperobjects 32–4, 176–7, 177n334; interpretation and 36; knowledge and 42, 44; magnitude and 52–3; mathematical 139–40; mental 122n238; metaphysics and 152–3; mind-independence and 28–30, 35–6, 170; nonbeings and 167–71; noncognitive 151; nonreal 170; nonrelationality and 10, 112n215, 144, 152–5, 167–8, 170, 172, 176; noumena and 103, 152; ontological individuality and 121–2; ontology and 12, 31; overmining and 19–20, 28; particulars and 33, 121; perceptibility and 121–2; perception and 14–16, 18, 26, 36, 51–3, 82, 144–6, 153, 159, 169–70; perceptivity and 51; phenomena and 50, 52, 84, 103, 106n205; properties and 14, 17–20, 29, 52, 105, 121, 144; qualities and 13–15, 19–20, 24, 27, 121; real 19–21, 24, 26–9, 33–7, 152–4, 168; reason and 51; reception and 51; recognition of xvi; reductionism/reducibility of 17, 172; relationality and 10, 17–21, 23, 33–4, 37, 83, 106n205, 107, 121–2, 145–7, 149–50, 152–5, 158–9, 166–70, 176; representation and 30, 109; sense/sensation and 51–3, 67, 78, 109; sensible 88–9; sensual 19–20, 24, 27–30, 36, 152, 168; significance and 152; space and 33, 67, 109–10, 176; subjects and 31, 82–3, 143–7, 151; substances and 121, 172; things-in-themselves and 84, 101; time and 33, 109–10, 176; as tools 152; transcendental ego and 111–12; two objects interpretation 108; undermining and 18–19; understanding and 79, 106n205; withdrawn 33; see also affectionability, transcendental and being and Dasein and ontology, object-oriented and world

ontic, the 41, 90, 122, 174n332

ontology: flat 12–13, 30–4, 37–8; fundamental xiv–xvi, 3, 8–9, 38, 43–8, 90–2, 106–7, 123, 178, 181–2, 184, 191; Platonic 26; realist 21; spectral xv–xvi, 8, 37–8, 177–8; transcendental 44–5, 106, 108, 181; see also ontology, object-oriented

ontology, object-oriented xvi, 2, 8, 10, 13, 17, 19, 19n28, 21–38, 149, 151–2, 167–8, 171–2, 176; emergence and 17, 19, 21, 171; flatness of 12, 30, 31–3, 38; materialist philosophy and 168; nominalism and 23–4, 26, 28–30; particulars and 29–30, 32–3; philosophical anthropology and 8; realism and 28, 32; speculative realism and xvi, 8, 13, 21–22, 24–6, 30, 32, 34, 36–7; universals and 29–30, 32–4; see also Harman, G.

overmining see objects

Parmenides 133–4, 136–7
particularity 26, 33, 49n66, 179, 185–6
particulars 14, 21, 26, 28–30, 32–4; universals and 34; see also ontology, object-oriented and qualities
Pascal, B. 54
perception 14–16, 18, 22, 26, 50–1, 51n72, 53, 56, 57n99, 65, 75, 78, 81–2, 87, 100, 102, 110, 122, 144–9, 152, 155, 159; mental 104; self-consciousness and 82; time and 62; see also objects
phenomena 3, 5, 7, 31, 50, 52–4, 56, 59, 77, 79, 82, 84–6, 98, 103, 106, 106n205, 108; affection and 103; perceptibility and 54; self and 84; as sensible knowledge 77; time and 54; see also Dasein and noumena and objects
phenomenology xiv–xv, 40, 182–3, 187, 190; see also Dasein
Plato 27–8, 94n173, 133–4, 174
Plessner, H. 130, 189
Poincaré, H. 28

positionality, excentric 189
Pre-Socratics 1, 132–33, 133nn278–9, 134
prioritization, ontological 152, 173–4
properties 13–15, 52, 110, 121–2, 143–4, 157, 161; dormancy and 16; emergent 16–20; epistemic 105; essential 15, 18; intrinsic 105; intuited 30; material 169; mathematical 23; nonessential 14; ontic 122; potency and 16–17; relational 16–18, 20, 105; universal 29; see also objects

qualia 86–7
qualities: aesthetic 35–6; essential 14, 124–5, 134; noumenal 152; particulars 29–30; primary 14–15, 19, 23, 29, 34; real 19–20, 24, 27, 29–30, 94, 152; relational 13, 27; secondary 13–15, 17, 19–20, 29, 52n77; sensible 13, 13n22, 14; sensual 19–20, 24, 27, 29–30, 152; universal 29–30, 35; see also humanness and objects

realism 12, 15, 21, 24, 28, 30–1, 34; Aristotelian 32; correlationism and xvi, 8, 18, 23; indirect 31; metaphysical 169–70; nominalism and 24, 26; nominalistic 24, 28; non-realist 24; Platonic 26, 28, 31–2; speculative xvi, 8, 12–13, 15, 17–18, 20–6, 30, 32, 34, 36–8, 159; true 26; universals and 31–2, 34; "weird" 24, 28, 30; see also nominalism and ontology, object-oriented
reason: antinomies and 71, 95–7; capabilities of 97; as category 76n133; experience and 55; finite 46, 50, 50n70, 51–2, 77; finite pure 46; finitude and 9, 49, 76–7, 111, 123n239; impure 49n66, 50, 74; infinitude and 76; intuitive 55n88, 56; knowledge and 101; limitations of 49–50, 56, 75–6, 105; logic and 74; metaphysics and 46, 184; nonfinitude and 55, 76; paralogisms and 56–9; practical 55; pure 1, 9, 40–2, 46, 49n66, 55, 55nn89–90, 56–9, 64, 71, 73–7, 92, 97; sensible 49n66,

55n88, 56, 74–6; transcendentalism and 55; see also Dasein and Kant, I.
receptivity 50–1, 109–11
reduction, eidetic 182n337
reductionism 19, 22, 26, 132, 169, 171–2; materialist 22, 172; see also objects
referentiality 155
regress problem 65
Reinhold, K.L. 3–4, 39, 40n48; see also Kant, I.
relationality 7, 16, 23, 33–4, 37, 90, 121, 145–50, 152, 154–70, 173–4, 174n332, 176, 181–2; cognitive 149; negative 155; nonrelational/nonrelationality and 61n107, 130n262, 154, 160, 165–6, 168, 176–7, 179; ontic 122, 144–7, 150–1, 154, 159, 183–4; place/position and 150; pure 146, 149, 158–9, 174n332; transcendental 165; see also being and Dasein and objects and world
relationality, world of 7, 47n59, 157–8, 162, 164–6, 174, 174n332, 177, 177n334
relations 2, 16, 18, 24, 26, 113, 120, 122, 152, 154–8, 161, 165, 173, 176; objects and 16, 18, 21, 33–4, 83, 121, 152; thing-in-itself and 23; world and 112, 117, 158, 180, 191; see also relationality
representation 3, 15, 28, 30, 40, 53, 57, 57n99, 58–9, 78, 80, 82, 87, 99, 110–11, 127; empirical 76, 81; Kant and 86, 88, 90, 104–5; transcendental modality of 109–11; see also objects
responding, act of 145–6
Robinson, J. 136

Scheler, M. 187–90
Schelling, F. 13
Schlegel, F. 4
Schulze, G.E. 5, 40
self: empirical 84; noumenal 84, 86, 108, 123; objective 87, 89; subjective 89; unifying 84
self-consciousness see consciousness
self-reflexivity 53, 83, 87
self, transcendental 6, 84, 89; see also noumena
sensation, transcendental 111

sense-data 110
scientism xiii
Shaviro, S. 171
Shepard, P. 180
significance 149–51, 151n314, 151n316, 152
singularity, ontological 183
Socrates 1
Spinoza, B. 11, 91
spontaneity 68, 70, 97; freedom and 68, 97; necessity of 97
Steiner, R. 188
Stoicism 26
Strawson, P. 99–100
subject–object distinction 11–12, 12n20, 31, 31n37, 32, 143, 147–8, 151–2, 167, 189
subjects 31, 64, 82–3, 143–7, 151; see also objects

Thales of Miletus 132
thing-in-itself 5–8, 18, 20, 23–4, 27, 29, 34, 37, 48, 57n99, 78, 78n139, 79, 81, 84–5, 87, 94n173, 99–101, 101n194, 102–11, 120, 161, 168, 174n332; affection and 103, 109; appearances and 105, 108; Kant and 20, 24, 27, 57n99, 87–8, 94n173, 99–100, 102–3, 107, 109–10, 161; knowledge and 85; mind-independent and 102; nature of 6; necessity of 6–7; objects and 84, 104, 108; perception and 102; problem of 8; senses and 102–3, 109; space and 105, 109–11; time and 105, 109–11; transcendental sense of 111; see also Dasein
transcendentalism, metaphysical 170

undermining 17–20, 22, 28; see also nominalism and objects
universality 4, 68, 179–80
universals 4, 21, 26, 28–30, 32–5, 179–80; correlationism and 34–5; objects and 29, 35; see also properties and qualities and realism

value-being [Wertsein] 189
Van Cleve, J. 100–1
Vorhandenheit 7, 91; see also Dasein

Whitehead, A.N. 171
world: conceptual 154; experientiality and 154; infinity and 60–3, 96; nonbeing and 156, 169, 172, 180; nonrelationality and 123, 151, 153, 155–8, 160, 162, 164–5, 167–8, 172, 174n332; noumenal 94n173, 99, 120; objects and 2, 10, 23, 65, 87, 94, 103, 107, 120, 141, 145, 151, 154, 158, 167–8, 172, 176; relationality and 7, 113, 120, 123, 149–50, 152–4, 156–8, 158n320, 159–62, 164–5, 174, 174n332, 177n334, 181, 191; worldhood 140–3, 150–1, 154, 158, 162; world itself 61, 156–69, 172–4, 174n332, 176, 177n334, 179–81, 191; world of sense 65–6, 71, 93–5, 98–9; see also Dasein and Heidegger, M. and Kantian system

Zeno 26
Žižek, S. 23
Zuhandenheit 7, 91, 119; see also Dasein

www.ingramcontent.com/pod-product-compliance
Lightning Source LLC
Chambersburg PA
CBHW050556170426
43201CB00011B/1721